1 MONTH OF
FREE
READING

at
www.ForgottenBooks.com

By purchasing this book you are eligible for one month membership to ForgottenBooks.com, giving you unlimited access to our entire collection of over 1,000,000 titles via our web site and mobile apps.

To claim your free month visit:
www.forgottenbooks.com/free97727

ISBN 978-0-483-53929-7
PIBN 10097727

Joseph Leckie

Photogravure by T & R Annan & Sons Glasgow from a Photograph by Jas. Magill Belfast

LIFE AND RELIGION

BY THE LATE

JOSEPH LECKIE, D.D.

AUTHOR OF "SERMONS PREACHED AT IEROX"

WITH BIOGRAPHICAL SKETCHES

EDITED BY HIS SON

GLASGOW

JAMES MACLEHOSE & SONS

Publishers to the University

1891

PREFACE.

THESE Discourses do not challenge criticism from the purely literary standpoint. They labour under all the disadvantages incident to posthumous publication, having been neither selected nor revised by their Author. With the exception of the two Sermons entitled respectively "Worship" and "Christianity and Literature," they were all composed rapidly in the course of Dr. Leckie's ordinary week-to-week ministrations, and are fair examples of his regular style of teaching.

The plan of the book throughout is memorial. Its design is to represent as fully as possible the different sides of Dr. Leckie's thought, and the various characteristics of his preaching. This explains the miscellaneous nature of the volume as a whole, and justifies especially the inclusion of that section entitled "Thoughts and Illustrations."

The editor owes warmest thanks to the Rev. Fergus Ferguson, D.D., for general supervision and advice; and to the Rev. D. W. Forrest, M.A., for help in choosing the Sermons.

J. H. L.

CONTENTS.

BIOGRAPHICAL SKETCH.

THIS is a memorial volume, and as such, makes appeal chiefly to those who knew its author, either personally or as a teacher. On this account, it has been thought well that the book should contain a short biographical sketch. Those who were acquainted with Dr. Leckie personally will be pleased to have the main points in his life recorded; while those who were attracted by his teaching or at any time gained inward help or stimulus from him, will not be indifferent as to what manner of man he was, or learn without some degree of interest what were the elements in his character and experience which gave to his message its characteristic form and drift.

Joseph Leckie was born at Falkirk in the year 1826, and spent his boyhood there. Of these Falkirk years it is not possible to write with any degree of fulness, for he himself spoke little of them. But this at least is certain, they were hard and unkindly years. His father died when he was but an infant; and during childhood he was, through circumstances which need not be dwelt on here, subjected to the control of a hard and tyrannous nature. This, along with straitened circumstances and the having to work early in childhood, robbed him of much which usually goes to make the freshness and vigour of youth.

In these days, when we wish to account for a man's characteristics we always seek first to know what sort of people his parents were; and in the case of Dr. Leckie this inquiry is not without profit. His father was a man of intensely devotional nature; quiet and reticent as a rule, but given to great outbursts of religious feeling, to long periods of retirement for fasting and prayer. He secluded himself in this way for an unusually long time shortly after his son's birth, and on being questioned about it by his wife, explained that he had been dedicating their child to the ministry of Christ. We cannot but regard this act of his as peculiarly solemn and pathetic when we remember that he at this time already stood, not unconsciously, in the near presence of death.

Mrs. Leckie was of a more practical turn, and never quite understood her husband's strange moods and enthusiasm; but she had much force and gentleness of character, a happy spirit that took the burden of things lightly, and withal a great love for the ballads and poetry of the Scottish tongue.

Who that knew Dr. Leckie does not recognize his

kinship with these two? With his habit of mental brooding over things and his profoundly devotional spirit, on the one hand, and his gleefulness, his unconquerable hopefulness of outlook, on the other—he was the worthy son of a father who spent long hours in fasting and prayer, and of a mother who went about the house in dark days singing the old Scots songs.

While he was still very young an incident took place which admirably illustrates the uncompromising strength with which he at all times held to any position which seemed to him the true one. It was the time when many were leaving the Secession Church and going over to the Evangelical Union, and among these was Mrs. Leckie. Her son, however, although considering his age one would hardly have expected him to hold strong theological views, absolutely refused to go with her, and continued to attend the old place of worship. It is interesting, in connection with this, to recall the fact that the Ibrox pulpit was the first one belonging to the United Presbyterian Church in which Dr. Morison preached after his expulsion from the Secession body.

In 1842 Dr. Leckie went to Glasgow University. Of the time spent there he never spoke with any great enthusiasm. It was perhaps not so very important a time in his life as it is in that of most men. The only teachers in the College who made much impression upon him were Professors Lushington and Ramsay; and in their classes only did he take honours. He had a keen love of scholarship in general, and an enthusiasm for the study of languages; but he never had the peculiarly academic spirit. University distinctions did not attract him. He never could submit to rules and regulations as to mental work, or limit himself to the line of study prescribed for any given class. His application was hard, continuous, prolonged; but it was not determined as to its object or manner by the requirements of the University. It is not, however, to be supposed that he did not take a good place in the classes. He was, as before said, a prizeman in Latin and Greek, and, as he used to tell with some amusement, twice lost prizes in Mental Philosophy through his having to leave College before the end of the session from sheer lack of funds.

During this college time he read widely in the classics, acquired a good knowledge of French and Italian, and laid the foundations of a solid German scholarship. At this time, also, began his lifelong habit of carefully studying the Greek Testament. It was probably, however, not till a little later than this that he began to read deeply in metaphysics. The teaching of the university on the subjects of mental and moral philosophy seems to have made but little impression on his mind. The position of the Scottish school on these subjects was never his. If it be true that all men belong implicitly to one or other of the

Philosophic schools, Dr. Leckie was a transcendentalist by nature.

As was the custom in those days, he entered the Divinity Hall while still attending the University. During the earlier part of his theological course he was a student of the Secession Church, but during the last two years he attended the United Presbyterian Hall. Many valuable friendships were formed there—some of these remaining for long, but nearly all being dissolved by death before his own life ended. He was always able to repeat the roll of his year, and used to dwell with affectionate characterization upon the different men.

The theological session at that time only lasted for two months, and, after the University course was finished, all the rest of the year was given up by the students to hard work, teaching and studying. Dr. Leckie at this time taught a school in the village of Airth; but of that school and of his teaching experiences there he never spoke with any degree of satisfaction. It was at Airth, however, that he met the Rev. Dr. Andrew Gardiner, of Dean Street, Edinburgh, who was through life one of his kindest and most faithful friends.

About the end of his student days he was prostrated by a severe attack of fever, which permanently enfeebled him and prepared the way for that oppressive, thwarting weakness against which his whole later life was a struggle.

In 1849, after being a probationer for a few months, he was called to Muirton, a weaving village in Kincardineshire. This call he accepted, though not without considerable hesitation and fear. " I have much need for direction," he writes at this time, " that darkness may be light before me. I hope that I shall be enabled to take the path of duty and to be without anxiety. I tremble to think of being minister of a church, however small—now that the matter has come to be a reality—and yet what can I do but go on. I have not put my hand to the plough to look back. I trust I have not so learned Christ."

" I have not put my hand to the plough to look back "—there could be no saying more characteristic of him than that. It might almost be written as the motto of his life. He never looked back. In the darkest days, he never once hesitated in his devotion to the ministry of Christ, or wished for anything better than just strength enough to go on with his work.

The years of his ministry at Muirton were filled with strenuous physical and mental labour. He read widely and intensely in general literature, and made a careful study of the Calvinistic theologians, especially Jonathan Edwards. The hardness of his application may be gauged from the fact that he made it a rule to begin reading at whatever hour in the morning he might first awake, be it ever so early. Then, the work belonging more closely to his pastorate was exceptionally hard. The congregation was very scattered, drawing its members partly from outlying farms and small hamlets, and partly from other more considerable villages, such as Laurencekirk and Fettercairn. In one or other of these latter, the young minister used to conduct a meeting every Sunday after his two regular services—and this involved a walk of about ten miles. Besides all this there was the labour involved in pastoral visitation among a people whose dwellings were scattered all round a wide countryside. What wonder that with work like this his already weakened constitution showed signs of giving way. The possibility of having to resign his pastorate began to haunt him in a few years after ordination ; but he struggled hard to hold to his post. The battle lasted for several years, but it was a losing battle all the time. First he gave up all general study, and concentrated himself upon the work connected with his charge ; then he stopped writing and committing sermons, and spoke from notes merely ; then he tried change of air and a little rest. But at last the futility of further struggle became apparent, and he demitted his charge in 1858. The Muirton congregation tried in every way to keep him ; they even offered to allow him to sit in the pulpit and read to them his old sermons, if only he would stay. But the same spirit that made him come to Muirton made him leave it. Having put his hand to the plough he would not look back. He would not hold a charge, the work of which he was unable to do —nor would he shrink from any sacrifice which offered hope of his regaining strength enough for the full service of the Christian ministry.

It was towards the end of the Muirton ministry that Mrs. Leckie died. Indeed, it was the great grief and anxiety connected with his mother's last illness and death that dealt the conquering blow to his already failing strength. He was not a man who spoke much about his sorrows; but there can be no doubt that the loss of his mother was the supreme grief of his life. Even in his later years, he spoke of the extreme difficulty which he sometimes had in realizing that she belonged now to another world, and had no more need of his support or his prayers. "I trust," he said to a friend once, "I trust God will forgive me if sometimes even yet I ask Him to have her in His good keeping."

If at Muirton, however, much was lost, much also was gained. There he first became acquainted with the great metaphysical teachers who afterwards chiefly influenced his mental life; and there he made his closest personal friendships, such as those of Rev. E. F. Scott, Dr. Fergus Ferguson, and Dr. John Ker. Of his meeting with the latter, Mr. Scott writes—"We remember his coming home after his introduction to Dr. Ker, and the enthusiasm with which he spoke of him, adding, 'And he doesn't know that he's a

genius.'" Thus began a friendship which was one
of the greatest treasures of his life. There have rarely
been two men who knew each other so well as these
two did. Differing greatly in temperament, and
perhaps sometimes in opinions also, there was yet a
most profound sympathy between them and a most
subtle understanding—an intimacy which was close,
and yet, at the same time, respectful and almost
reticent. The death of Dr. Ker in 1886 was the
greatest trial of Dr. Leckie's last years. Of other
men, eminent and well-beloved, who were taken away,
he had been able to speak in the pulpit with fulness
and feeling. But in this case, he spoke with reserve
and briefly. The memorial notice, also, which he
wrote for the *United Presbyterian Magazine*, at this
time, scarcely revealed his deep knowledge of Dr. Ker,
or the full tenderness and depth of his thoughts concerning him. But this reticence regarding the things
which he held most sacred was characteristic of the
man. He never spoke much of his mother; and he
could not write eloquently of his friend.

After the Muirton period came a long time of wandering about in search of health. He travelled in
Germany, Italy, Switzerland; stayed in Glasgow for
some time undergoing various kinds of medical treatment; took a voyage to Canada in a sailing ship, and
in all possible ways strove to recover his lost strength.
This was a period of weariness and frustration—of

disappointment and loneliness—a period in which all
his special tendencies and inclinations seemed to be
thwarted. Preaching was his very life, his joy and
strength ; yet for nearly six years he was condemned
to silence. His whole bent was towards reading and
production ; yet he was for the most part forbidden
either to read or write at any considerable length.
Of an active, energetic nature ; he was during nearly
all this period unable to walk beyond a few hundred
yards. A lover of quietness and home ; he yet was
compelled to continually wander about, having no
fixed dwelling place.

There were, however, large elements of compensation
hidden beneath the plentiful sorrows of these years.
They contained much experience of the kindliness of
the world ; for the worn-out and homeless preacher
received nothing but kindness on every hand. Again,
they gave large opportunity for the cultivation of that
conversational faculty which was latterly a peculiar
characteristic of his. The very fact, too, of his being
unable to read much encouraged his habit of studying
closely the types of character met with, and thus
greatly advanced that close knowledge of human
nature which was afterwards such an important
element in his preaching power.

Of his travels abroad during this period he used to
speak with great pleasure. All elements of pain and
trouble disappeared in the retrospect, and there re-

mained only the memory of stir and change, of "passing faces" full of kindness, of rich and responsive fellowship. Dr. Ker was at that time also unable for work, and the two friends went much about together in search of health. Many a happy day they spent in German university towns and Italian watering places, less occupied in sight-seeing than in observing and knowing the people around them. Dr. Leckie used to say how convinced his travels made him of the number of good people there were in the world.

Dr. Ker's power of adapting his conversation to any society in which he found himself, and his gift of repartee, greatly impressed his friend. He used to tell how once at dinner, a German, on happy thoughts intent, said to Dr. Ker, "How is it that you English have a hundred and twenty-four religions and only one sauce?" to which Dr. Ker replied, "How is it that you Germans have a hundred and twenty-four sauces and no religion?"

To these years of wandering Dr. Leckie owed a great increase of his love for the German tongue, its poetry and folk-songs. A great favourite of his through all after years was the ballad, "Es zogen drei Burschen wohl über den Rhein." He was never weary of repeating it and pointing out its beauties, often dwelling with dreamy delight on the last verse—

"Ich liebte dich immer, ich lieb dich noch heut',
    Und werde dich lieben in Ewigkeit."

It is not to be supposed, either, that no reading was done during these years. He always had one book with him wherever he went—perhaps Emerson, or Tennyson, or Heine, or Kant's Kritik—and this book he would read by short passages at a time. Wherever he went, also, he was sure to get some one pressed into the service of reading aloud.

In estimating the hardship of this period, one has further to bear in mind Dr. Leckie's peculiarly hopeful constitution. He might be cast down for a little; but he never desponded long. The slightest sign of improvement in health would raise him to the heights of elation; and he never looked to the future. Where money was to come from, or what was to happen if he did not grow strong, troubled him comparatively little. He lived in the present—partly through natural temperament, and partly by reason of his simple, unobtrusive trust in God. He talked less of piety and prayer than most men; but he had a peculiarly vivid, persistent realization of the present God. He preached much about the duty and the joy of this trust in the Highest and communion with Him; and he spoke that he knew and had seen.

Towards the end of these six years he began to preach occasionally, as his strength would allow.

And the joy of this return to work it is hard to estimate. The doors of the prison house were opening at last; the long period of silence was coming to an end. He went forth from his retirement, not indeed with the old physical strength, but with a richer, fresher message, with a subtler knowledge of men, with a deeper, fuller spirit of devotion. Henceforth there was to be struggle and weakness enough; but never total inability for labour. He went forth to his work and to his toil until the evening.

In 1864 he was called to Millport, where a new congregation had just been planted. So doubtful was he about his strength that he refused the call twice before finally accepting it. His ministry at Millport, however, was most vigorous and successful. It is doubtful whether he ever had an audience which suited him better than that which crowded his church there in the summer time. It was a shifting audience, it is true, but varied and intelligent; affording stimulus by its freshness. There, as during the first ten years of his Ibrox ministry, he did not write and commit, but spoke from notes. Many people say that he reached heights sometimes in these extempore sermons which he never attained afterwards; but, on the other hand, he felt that the strain of preparing for this kind of preaching was too much for his strength. He used also to speak of the feeling of defeat and despair with which he often left the pulpit after extempore speech.

b

And it is doubtful whether he would ever have adopted this style after his return to work, had it not been that for a long time he was physically unequal to the task of writing. In his latter days he always maintained that while every one should be able on occasion to speak extempore, he should make it a practice to write his sermons—and so avoid the danger of falling into repetition and commonplace.

At Millport he had opportunity of indulging that taste for sailing which he had formed in Italy. "He would sit oot in a boat for hoors looking at the clouds. He was an awfu' thinking cratur!" were the words in which the Millport beadle afterwards summed up his reminiscences of him. This saying has the patronizing tone proper to beadles, but it is strictly true to facts. Then, and up to the very last summer of his life, he was an enthusiastic sailor. No weather daunted him, no breeze was too fresh. He loved to feel the salt spray flying, and to have the boat burying her side deep in the foaming water. Many a text and many an illustration he got, in later years, during long sails about the Kyles of Bute and the Firth of Clyde. It was his delight to get comfortably settled in the boat of a bright summer evening, and let the influence of sea and sky, with all their subtle suggestion, have full sway over him. At such times he would repeat, in half conscious monologue, ideas for sermons, reminiscences of old days, scraps of German

Lieder, and Scots songs and ballads.   The constant reference to natural scenes and objects in his sermons rises out of one of his most striking characteristics— his intense love of nature and power of associating its varied moods and forms with things belonging to human life and spiritual experience.   It was not that he consciously sought for parallels so much as that they were always suggesting themselves to him.   His mind was essentially unifying, reconciling, mediatorial —sensitively responsive to all that spoke of the unity and harmony of things.

Just before going to Millport he had married Eliza Hannay Meikle.   Of her it may be out of place to speak much here.   But if Dr. Leckie was enabled, in spite of weakness, to hold a city pastorate for so long a time, and to accomplish some good work in his generation, it was largely through the sustaining, stimulating power of his wife.   Herself an entire invalid for nearly twenty years; she was yet, more than most strong women, able to help and to cheer.   Out of the depths of her own weakness she was always able to bring strength for others.   Whenever the heavy grasp of pain was relaxed a little, the natural joyous- ness of her spirit leaped up with unconquerable brightness.   She was not able to go about among the people, her voice was not heard in their homes or their gatherings ; but a wide and subtle influence proceeded from her silent ministry of suffering, and no one could

enter that sick room without receiving a lesson impressive and elevating beyond the common eloquence
of men. Of her Dr. Ferguson says: "It was not
merely that she was patient and unmurmuring, but
rather this, that the essential activity of her mind and
the cheerfulness of her spirit so triumphed over the
enforced passivity of her condition, as to leave no
trace behind of any morbidness of feeling, but a most
healthy tone and ring in all she said and did; with a
brave and loyal acceptance of the will of God. She
looked.out with a broad and clear intelligence upon
all that was going on in church and world, and was
in full sympathy with progressive and liberal ideas."

The introducing of this reference to Mrs. Leckie
is justified. For there could be no true account given
of Dr. Leckie's life and the influences which shaped
his teaching, without reference to this strongest influence
of all.

In 1866 Dr. Leckie received a call from the new
congregation which had just been established at Ibrox
—then the extreme outpost of Glasgow to the south-
west. There were less than thirty names appended to
the call; and for a year or two after he went to
Ibrox the congregation worshipped in a little wooden
church, holding two hundred or so. In the year sixty-
eight, however, it removed into the stone building
which it still occupies. At the opening of this new
church, there preached Dr. W. B. Robertson in the

morning, Dr. Leckie in the afternoon, and Dr. Ker in the evening. It was a great day in the church, and a great day in the minister's house. The social intercourse between the three at that time was, to one of them at least, an always pleasant memory.

The principal public incidents in Dr. Leckie's Ibrox ministry were the receiving of his degree in 1876, his work in connection with the Revision of the Standards, 1877, and the publication of his volume of sermons in 1884.

The second of these was almost the only public work of an ecclesiastical nature which he allowed himself to enter upon with enthusiasm. And it did absorb him for the time being heart and soul. The intensity of his conviction as to the worthiness of the cause for which he was fighting, and the care with which he had studied the whole question involved, are clearly shown in the long notes on the subject which are found among his papers. The objects he had in view in his action at this time were (first) that ministers and elders should not be made to subscribe to a larger creed than that which was required of ordinary members; and (secondly) that it should be no longer necessary for men to profess a belief in any formulated solutions of the hard and abstruse problems connected with the Foreknowledge of God. His position is clearly laid down in the "Remarks" which he appended in Committee to his written suggestions as to Revision.

"Reconstruction better than Revision: We should have a brief creed, containing only essentials, and binding on members as well as office-bearers.

If neither reconstruction nor revision be entered upon, the terms of adhesion should give freedom as to the points objected to. The three following propositions should be put in a prominent place:—(1) God loves all men and desires the salvation of all; (2) Christ is the propitiation for the sins of the whole world; (3) the Holy Spirit strives with men, and seeks to convert all to whom the Word of God comes."

The following passages taken from his note book will further explain his attitude.

"There are many minds who will not be bound by logic. It is not the logical understanding that is the main power with them, but what some might call the pure Reason—others, the Synthesis of the whole being. They respect Aristotle, and may call him, with Dante, 'the first of those who know,' but they follow Plato by instinct. Their convictions on anything in the sphere of Spirit never rest on mere logical proof, but on the assent and consent of their inward nature as a whole.

"People of this sort, of course, never can receive any elaborate creed except in its general spirit and essence. They may be as loyal as others—but it is after their own fashion. Now, should there not be room in an orthodox church for people of this sort?"

Again : " Logic has its sphere only in regions where all the terms are known and capable of definition. *E.g. The Will of God*—who can define that thoroughly so as to be sure that he has presented it fairly ? (What does 'purpose' mean in a Being whose relation to time is so different from ours ?) Are we really capable of taking up that grand word and making triumphant, inexorable, unanswerable syllogisms with it ? I am afraid of syllogisms where they have such awful, vast, mysterious quantities in them. It is the x in an algebraic formula. You may be very skilful with $+$ and $-$ and $=$; but what is your result after all ? It is merely x."

Again : "I only want a few things fixed and clear— but these must be very fixed and solid. I want to have no doubts or clouds about them at all. But I have little concern about the rest being shapeless. Indeed they are better so. When there is anything like a closed-in system, I feel as if I wanted to be out—to get breath and freedom and reality."

Certain great truths stood always out before his mind with unmistakable reality—as the Fatherhood of God, the Sacrificial Atonement of Christ, the possibility of a direct Communion with the Divine. Of such things he was entirely, passionately convinced. In talking of these his whole face used to light up with the great joy of an enthusiastic belief, and his voice to tremble with emotion. His hope for humanity, and it was great, centred in the Cross of Christ ; his belief in the essential goodness of the world and of life, a belief which grew more assured with every year, rested upon the Redeeming love of God.   A few weeks before he died he said, "The longer I live the more does the ultimate triumph of good become for me a necessity of thought"; and about the same time he confessed that he grounded all hope of acceptance in the hour of death upon the merits of Christ alone.

It will be thus seen how Dr. Leckie's hostility to some parts of the Confession of Faith was rooted in the deepest elements of his nature.   His peculiarly tender sympathy with the various types of men led him to dislike all such over-theorizing as would tend to alienate minds of a certain class ; his mystical turn caused him to distrust instinctively all play of logic in these higher fields of thought "where logic is but a game in the dark"; while the very depth of his belief in the great Catholic doctrines of Christianity made him an enemy of all such teaching as seemed to obscure these and hide them in their full breadth and grandeur from the eyes of men.

Concerning his every-day life and pastoral work, there need not be much said here.   He was never able to walk a great deal, and this hindered him from visiting the people so frequently as he would have liked. But in any case of serious illness he was most faithful and unremitting in his care ; and many who passed through bereavement during his pastorate can bear witness to the peculiar tenderness and power of his ministry to the dying.

His most characteristic gift as a pastor, however, lay in his faculty of meeting those who were in moral or intellectual doubt. With dramatic and sentimental doubters he never, indeed, had any sympathy; but if a man was really in difficulty his patience with him was inexhaustible. Many a long hour which could ill be spared was given up in this way to the helping of people. Sometimes his help was given in a simple sentence or two which lingered long in the memory. A lady who belonged to Ibrox Church during the first year or two of his ministry tells how she once went to him in difficulty as to the question of the salvation of infants, and received the simple answer, " Never believe any ill of your Heavenly Father, He is better and kinder than any one else you know." On another occasion this lady came to tell him of an old friend who "had passed her that day without recognition, on account of some fancied wrong which could have been explained in a word." " Ah, well, just have patience. It will all be explained some day. And your friend will be very *magnanimous* ·in Heaven. There is wonderful magnanimity in Heaven."

In one case, an enterprising student of divinity came to ask if the orthodox belief did not involve that so-and-so (a religious teacher of the Theistic school) must be lost ? and was met with the counter-question—"Do you think any one can be lost that loves God ? "

His mode of preparing for the Sunday's work is well described in the paper appended to this notice by Mr. Forrest. In one sense he was always making sermons, in another sense his pulpit work absorbed only from two days to one a week. Often he had not chosen his subject for the evening sermon till late on Saturday night. The finding of a text in such a case was the finding of a treasure—a triumph to be announced with beaming face and exultant spirit. Once a good text was got, the way was clear. He wrote with incredible rapidity, some of his best sermons being produced in less than four hours.

The social side of Dr. Leckie's nature was very strong. Often, indeed, in a company of people he would, either through physical depression or absent-mindedness, be almost entirely silent. But when he was well and in the mood, no one enjoyed society more. Meeting with a few brother ministers of kindred spirit was a great delight, and often he said things at such times which were perhaps better than any saying in his sermons. But it was not by any means in 'intellectual' society only that he found pleasure. If men were open and frank and broad-hearted, though their mental power might be little enough and their culture less, he was at once drawn to them, and would spend a long time in their society with the most entire satisfaction. In

such company he often showed a side of his nature
which was hidden from the wise—a joyous, even
rollicking strain, little suspected by those who knew
him only in the sphere of theology and thought.
Nothing broadly human came amiss to him. The only
things on which he was really hard were narrowness
and dramatism and insincerity. Sentimentality and
pietistical talk he also fervently disliked.

But while he loved and entered into the healthy
happiness of men, the pathetic side of human life was
always before him. " After a long ministry my prevailing feeling for my people and friends is one of deep
compassion," was a saying of his in one of his later
years. He had a deep and growing pity for the whole
race of men with its labour and pain; and spite of
the faith and hope which he had, his restless mind was
forever working and puzzling over the painful riddle of
things.

This deep realization of the negative side of life was,
no doubt, greatly strengthened by his personal acquaintance with pain and defeat. That struggle with disease of the nervous system to which reference has had
to be made so often, went on till the end. And the
full extent of this struggle was known to few—partly
because he was very reticent as to his ailments, and
partly because the weakness was not such as shows
itself in emaciation or pallor. One of the chief trials
connected with this sort of trouble is that people do

not understand it. If a man looks well he must in popular estimation *be* well. And hence Dr. Leckie, naturally one of the most energetic of men, was constantly throwing himself open to the charge of indolence. His congregation, however, showed him throughout the greatest kindness and consideration. Few congregations can have less to regret in looking back than have the Ibrox people in reviewing their dealings with their late pastor.

In the early part of 1887 Dr. Leckie's strength began seriously to give way. That summer he went to Norway, but returned no better. His holiday was extended, and he spent the rest of the year at Crieff Hydropathic. There he gained strength enough to begin preaching again on the first Sunday of the new year. But it was evident from the first that much of his old power was gone, and he had actually to be supported by external means during the delivery of his sermons. Yet he managed to struggle on, with one or two breaks, until the Communion Sabbath in June, when he left the pulpit never to return. Had he been able to realize that his work was done, as he left the church that day, his remaining time on earth would have been darker than it was. For his work was his life. When at the end of the summer it was resolved that a colleague should be got, an incident occurred which showed touchingly this love of his for the service of the Christian ministry. He was composing a letter to his congregation on the subject of the contemplated change and, being unable to write, was dictating it to his daughter. In course of the letter the phrase occurred—" The work which I have loved so well." " Are you sure you have that in,—' The work which I have loved so well'?" he asked ; and two or three times repeated the words, " that I have loved so well." It seemed as if that phrase expressed the whole burden of his life—the joy of his manhood, the regret and pathos of his evening time.

After this, the disease advanced with rapid strides. He soon became completely prostrated and lost all physical power. But he kept full control of his mind to the end, and remained keenly interested in all the topics which had been wont most to occupy him. Only a few days before his death he dictated some notes regarding two of the elders who had been taken away ; and, although his voice was very weak and broken, the old insight into character and the old power of vivid statement were clearly apparent in his words. In the long conflict of his strong will and intellect with the weakness and unresponsiveness of his body, the inward powers remained triumphant to the end. But on the 2nd of January the struggle ceased. He fell into a state of unconsciousness, and passed quietly away next morning—January 3rd, 1889.

These are the main points in the life of Joseph Leckie. It is hoped that acquaintance with them may help those who knew him a little to understand better any elements in his character which seemed to them strange, and may also cast an interpreting light upon his teaching, for those to whom that teaching is of value.

We have called this book " Life and Religion," because the title seems well to convey the general drift of the volume. And, indeed, these two great words standing together indicate the whole content of Dr. Leckie's message. He spoke much of religion— the truths on which it rests, the devotion which supports it, the conditions of its growth and power. Much also he spoke of human life—its vast mysteries, its pathos, temptations, weariness, pain, and joy. But he never took either of these by itself. Life needed religion, and religion was determined in its nature by the requirements of life. No truth was true except in relation to life. No life was real except as founded on truth.

Between two great points his mind continually moved—God and Humanity. Not God the absolute, the Idea; but God the living, the moral, the incarnate in Christ. Not man in the abstract—but as he actually is, with his strange complexity of nature, his "grandeur and gloom."

And whatever may be thought of the teaching and its form, this at least is true: it was no traditional telling of an old tale, no mere exposition of a time honoured system of doctrine, but the genuine message of a strong and sincere personality—a real voice of faith and hope rising out of a life more than usually burdened with care and yet more joyous and unaffected than is common, a life which was very much at home in the world, and yet had a true and direct relation to the unseen Life which wraps us round.

J. H. L.

NOTE BY REV. FERGUS FERGUSON, D.D.

IN offering a contribution to this volume, at the request of the Editor, I feel that I cannot do better than submit the following statement, taken from the close of a sermon preached in Ibrox United Presbyterian Church, on Sabbath forenoon, January 13th, 1889.

Of Dr. Leckie's ministry in your midst, I am called to speak to those who have had experience of his worth and work as no one who was not in constant attendance upon his ministrations could have. I cannot presume to say all that ought to be said, or that might be said ; and this is not the place for vain eulogy or extravagant praise. But I know that I have your indulgent sympathy, in addition to the claim of a deeply attached friendship of thirty years' duration. Knowing, too, something of what work in a great city implies, I can bear witness to the fact that those twenty-two years of your late lamented pastor's life meant a struggle of which very few indeed could have any adequate conception. Even robust men have found the half of that time in a city charge, where they put their heart into their work, sufficient to take out of them the whole freshness and vigour of life. To labour on for twenty years, at such a high level, with fluctuating health, was no common achievement. Your beloved pastor had a great and constant struggle to maintain against weariness and inadequate strength. No one knows what the mental strain and spiritual drain of the pulpit amounts to in these days but he who has to sustain it. It is impossible to sustain it, if one has not the constant presence and help of the Master, a heartfelt interest and even keen enjoyment in the work itself, and the confidence and sympathy of one's own congregation, with the assurance that one is not labouring in vain. Your revered pastor had all these elements of strength and satisfaction ; and therefore he was enabled to labour on. His whole life and strength were put into his work. It was the joy of his heart, the sole and supreme endeavour of his life, to bring forth to you in their most striking and attractive form those treasures of grace and truth with which his own soul was enriched and made glad; and if he sometimes seemed to husband his resources, or to avoid other forms of labour during the week, need I say to you that it arose from his anxiety to be fresh and well for his spiritual task on the Lord's Day.

I have said that he put his life into his work, and it is to some of the characteristics of that work that I would now recall your thoughts. To speak of his work as a preacher of the Gospel is to speak of his

life. The deep inner current of his whole being ran
steadily in this direction; so steadily as to withdraw
his attention from a thousand things in which a less
absorbed and concentrated spirit might have taken
an interest. His reading and conversation, rich and
broad and varied as they were, especially when in the
company of other preachers and students, always con-
verged more or less upon the work he had to do, not
at all as a professional matter, but as a profoundly
spiritual reality in which all men ought to feel an
interest. A shrewd observer of human nature, he had
a very exact knowledge of men and affairs, in so far
as he cared to look at them; but the whole burden
and emphasis of his life and thought were cast upon
the other side—upon the spiritual side—and this gave
to him sometimes an air of abstraction and an appearance of indifference, in relation to ordinary affairs,
very apt to be misunderstood. The mystical element was strongly developed in him—an element not
at all essentially morbid or unreal, but lying rather
in the direction of all that is most real. In his
preaching he taught, what the Scriptures in their
inner meaning also disclose, that the outer material
form of existence is not the reality at all. It is
at best but the husk or shell within which the kernel
of truth is to be found. The death of the outer form
is but the breaking of the shell, by means of which we
are brought all the more into contact with the living

truth.   The spiritual element in which he moved was more manifest in his case than with many Christian men.   This seemed to arise from the degree to which his life was one long thought; for thought to him was spirit and life.   It was the fountain-head of all high, pure feeling—what we call emotion, as distinguished from mere sensation.   He was not at all a sensational preacher, in the ordinary sense of that word, playing upon the mere surface sensibilities of others, and studying those effects that appeal to the senses alone, as distinguished from the mind; but he was an emotional preacher.   The very tone of his voice when beginning a religious service put one into a devout frame of mind, as a worthy member of the congregation, now deceased, once said to me. To read attentively his volume of published sermons is to see how charged his preaching was with deep, pure feeling.   This feeling runs high in all his discourses.   It seems to be the uniting element in them all, and it implies the profoundest thought. Sometimes, indeed frequently, it flows between two opposite poles of thought.   In all profound and accurate thought there is this recognition of two sides, between which, especially in view of our inability to reconcile the seeming opposites, we are nevertheless bound to recognize, there springs up in the soul those fountains of pure feeling, of sanctified emotion, and of " thoughts that lie too deep for tears," in which the very essence of worship and the very soul of devotion are to be found.

Between those seeming opposites, both of which are true, the soul need not be driven to scepticism, nor need it be lost in an abyss of doubt. It is filled rather with wonder and awe, with reverence and aspiration and humility such as could not be felt at all from a merely one-sided view of life, or from the vain confidence that one has mastered the whole matter. This two-sidedness, giving rise as it does in a believing mind to profound emotion, is opposed to the narrowness and bigotry of the purely sectarian spirit, which sees only one side of a question, and will not look at any other. Hence the catholicity of Dr. Leckie's spirit. Faithful to his own Communion, he none the less belonged to the universal Church. He was supremely interested in the essence of things rather than in their accidents. One has only to name his favourite authors in order to see how immense was the range of his intellectual sympathics. Emerson and Martineau, Jonathan Edwards and Beecher, Wordsworth and Browning, Jacob Böhme and Hegel, Rothe and Lotze, not to speak of many nearer home, he read and studied. He had not much interest in theological systems as such. Even at their best, they seemed to him a mere temporary framework, or scaffolding of truth. He had no difficulty at all in holding firmly and clearly to all the essential doctrines of Christianity, to the Incarnation and the Atonement,

to Justification by Faith and the Sovereignty of Divine
Grace, and at the same time keeping his mind open to
the movements of modern thought.   Those movements
of thought, with all the dogmatic changes they are so
sure to bring, did not seem to him to imply any dis-
turbance of the centre upon which we rest, and from
which we can never move—the centre of a living and
glorified Christ.   His mind was so frankly open to truth
under all its forms, and so essentially eclectic, that like
a magnet, it drew from all systems, and gathered even
from an otherwise poor book such grains of gold as it
might contain.   Corresponding to this was the character of the influence he had over others.   He had at
once the confidence of the orthodox and the ear of
those opening and ingenuous minds who do not belong
to any school or party. The attraction of his preaching
was selective in its character ; it drew people of culture
and refinement, and especially those who had sympathics akin to his own.

It was thus that your revered minister was all along
a fresh and original preacher, and never could be anything else.   Keeping so near the centre, to which he
was held by the spell of a supreme attraction, he
sunned himself all around in the light of truth, and
never went off at a tangent from his own true orbit.
In this way he brought forth the fruits and flowers of
a truly original mind, which knew the secret of keeping close to all that is good in the past, and abreast of

all that is good in the present ; neither stereotyped
on the one hand as clinging to the old, nor eccentric
on the other hand as going with the new ; but like a
wise householder, bringing out of his treasures that
which is at once old and new ; old as the morning of
creation, and yet new as this present morning of God.

His simplicity of mind was a marked feature of his
character, by which I mean his singleness of eye and
purity of aim. Amid the warring crowd of paltry
ambitions one meets with in daily life, he never lost
sight of the one great and holy end of human life.
This gave insight into the character of others. Ob-
livious as he might seem to the mere externalities of
life, he could read off a character at a glance, and dis-
solve by a single word the most pretentious sham.
Affectation and insincerity were the objects of his
implacable disgust. The one word that covered his
deepest characteristic—and with this I shall close—
was his passionate love of reality. Alas, " what
shadows we are, and what shadows we pursue," if we
are not smitten by this same love of the Eternal
Real. The one text from which he always seemed to
preach was this : Be real, be true, be sincere. He did
not think it an easy thing to be sincere in this world
of compromise, conventionality, and all kinds of polite
falsehood. He knew that it meant a struggle and involved a sacrifice ; but he thought it was worth
the struggle and the sacrifice to keep one's soul

unstained by pretence; and rather than run the risk of appearing to be interested, or to believe in that which had no merit in his eyes, he suffered himself many a time to be grievously misunderstood; and yet there lay in his inmost nature and spirit the finest essence of courtesy.   Across the uniform solemnity of his life there played occasionally the sweet radiance of a childlike mirth, reminding one of those sunny ripples that sometimes flit across the surface of the calm, sad sea.   Can we wonder that a man so divinely gifted and so variously endowed was great in prayer?   You know, my friends, better than I can tell you, with what freedom and elevation, with what majesty and pathos, he touched and lifted your souls.   And now he who arose so frequently from this very spot on wings of supplication to the gates of heaven has wholly passed within the veil to look upon the Beatific Vision, while we are left, with sorrowing hearts, upon the footstool still.   Let us learn the lesson of a saintly life.   The message has been delivered and the burden laid down.   Be it ours to lay to heart the call to a life of faith and hope and love.

NOTE BY REV. D. W. FORREST, M.A.

IT is not for me to attempt an estimate of Dr. Leckie's work as a whole.   My acquaintance with him began in 1883, so that I can only speak of him as he appeared in his later days to one who, though belonging to a younger generation, had the good fortune to be admitted to a close intimacy. During those six years I had every opportunity of knowing what manner of man he was, and what were the thoughts that most attracted and possessed him, as the end drew near.

His personality was very pronounced, both in its strength and in its limitations. He had almost nothing of the practical gift—the energy, the alertness, the love of details, the ambition for 'managing things,' that distinguish the man of affairs. His interest lay in the wider problems of man's life, in the motives that sway his action and the laws that govern his destiny. The predominant characteristic of his mind was its *inward* quality : but the inwardness was speculative, not introspective. There was no morbid self-analysis. No one took broader or saner views of life. The world on which he brooded so much, was not the world of his own moods and feelings, but the great objective spiritual world which lies everywhere at the heart of the visible.

The influence which he wielded over his congregation came simply from the power and freshness of his message. He was not able, from physical causes, to overtake frequent or extensive pastoral visitation ; and the arts and methods of church organization were not his. Week by week, however, his preaching braced and soothed men by its elevation and its fine insight.

It owed nothing of its effect to rhetoric.   His delivery
had a direct and veracious impressiveness of its own, ·
and there were searching tones of pathos in his
voice.   But he never seemed to alter a sentence
for euphony or flow.   At times indeed, one might
have wished a greater regard to artistic demands, a
more pliant adaptation to the needs or weaknesses of
the ordinary worshipper.   For a long period it was
not his practice to write out his sermons beforehand.
He pondered over his subject for days, till it grew upon
him and possessed him, and then he spoke out of the
fulness of the treasures he had gathered.   This method
suited a mind of his intense absorbing temperament.
But it cost him so much nervous strain, that he ultimately abandoned it, and for the last ten years or so he
both wrote and read his discourses.   Yet the former
spontaneous, almost colloquial, manner of expression
remained.   He composed quickly, as if he were con-
versing ; set down his thoughts just as they came.
There was no *labor limae,* no effort after an exact dove-
tailing of parts, no complete working out of any single
idea.   From a literary standpoint the sermon might
easily be open to criticism as somewhat unbalanced.
Repetitions occurred in it, like the refrain in a song.
But then it was not meant as literature ; it was the
testimony of a soul that had communed in the deeps
and on the heights with God, and learned much concerning His ways.   And the same was true of Dr.

Leckie's public prayers. They were the natural out-
pouring of a rich and devout nature, a personal colloquy with a personal Lord. A fixed form of prayer,
however beautiful, seemed to him to secure the aesthetic
at the expense of the religious, because it did not adapt
itself to the ever new and varying character of the
soul's necessities. He himself sought to obtain this
freshness of devotional expression by drawing his inspiration from the Book of Psalms. He would choose
a Psalm before service, and make a few of its leading
ideas, not always in the order in which they stood, the
basis of his supplications and intercessions. By thus
following freely the lines of the great devotional book
of the Christian Church, he believed that the spirit of
prayer in all its richness and directness was best maintained and fostered.

Personally, he was a man of many reserves, and was not
always easy to know. Those who only met him accident-
ally or occasionally, might come away without the least
impression of his power. If the question discussed did
not attract him, or if his companion were of a narrow
and disputative turn, he would possibly take refuge in
silence. And so he had often a withdrawn look, as of
one whose thoughts dwelt in a world by themselves.
Something of this was due to bodily depression: partly
it was the result of habits formed in the retirement and
solitude forced upon him by prolonged ill-health. This
frequent irresponsiveness in ordinary society was the

'defect' that attached to his meditative 'quality.' On the other hand, when he was in harmony with his surroundings, he revealed himself with astonishing frankness. He would talk of the deepest things of life with a certain personal accent and reference. You felt how absolutely free he was from all trammels of traditionalism. He had travelled by a way of his own, and was not at all anxious to square his experiences with prevalent opinions.

Dr. Leckie belonged essentially to the type of the Mystics. Both outward nature and the activities of mankind were to him parts of one spiritual order. He was "haunted for ever by the Eternal Mind," and he had no high opinion of mere logic as an organon either of discovering or of verifying its sacred messages, which bore their witness not to the formal reason but to the whole being of man in its breadth and depth. Emotion, aspiration, conscience, were factors in the process as really as thought. The knowledge of the Divine was not a prize to be won by the victorious militant intellect, but a heritage to be *received*, a vision granted to the soul through its richest experiences.

"The best kind of meditation," he says in his first volume of Sermons (p. 307), "is closely akin to reverie. I know that reverie is accused of many faults, and that it finds little mercy. Still the light, soft, gentle way in which reverie deals with subjects, is the best for moral purposes. Begin to examine a subject more formally, and the mental interest becomes stronger than the spiritual.   The greatest subjects refuse to give off their aroma, they utter no music to the soul, they shine in no splendours, they touch with no pathos, when they are pressed and scrutinized.   You must touch them, almost at unawares, taking them by a kind of surprise. .   .   .   .   The more you lose yourself in the great themes the better.   He who never loses himself in these, never truly finds them."

No words could more accurately describe his own method.   He laid himself open to all influences, whether from nature or men or books, that proved their right of entrance by their power to nourish the higher life. For he felt that the Spirit of God chose many avenues, and that the impatient or heedless closing of any of them might imply serious impoverishment.   It was impossible for him to believe in the adequacy of those categories in which many sought to sum up in regular detail the entire Christian verity.   He was indeed, and ever claimed to be, an Evangelical, in his profound faith in Christ and in the necessity of Christ for souls. This was a matter to him absolutely central, and he never swerved from it.   He accepted also the substitutionary theory of the Atonement as an explanation of one part of the truth, because, as he said, the principle of substitution ran through life.   But his Evangelicalism was rather affirmative than negative. He preached Christ not only as indispensable to the individual, but as standing in organic relation to Humanity, and as the prophecy and sure condition of a regenerated world. The life and death of Christ were precious to him as interpreting and making clear the Divine which enveloped and permeated man everywhere.

His instinct for Transcendentalism was quickened by two chief influences. The first was Jacob Boehme, whom he studied early in his career, and whom he knew as very few men in this country have done. The second was Emerson, whose essays he so completely absorbed that latterly he ceased reading them, " for he was laying too great a spell upon me." Even a slight critical gift may still see the stamp of Emerson in the style of the sermons, the short self-contained sentences, the surprising imaginative touches, the penetrating spirituality. One of his noblest discourses—that on *Compensation*—was inspired from the same source.

A man who so lived and moved in the spiritual, to whom fellowship with God in Christ was the most indubitable of all experiences, had no room or cause for panic as to the future of the Church. The modification of dogmatic forms in accordance with the changing customs of generations and the fresh lessons of Providence, was in his view rather a ground for gratitude : it meant another stage in man's apprehension of the Infinite Goodness. It was a loosening of the things which can be shaken; that the things which cannot be shaken might remain. He realized as clearly

as any the immense forces which to-day array themselves not only against Christianity, but against any
Divine rendering of human life. But this neither
dimmed his vision, nor chilled his ardour—

> " Whoso hath *felt* the Spirit of the Highest
> Cannot confound, nor doubt Him, nor deny."

Not in defiance, but in quietness and confidence, he
anticipated the issue, staying himself upon his God.
Thus at peace himself, he had the tenderest sympathy
with those who were in religious bewilderment, and
were crying out for light. And he had just the
qualities that make a good confessor for a perplexed
soul. He had no cut-and-dried formula to prescribe as
the test of truth and the condition of salvation. The
approaches to souls were, he knew, as various as life
itself, and the finest wisdom is needed to discover
where the approach lies. Help is often best given
where the intention is least apparent, where there is
no obvious determination to drive to a particular conclusion. It is said of Bushnell, who in his earlier days
had been the hero of many a fight, that latterly " he did
not wrestle with or for the truth so much as before : *he
waited rather for it to shine.*" That was true of Joseph
Leckie also. He did not dispute or argue. He suggested, widened, uplifted. As his own convictions
were arrived at not by logic, but by brooding over
many thoughts, by receptivity, by assimilation ; so in
dealing with others he did not strive or cry, but sought

to raise them gently into the same calm atmosphere, as of the Divine Presence. Sometimes it was astonishing to watch his patience in listening even to one who prided himself on his aggressive scepticism. He once remarked to me, " If a person talks blatant or foolish heresy, or intimates with a superior air that Christianity is played out, and that science has proved there is no God or future state at all, I never look startled or hurt. It is a great mistake to show irritation or alarm. Leave him alone, and he will soon settle down." With some men that might be a mere dictate of prudence and shrewdness : in his case, it was the natural outcome of an assured religious conviction. All the violence and rabidity in the world, he felt, could not alter facts.

This fearless faith was the deepest thing in his character. It grew and strengthened with the years. Nothing was more touching than to find, during his last weeks of sad bodily oppression and infirmity, that its flame shone as brightly as before. Never was he less inclined to tremble for the Ark. Nay, he dwelt more than ever on the thought of final Restitution as the goal to which God's revelation pointed. It was with this feeling that on the Sunday before he died, he desired to have read to him the eighth chapter of Romans. That had always been a favourite passage with him, gathering up as it does all things in heaven and earth, and illuminating them with the glory of

Christ's Redemption ; beginning with " the groaning of the creature " and ending with the *Quis separabit ?* So also the hymn, which perhaps of all hymns he best loved, was that noble one of Faber's, " Souls of men, why will ye scatter ? "   He was wont to say that, if he should recover, he would have it sung in church. It is easy to see why it charmed him—

> " There's a wideness in God's mercy
> Like the wideness of the sea.
>
> . . . .
>
> For the love of God is broader
> Than the measures of man's mind,
> And the Heart of the Eternal
> Is most wonderfully kind.
> But we make His Love too narrow
> By false limits of our own ;
> And we magnify His strictness
> With a zeal He will not own.

Thus he passed from us into his own land of Spirits, with a Hope, in God and for man, "full of immortality." .

SERMONS.

WORSHIP.

"The hour cometh, and now is, when the true worshippers shall worship the Father in spirit and in truth: for the Father seeketh such to worship Him. God is a Spirit: and they that worship Him must worship Him in spirit and in truth."—John iv. 23, 24.

IT should not surprise us that Jesus uttered such elevated truths in circumstances so humble and obscure. You have seen in a dull cloudy day, when sunshine seemed gone from the earth, a streak of brightness breaking through a rift in the leaden expanse, and resting on some distant moorland farm or shepherd's hut; and perhaps to some sad eyes there the golden flood was as welcome as it could have been in places more prominent. Some of the greatest utterances of our Lord were drawn forth in a purely incidental way. What we would deem isolated outstanding incidents in life are often points of attraction for great ideas or strong influences, avenues for which God, who besets us everywhere, waits to disclose Himself. Here the point of contact was found in one who seemed not sympathetic, but whose whole interest in religion was centred in a traditional controversy about Gerizim and Jerusalem. But our Lord has reminded us that the spark of devotion lies sleeping in every human heart, that the sublimest truths are not thrown away when presented even to those who seem enclosed in a husk of earthliness, that it *needs* the highest ideas to reach the lowest, and that such ideas may have an awakening power though at the time they seem to be ignored and turned aside. If there is a spirit in man, it can never quite shut itself up from the touch of spirit and the call of thoughts which are akin. It is the individual that God seeks, and when the soul is made to feel itself singled out and known, sought for and valued by eternal love and wisdom, it begins to look homeward. What a great day dawns for a soul when it feels that the grandness of truth, and the loftiest heights of experience, have a real birth relation to itself, are open to it, and belong to it. It is this contact of great heavenly truths with the very concrete realities of our personal condition, lot and history, which touches us to the core.

The truths on which all the rest depend are two— God is a Spirit, and God is a Father. On the Fatherhood of God worship depends; it is because God is a Father that he *seeks* to be worshipped. By the spirituality of God the character of worship is determined; because God is Spirit they that worship Him must worship in spirit and in truth. Spirit is the reality, the only reality. Matter and form are but passing shadows. He only who worships in his spirit worships in reality. We are to speak then of the *Worship of the Spirit,* and of *God's Requirement of Worship.* They that worship the Father must worship in spirit and reality. The Father seeketh such to worship Him.

The character of worship is determined by the nature of God. God is a Spirit. What then is Spirit ? Spirit is the ultimate, indestructible, unchangeable, intelligent principle that lies behind all visible things and is their origin and explanation. It does not seriously affect the position though we say that there is only one substance, and that matter and spirit are its two sides, if we only see that it belongs to spirit to be self-conscious and to preserve the sense of continuity and identity. Of the two substances or the two sides of the one substance, matter and spirit, only the former is cognizable by our senses. Spirit cannot be seen or touched or weighed. The lightest and most imponderable forms of matter, such as electricity, the magnetic fluid, gravitation, can be in some way tested and made apparent to the senses, they can in some way be estimated by external means ; but spirit eludes our grasp. There are no instruments fine enough to appreciate or reach it. And yet we have a better conception of what spirit is than we have of the most familiar material objects. Why ?

Because we are spirits. Spirit is that which knows itself separate and whole, which grasps, surveys, analyzes and weighs itself, which approves or condemns itself, which aspires and longs and yearns and forms the picture of another self which it prefers to the actual and present, and which, whatever its experience, can never free itself from a sense of the boundless and endless. We know spirit in its working, in its struggles, in its pain and joy, in its hope and fear. No material thing can ever be brought so near to us as this. We cannot indeed be said to know matter at all when we compare our knowledge of it with our knowledge of spirit. However clearly we see, however firmly we grasp, still matter is outside of us. It is not in the inner circle. Spirit only is ourselves. We are conscious of it, we know it, and by knowing it we know all other things. It is only by doubting his own consciousness, that is, by doubting all things, that a man can rationally doubt the existence of spirit, or that he is spirit. That spirit is something wholly different from matter we know, for it is swayed, nurtured, coloured, incited and transfigured by that which has no influence on matter. The spirit is depressed or elevated by ideas. They are a world to it. Abstract truths, or the imagination of that which it never was and never can be, rouse it. The spirit revels among things of its own creation or the creation of others. If spirit were any form of matter, it would need matter in some form to sustain and rouse it. Abstractions or imaginations would not thus master and satisfy it. The consciousness of freedom is equally alien to matter. All through nature there is uniform, necessary action. There is no such thing as freedom in any particle of matter, from a planet or sun to a flake of snow. Even in the comet, the apparently wild wanderer of the sky, freedom there is none. If any particle of matter were free to take a way of its own, to act after some fashion of its own, to select some new career, to deviate in any way from the path assigned to it, there would be an end to the order of the universe. But that freedom which is impossible to matter the spirit is conscious of. It is conscious of choice, of deliberation, of weighing, hesitating, determining. It is conscious of pain, very agony, in deciding, conscious sometimes of deciding against weighty reasons; of deciding in spite of feeling and inclination; of turning resolutely, though with many an inward tremor and qualm, and taking a fixed road. If the spirit is conscious of anything it is conscious of this freedom, of a freedom that shows itself both in inward fighting and anguish and in a constant elevated sense of being free and not bound as matter is. The consciousness of freedom is attested by all the pangs of remorse and by all the joys of a sense of rectitude and sincerity. Man's best and holiest and highest would be a delusion were he not free. And all that attests his freedom attests that he is not matter, that spirit is something wholly different from anything in the material universe.

We begin then with this : Man is a spirit. He knows himself to be mind, spirit. He knows himself possessed of that which is wholly contradictory to the nature of matter. He knows himself capable of being moved, fed, sustained by ideas which would have no influence on any form of matter. There is nothing of which a man can be so sure as this. If he is not sure of it, he is sure of nothing. It is by his own spirit that all knowledge comes; and if he begins by doubting its main, invariable testimony, he must doubt as to everything else ; his knowledge is at an end, and universal darkness reigns.

Every man then must begin here. He knows himself a spirit. He has immediate direct knowledge of it, and he knows *what* a spirit is better than he knows anything. Every man has in his own consciousness a direct road into the spiritual world. He knows that his spirit does not belong to the material world. But he cannot stop here. This spirit of his, whence did it come ? It has a sense of weakness: it is overwhelmed by a sense of weakness at times. It has a sense of sin. There is something wrong and wanting in it; and yet it aspires for perfection and the boundless. Certainly this spirit, so weak and sinful, did not originate itself ; and just as certainly its longing for the perfect, its sense of the infinite, its craving for rest and a home declare that it comes from an infinite Spirit· Whenever I am certain that I am a spirit, I become certain that there is an infinite Spirit from whom I have come. I know it both by the weakness of my spirit and the greatness of my spirit. I do not suffice for myself. I need help. There must be a perfect and infinite Spirit in whom my spirit can find a home and rest.

I seem to hear some one saying, " But men do not go through any such process of reasoning in order to believe in the Father of their spirits. They attain the knowledge in a more direct way." A more direct way —where is it ? Nay, my friend ; this is the directest way of all, that I have been describing. This is the way that men take without being conscious of it or analyzing it. There can be no shorter way than this, whether you travel it consciously or unconsciously :— knowing yourself a spirit, by the freedom, the horizon of thought, the pains and joys, the struggles, regrets, hopes and fears of a spirit ; and knowing, both from the weakness and the greatness of your spirit, that there is an infinite Spirit from whom you have come. There cannot be a shorter way than this or an easier one.

I know what the infinite Spirit is by knowing my own spirit. He is all, perfectly and boundlessly, which I am imperfectly. He shows Himself in the whole material universe. He gives an idea of His power and wisdom in the grass growing on the mountains, and the millions of suns blazing in space. But He has revealed Himself a sspirit, as a Father, as righteousness, love and mercy in Jesus Christ. "He that hath seen Me hath seen the Father." The utterance always fills us with new surprise. Often as we have read it, it comes over us at times with a startle and thrill of amazement —seen the Father, the Infinite Creator of worlds, the Eternal One—seen the Father. How can we see the Father in a weak human form ? Ah, yes, we see the Father there as nowhere else. We see His tender love —His inflexible purity—His patience—His yearning pity. We see even His power interpreted as the servant of His love. We see that He is truly a Father— the tears and sighs and groans and pleading and wrestling of Christ interpret His heart—and the miracles of mercy, wrought never for Himself but for others, show how the Father's might runs.

As our spirit, then, wills, loves, is free, holds colloquy with itself—so it is with our infinite Father.

And here we find the place for worship. It is the colloquy of our free spirit with the infinite free Spirit. It is the colloquy of the needy spirit with the compassionate, bountiful, almighty Spirit—it is the colloquy of the struggling, imperfect, anxious spirit with the almighty, sympathetic, helpful Spirit—it is the colloquy of the child with the Father, the child that

knows his sin, and knows also his longings and yearnings for higher things. It is the colloquy of the loving
heart with the Infinite Heart of love,—its lamentation
and beseeching, crying and groaning. It is the heart
that knows its own misery and plague, bringing it
out before the Infinite Eye in order to know it still
better, and in order to have it healed. This is worship
such as it exists in a sinful, struggling spirit. Worship
of the infinite Spirit always springs from a heart that
knows itself and is conscious of its burden and greatness. It is the worship of a spirit that knows itself a
spirit.

But worship is highest when, springing out of this,
it forgets itself in the thought of what God is. The
worship of the spirit is the realizing what God is. It
is not worship to bow before a vast Presence, mysterious
and dark. This may be awe—but not worship. It is
not worship to tremble before a terrible Majesty—for
that is destitute of love and confidence. Worship is
the awe, the reverence, the love, the tenderness of the
soul that believes in the Justice, the Love, the Mercy,
the Patience of God. It is when these qualities are
dear to us, wherever they are, that we truly worship
them in God. We see them all united in God and
perfect in God. Whenever we see this—all beauty,
excellence, grace, united in Omnipotence and Eternity
—we cannot but worship. It is vain to ask, Of what
use is worship, what purpose does it serve? We must

worship what we see to be infinitely high and loving and true, righteous and tender. We cannot worship the opposite, but must turn away : but love, righteousness, truth in perfection and splendour we must worship. Not to worship these united in one will and heart must be to degrade and corrupt ourselves—not to worship the perfect, is to throw contempt on every approach to the perfect—not to worship perfect right and love, is to contemn and lower and injure every imperfect, struggling approach to these. Worship, then, is no artificial thing. There is nothing so in accordance with the whole nature of man. There is a hint of it and approach to it in every joy, in every admiration, in every rapture of the soul, in the beholding of the great, the noble, the true, the enduring. He whose heart has ever swelled with emotion at the sight of the sky or the sea or the mountains, who has ever been thrilled with music or beauty of form or deed or thought—he has a knowledge in himself of what true worship is, and of the need of it. As long as man must admire and love and trust, as long as man must hope and fear, so long must he worship, for it is only the thought of the infinite Father that can truly rouse and satisfy all of these. And because worship is so in accordance with the deepest nature of man, it will express itself in a great variety of ways. It will find expression in look, the rapt look of devotion—in the sigh and the tear—in the deep silence, subdued and solemn—in crying and singing aloud. It will feel that there is no silence too deep to express its awe, no noise loud enough to express its thanks and joy, no music rich enough to utter all its triumph and hope, no melody plaintive enough to utter its grief, no prostration low enough to express its humiliation. Yes, worship is in the spirit. But the spirit seeks appropriate form to utter itself, and by uttering itself it grows. It calls for words and sounds, the best, deepest, strongest it can find, to express itself and to rouse itself. The spirit of a man is often sleeping till some outward sound wakes it up. There is a seed in him, but it might sleep on for ever if it were not roused up by outward things.

The spirit truly is all; and because it is all it should use the best means in its reach to bring it to its full range and power, to bring out all its tenderness, sublimity and fervour.

Spiritual worship may be said to be the central thing in life. If a man has his spirit of worship kept alive, and *all* alive, all will go well with him. Earnest worship keeps alive *belief*. It is easy for a man to believe all the mysteries of the Christian faith who has a devout, fervent, penitent spirit kept alive by worship. When is it that you feel as if the doctrines of Christianity were too grand for belief? It is when the pulse of your spirit is weak, feeble and low. When the spirit rises on the wings of devotion, the grandness of religion, the mysteries of redemption, are congenial to it.   These things are like its native air.   Worship is a luxury, the greatest luxury of life, but it is also the deepest necessity.   It breathes courage and joy into all life.   It nerves for battle.   It sustains daily toil.   It brings up the bright scenes of home to the pilgrim far away.   It makes man feel that he has a spirit and how vast and awful his spirit is.   It dwarfs the difficulties of life.   It magnifies the duties of life.   It makes sacred all the relations of life.   In worship man feels that he has wings, that he belongs to Eternity, and then sorrow grows light.   Burdens fade away.   He grows young again, but with a youth richer and stronger than earth ever knew.

Do we ask then *why God seeks to be worshipped?* The answer is virtually given in what has been said as to the sphere of worship.   But the question is sometimes put in a doubting or hostile spirit, and requires a more explicit answer.   "The great God," it is often objected, "does not need any man's praise.   Are we to think to flatter God and win His favour by loud sounding proclamation of the splendour of His character?   He knows and alone knows what He is; why should we tell Him our poor conceptions of Him? It is well—it is right—it may be necessary to have reverence for God.   Adore God in your heart, cherish lofty feelings about the Eternal and Absolute One.   Be humble and lowly toward Him and maintain perfect confidence in Him; but do not think to please Him by uttered praises. That is wholly a human conception, originating in a dark era, and is quite unworthy of God or of an enlightened mind. It would be degrading even to a man to think that he would be gratified with direct and reiterated praises."

But the Great Father seeks to be worshipped— seeks worship because He is a Father. As a Father He seeks to be loved. He is content with nothing less than love. If God were not love, He would not care for our love; but since He is love, nothing but love can ever satisfy Him.

Do you think then that love to God can exist or grow without expression? You might as well think of the seed living without sending its shoots up into the light. It is in vain to distinguish between love, grateful adoring love, and the expression of it. They are as fire and flame. Man must, constituted as he is, strive to utter his feelings. In the utterance they become clear, distinct, and strong to himself. Never uttered, they die away—become vague and shadowy. Utterance turns them into solid structures. Utterance gives them wings of fire. Utterance multiplies grateful feeling and makes it at once substantial and ethereal. If it is right to have gratitude and admiration, it is equally right and necessary to express them, for it is in expression that they become consciously real and acquire permanence. It is quite true, then, you do not need to tell God what He is, but you need to love God, you need to grow in love to God— you need to tell God of your love to Him. There never was sincere love to God that did not yearn to utter itself. It felt a necessity to say to God what it felt and thought regarding Him. You need not tell fervent love not to speak—you need not say to the burning heart, " Be quiet." It must speak. It must cry aloud. It must sound out the praises of God. And do you think that God, being love, despises this, that He does not care for it? What! the Infinite Lover not care for the utterance of love because it comes from a poor creature—the Infinite Heart of Love not care to have the utterance of love because it comes from stammering tongues that shall soon be dissolved in dust? Ah! you surely do not think what love is. Love is not a proud but a lowly thing. There is nothing so lowly as love, and if the great God of Heaven is a Father, if He is Love, then the praises of loving hearts are unspeak- ably dear to Him just because they are the necessary expression of love and the necessary means of ris- ing in love. What! the Infinite Father think less of the expression of love because it is so defective, because it comes from minds so limited and weak, dwelling in mortal bodies? That is not the way of love, it thinks most of the efforts of weakness. It values most the praises that rise out of mist and darkness and pain. He remembers that we are dust, and He values most the love that rises to Him out of the battle between life and death—the love that defies even the prospect of the grave to quench it. Ah! do not imagine that the Infinite Father can think lightly of the poor efforts of love to utter itself. You dishonour Him by the thought. You forget the very meaning of the word Father. You are thinking of something quite different from love, and a Father. You are really attributing, are you not, something hard, superficial, supercilious and unreasonable to the Infinite One when you conceive of Him as making man so that he needs to express his love, and yet caring nothing for the expression, setting no value on the tribute of full hearts because it is offered in words, words which yet are the vehicle of man's highest and best in everything?

God wishes as a Father the society of His children—He wishes them to be acquainted with Him and to live habitually beside Him. If you ask why, it must be enough to say, because it is the nature of love. It is its nature to desire the society of the loved. This living near to God, this dwelling in fellowship with Him, is the grand means of educating and purifying the soul. When we associate with God, He penetrates us. He warms and vivifies our whole being, and puts hope and joy and courage through us. But all this is utterly impossible without utterance on our part. We have no conception of society or fellowship without speech as far as it goes. It may be a whisper in the heart, but it takes the form of speech. The great subject of our intercourse with God is what He Himself is. At times indeed the burdened heart must speak about itself. Speak about yourself not much to men, but much to God. But you are in your best state when you wish to speak to God about what He is, and to tell Him all your thoughts about Him, all your longings for Him, and all the joy and rest you have in Him. Speaking to God about what He is is the medicine of the soul. It is the soul's gala day, it is a time of triumph, it is the bursting of all prisons, it is the ascending to the mountain tops, it is the walking on the shore of the infinite sea, it is the plunging into the sea, it is the rising into the boundless empyrean, it is the being like the lark that soars and sings, like the eagle that wings beyond the gaze. Yes, while you sit in your place all this is real to your soul through the words of devotion.

It is false, then, that our God and Father cares not for our words. If He did not care for our words He would not care for ourselves. He would be setting at naught the very nature He has made. Not to care for our words would be not to care for the elevation and fervour of our souls, not to care for our words would be not to care for our strivings and aspirations, for our burdens and fears and sorrows. Words bring out the very quintessence of man's nature; they are his discipline and crown. And to say that our words are nothing to God is to say that He disregards the most essential things.

Nay: the Father seeketh to be worshipped. He is Love. He is no cold motionless abstraction, but a living Heart. He seeks to be worshipped because He seeks the heart. Therefore, men and brethren, pour out your hearts before Him.

THE SPIRIT IN MAN AND THE INSPIRATION OF GOD.

"There is a spirit in man: and the inspiration of the Almighty giveth them understanding."—Job xxxii. 8.

ELIHU was a young man, and Job and his three other friends were old : therefore he waited till experience had uttered itself through them. But the result was not satisfactory to him. Neither Job nor his friends spoke wisely concerning God and human life in his estimation. So he took courage, notwithstanding his youth, on the ground of the spiritual nature of man and the common inspiration from God, to utter his opinion. Whether Elihu was nearer the mark than the others must be left to every one to judge, according to the standard which he himself sets up. But whatever may be thought of the *use* he made of the idea, there can be no doubt of its soundness. Man is a spiritual being, and therefore his nature lies open to the direct teaching of God. He is spirit, and as such the infinite Spirit has direct and immediate and constant access to him. Experience, to which the appeal is often made, may be only a confounding and drowning of this inspiration. How often have the results of experience been employed to deaden all high aspirations. The enthusiast has been told—" These are only fine dreams of yours: experience has falsified them a thousand times." Experience has been pleaded against every man who fell back on first principles, against every man who broke through custom for the sake of eternal truth and trusted simply and boldly on what he saw to be the reality. What is experience in such a case but a collection of ruins, a number of broken and fragmentary perceptions, a mass of observations more or less perverted by indolence, self-interest, or fear. Every new widening of human thought, every new discovery has been in the face of this kind of experience. Experience shook its head gravely at Galileo, as it had before done at Columbus. It was sure that steamboats never could cross the Atlantic, just as no doubt it stood on the shore and bewailed the folly of the first mariner who ventured out of sight of land, trusting to a tiny needle or a minute star in the northern sky. We would be the last, indeed, to deny the value of Experience in its own place. Its lessons in the way of application of truth and the discerning of circumstances and men are invaluable. He who does not learn sympathy and helpfulness as well as caution and courage from experience has missed one of the great uses of life. But experience has often dared to place itself between the soul and truth, and to dilute and degrade genuine convictions. It has often been a substitution of the weakness, folly, timidity, guessing and reasoning of men for the wisdom of God. Many a man would see far further, and be far better, if he would only hearken less to the confused voices of his own experience and the world's, and listen with all his soul and heart to the clear voice of Revelation, or even the ample testimony of his own conscience.

But we shall not seek further to adjust the controversy which Elihu starts between the dictates of experience and the lessons of inspiration—the inspiration which each man derives from the Almighty in virtue of his spiritual nature. Let us rather turn to the *Fact and Evidence* of this spiritual nature and the *Fact and Character of the Inspiration.*

I. *How do we know that there is a spirit in man?*

We know it first of all by *his capability of tracing the working of the infinite Spirit.* Spirit recognizes spirit. Man understands the principles that underlie the divine work. Even when he only dimly guessed that there were principles, that things were not just what they appeared, that there were laws uniting the most distant objects and the most diverse in appearance, he gave evidence of a divine spark in him. But now that man has found out that God has made things by weight and measure, that the pebble on the shore, the wave that beats it, and the farthest star are pervaded by the same principle, now that he sees the same laws at work everywhere, and can reduce their operations to fixed modes, how plain it is that he is of the same nature with the mind that constructed all. He sees mind at work everywhere, and he can follow in the track of this mind. It is not a mind that goes on different principles from his own. The arithmetic and mathematics that he has worked out from his own mind are the very same that he finds in the universe. If he came across a different application of numbers or a different geometry, something that contradicted all his arithmetic, then he might conclude he had come into the realm of a different kind of mind—but this he never does; light and gravitation can be calculated by him to the farthest verge that can be reached. If he were totally unable to comprehend the plan of the universe, if he could trace no connection, see no interior meaning in things, if he gazed on all things with dull uninquiring eye, not even seeing that there was a problem to be solved, then evidently there could be no bond between him and the creative mind; but the fact of such a bond, nay even of sameness of nature is established between him and the Infinite by the fact that he can comprehend the principles of His operation.

The same thing is shown by *his capacity of making*

himself and his thoughts the subject of his study. Man realizes himself and puts the question, What am I? He analyzes and watches himself; starts the question whether he is free or under a law of necessity, as he sees all other things to be. The testimony of his own consciousness is that he is free, and that therefore he is a being above nature,—strictly speaking super-natural.

There are some who reply that man is not free, that he is simply a portion of nature, and under the same law of necessity. But such men have always contradicted themselves by their indignation at wrong, by their admiration of goodness, by their whole be-stowal of praise and blame. A better example of their position could not be found than Professor Huxley. He argues strongly that there is no such thing as freedom, and that man is simply a machine; and yet how strangely he speaks at times. "A human being," he says, "though a machine, is capable, within certain limits, of self-adjustment." And again, "Our volition counts for something as a condition of the course of events." Now, no reasoning, however subtle, can make such a position consistent or save it from being a virtual giving up of the whole question at issue. If a human being is a machine, how can he be capable of self-adjustment? Self-adjustment is just another name for freedom. We contend for no other freedom than that. It is quite true that he qualifies his statement by saying, *self-adjustment "within certain limits."* But nobody that I ever heard of has claimed for man an *unlimited* power of self-adjustment. Man cannot adjust himself so as to make himself something else than man. Enough that he can " adjust himself," as Professor Huxley admits, " within certain limits." The least power of self-adjustment is fatal to his whole theory. There is no other creature to which one would for a moment think of conceding a power of self-adjustment. Every other creature is fixed absolutely by laws of necessity which cannot be infringed. Man is a self-adjusting being : he can alter himself : he can better himself or degrade himself—he can reform or ruin himself. He can deliberate and take a course in direct opposition to inclination, and persevere in it in spite of the continued struggle of inclination, because he recognizes an *Ought*, a something that should be obeyed, whatever inclination says.

Again, man is a spirit because *he is capable of thinking of the Infinite, conceiving of the Perfect, and seeking intercourse with this Being.* This capability is admitted to be a universal characteristic of man ; and it marks him off absolutely, even in his most degraded state, from all lower creatures. Not even the highest of the animals exhibit a trace of religious ideas—it is impossible to conceive of such as belonging to them— but the very lowest and most ignorant of men are capable of these, and may at any time, by the adoption of noble views of God, be lifted even out of savagery to a high level of human virtue. Many of you may have heard of the old Greek mathematician who had been working hard at a problem for long. One day the solution broke upon him. His delight was beyond bounds. He leapt up in exultation, and exclaimed, " I have found it : I have found it." This is but an example of the delight of man in truth. How much greater is his delight in God, in the thought of the eternal and infinite Father. The thought of God is capable of giving such a delight to man as even to drown the sense of pain, and make him face all dangers with joy. How clear it is that a being who is capable of such joy in truth for its own sake, and such supreme joy in God—a being who can trace the working of spirit everywhere, and discover the very laws on which the Almighty Architect has constructed the universe ; a being who can rise to the heights of self-forgetting goodness and reckon all things but nothing compared with truth and righteousness and the fellowship of God ; a being who can analyze his own nature, search his own heart, groan under a load of sin, and rise by this sense of sin nearer and nearer to God—how clear it is that this being is a spirit.

II. But how does it appear that man has *an inspiration from the Almighty ?*

The great fact in man's experience that has always seemed to him to necessitate this belief, is the occurrence of sudden thoughts and elevations that stand far above ordinary life. In all ages men have felt occasionally, especially in solitude, a movement, a rush, a deep awe in their spirits, a sense of superiority to all earthly things; and have had perceptions and ideas rising upon them which they never sought out. A wide horizon has opened upon them, and they have had impressions of grandeur, beauty, which they could by no means account for. At times a melancholy has seized upon them in the midst of mirth or business; a deep hush has fallen upon them in roaring tumult, an utmost penitence and anguish of heart and a keen, high longing for better things. There are traces of these experiences from the remotest times, and men have thought naturally that they came from God. They have not been able to conceive any other source for things which they did not produce. *Further*, men have been in the habit of praying for divine light and guidance. They have felt the need of a divine hand to guide them in the darkness of life, and to sustain their weakness. They have felt how natural it was to believe that what they needed, the infinite Source of Wisdom and Life would give. When man believes himself a spirit he finds it easy to believe, essential and necessary to believe, that intercourse between him and the infinite Spirit is possible. This feeling that there is an inspiration from the Almighty brings with it no sense of being a special privilege or being anything infallible. It is rather the feeling of an illumination or elevation which a man may use, of a voice which a man may heed and interpret in different degrees. With prophets and apostles it rises to a clearness, fulness, precision and certainty, altogether peculiar.

The fact of an inspiration of the Almighty in the spirit of man is full of suggestion.

First, since there is such an inspiration, then the closer man keeps to God the more he may expect of it. When a man is careless of God's will and is intent on following his own way, when his mind is the arena of noisy contending passions, he cannot expect this divine truth.

Again, since there is a spirit in man and the inspiration of the Almighty giveth him understanding, this must be the best interpreter of Scripture. Many things aid in understanding the word given by prophets and apostles. All learning is a help. Sagacity and patient application, research and the comparing Scripture with Scripture, help; but the direct inbreathing of God's Spirit is the chief source. A heart filled with the Spirit understands the written word. But such a heart must take care to free itself from prejudice; it must beware of listening to the suggestions of fancy or pride.

Again, since there is a spirit in man and the inspiration of the Almighty gives him understanding, some of the convictions of a man enlightened by God may rest upon grounds which his reason can only partially discover. A man may have a conviction of a truth which he is only able partially to justify to others. The roots are away down deep in his heart. The grounds and reasons are certain; but when he tries to put them into shape for the understanding he fails. He never sees any reasons presented by the understanding which are half as powerful as those he is conscious of in his heart. It is so with his belief in the existence of God. He *knows* that God is, and all the arguments brought to prove His existence seem to fall short of the unspeakable argument in his own soul. He knows too that the Bible is the Word of God. The arguments brought to prove it are very well—they are forcible and convincing—but they are not equal to the argument that he has received from God. He sees a glory, he feels a proof, an evidence, radiating from the Bible, that he could never express, and which he is sure never can be expressed. He feels as if all the arguments of sceptics never once came near the grounds on which his faith rests. It seems not faith at all that he has, but an absolute demonstration, a sure and fixed certainty like the consciousness of his own being. It is the inspiration of the Almighty that has given him understanding. Hence there is a danger that men who know the

reality of this direct teaching of God should undervalue ordinary reasoning and evidence. They are
so full of the higher evidence that can scarcely be
communicated, that they are apt to pay little heed
to all inferior things. This is a mistake ; for Reason
also is God's gift. It is only a lower degree of
the inspiration of the Almighty. No man can sharply
divide or define between the two. Reason has helped
many to faith in God and His word. Learning has
aided many. Research and investigation have shed
invaluable light on things. Let a man be unspeakably
thankful for that calm, steady assurance which comes
from the inspiration of the Almighty ; but let him have
sympathy with spirits who are more conscious of
the lesser lights.

And let not those who are only conscious of these
lesser lights look doubtingly upon men who walk
by the deep inner light. They may have an inkling,
from their own occasional experiences, of the power
and splendour of the direct testimony of God in
the heart. Let them believe that there are men in
abundance, able to say little even to themselves of
the reasons of their hope, who yet have most deep and
wide and sure grounds, whose convictions rest on
thoughts deeper than the foundations of their own
being.

But the man who rests on the inner light ought not
to be disappointed if other men are not carried away

by his deep convictions. His convictions are sure and unassailable, *for himself;* but when he tries to bring them to bear upon other men he must come to definite reasons, he must deal in forms that the understanding can appreciate. It was so with the Apostles. They certainly had the higher light themselves; they had in abundance the unction from the Holy Ghost; but when they sought to convince men they reasoned with them out of the Scriptures, they pleaded and wrestled with men in strong appeals to their understanding and conscience, " commending themselves to every man's conscience in the sight of God," and *proving* that Christ must needs have suffered and risen from the dead.

Again, since there is an inspiration from the Almighty, we see the ground of a rational independence of the individual believer. It is often said that the mass of Christians must depend altogether, or at least nearly so, on the testimony of others—that they can have no direct knowledge for themselves of the grounds on which their religion rests. And certainly there is a period with almost all believers when this is so. But this is not an unreasonable position. It occurs in reference to everything that man learns. The elements of knowledge must be taken on trust. We must believe or we shall not know : we must make the first steps in faith or not at all. It may be safely affirmed that religion from its very commencement requires much less of this trust in men than any other subject of knowledge, inasmuch as there is always a wide, plain, manifest appeal in it to knowledge that all men have. But if there is an inspiration from the Almighty to every receptive and earnest soul, there can be no room for the assertion that the mass of Christians are dependent on human testimony.

May everyone possess a direct inspiration, and know for himself the truth and certainty of his faith ?—then to say that he is dependent on man is a mere figment. His faith does not rest in the wisdom of men, but in the power of God. His faith does not rest on a church or any body of men ; it rests upon the enlightenment which God gives him. He sees by a celestial radiance the reality, the grandeur, the heavenly origin of the truth. He lives by direct communication from God.

GOD BEHIND AND BEFORE.

(NEW-YEAR'S SERMON.)

"The Lord will go before you, and the God of Israel will be your rearward."—Isaiah lii. 12.

THESE words refer primarily to the departure of Israel from Babylon, after the overthrow of that city by Cyrus ; but this return march to Jerusalem may be well taken as a picture of the course of the Church through the ages, and of the individual history of man in all times. It is always true of God's host, marching on to the conquest of the world, that God goes before it, leading, and preparing the way. He prepared the way for His Church by the spread of the Jews, by the diffusion of the Greek language and literature, and by the unifying, consolidating power of the Roman Empire. He prepared the way for the Reformation by the Crusades which broke up the hard narrowness of the Middle Ages. He accustomed men to a range of ideas outside their own by the fall of Constantinople, which spread Greeks and their literature afresh over the world—by the art of printing, and by the discovery of America, which startled and awoke men, and widened their horizon.   So He goes before His Church still, and prepares the way, in the shaking of nations, and the slow but sure influence of travel, commerce, and literature. Cyrus is but a type of those whom in thousands God girds and sends forth, even though they have not known Him, to break down the gates of brass, and to bring the captives out of the prison-house.   And so it is with the individual.   In proportion as he craves and trusts divine leading God goes before him, prepares his way, and removes difficulties, or else prepares the man for them.   Standing here, then, as it were, on the dividing line between past and future, with one period of time just gone, and another stretching out before us and known to us only by a day's experience, let us think of the comfort, strength, and direction to be got from the thought of God both behind and before us—our Guard in the rear, our Protector and Guide before.   Let us think, first, of the dangers and difficulties connected with past and future ; and, secondly, of God as Defence and Help.

I. *There are Enemies and Dangers both in the Past and the Future.*

Though the Past is gone, the dangers of it are not. A furious wind may attack the mariner from seas over which he sailed in peace.   His days and nights there

were free from storm, steady and moderate breezes
wafted him on sweetly; and yet, from that very latitude
may sweep upon him the tempest that shall toss and
wreck his ship. When the traveller is just leaving
Sahara, when already the green fields stretch before
him, the swift simoon from the far recesses which he
travelled safely may overtake and bury him. So the
blasts of winter may throw themselves across the
boundary of seasons, and cover the tender herbage of
spring with snow. Thus *memory* is big with danger.
There are blasts of sorrow from the regions of memory
that benumb and freeze the present, or overthrow its
rising structures. The memory of past years may come
as a burden that bows a man or even prostrates him.
Fierce *temptations* also pounce on many from memory.
Sins that have been forsaken may look seductive in the
romance which the past often throws round things.
The remembrance of false and ruinous ways often re-
vives and perpetuates them. It was so with the
revival of ancient learning towards the close of the
Middle Ages. When the study of Greek and Latin
literature became an enthusiasm, it quickened the
intellect of men, and broke the bondage of the dreary,
artificial scholasticism that lay across the world; but it
also poisoned many minds. Vice which had been dis-
credited, passions and maxims and pursuits, the dis-
grace and infamy of former ages, revived again and
stalked abroad with brazen front. Heathenism with

all its foulness, boundless license, and insolent selfishness, threatened to take its old place, and even popes
and cardinals were pagans thinly disguised. Many
earnest spirits cursed bitterly the day when the old
heathen literature spread its influence once more over
the world. So the memory of evil works with the
individual. There are thousands and thousands to
whom oblivion would be one of the greatest friends.
Shut the records of memory to them, and you deliver
them from more than half their danger and toil.

The *sins* of the Past also send their condemnation
on through the present. It is not merely memory
that is burdened with them, the man himself is laden
and chained with them. The past is real and cannot
be annihilated or altered. The sins of a man are a
great and inexorably hostile army in the regions of the
past. The man himself has created that host and
armed it. And though that evil army of his own
raising may seem dim and far off to him, it is yet
there, and its steady hostility is directed against himself. Each of its poisoned arrows is a deadly thing.

Still another terrible danger from the past is *habit*.
Habit is the cumulative influence of our past self.
Every action makes not only a history for itself in
memory, but puts a claim in for the future. A man by
every sin puts the past in danger, and mortgages the
future. He adds to his bondage and strife through all
the coming years. Habit forges chains for the future

man, while it also lessens his will and strength to break these chains. The imagination that has run on tracks of evil, that has been accustomed to take its unbridled flight through poisonous atmosphere, will not readily quit that region for pure and heavenly air. It has come to feel at home in the lower atmosphere, and, even though it may loathe it at times, it cannot and will not leave it. All desires and appetites and speech and action follow the same course. Thoughts, deeds, and tempers grow in persistence and ease, and incorporate themselves with the very nature. In this sense the past is never past. It is not mere history, it is no mere deposit in memory : it is present possession, present experience, present self.

Enemies and dangers pertaining to the *Future* are partly known and partly unknown. In a general way we know the future. We know that it will be composed of the same general elements as the past— joy and sorrow, labour and rest, hope and fear. The outward world will present the same broad aspects and relations. Its helps and its dangers will contain nothing quite foreign. And yet within this range of the known what terrible variety and newness may lie. With some the fear may be the perpetuation or the renewal of what they already know too well—of racking pains, of grief from friends, or of machinations of implacable and unresting enemies, of disaster that seems inevitable, of combinations of circumstances that

shall wholly shut them in and render all further effort
unavailing. Men that have once had bitter experience
dread its recurrence in the future. Every cloud
portends a storm. Sunshine will not last. Each
illness is deemed fatal. A sombreness from the past
settles over all the coming days.

Before every man the vast endless future stretches.
He is moving on to that, and cannot turn back. It is
this that gives the weight to life. What shall the
future be to me? Death may be soon. How shall I
meet it? Am I prepared for death? Am I standing
in right relations to the eternal world? Am I so at
peace with God, so reconciled and harmonized with
God, that I can look forward with confidence? It is
here, my friends, that we see the connection between
the dangers of the past and those of the future. A
man might look to the future with a serene front, were
it not for that hostile army which he has raised up
against him in the past—for behold, it has gone on
before him. It has travelled swifter than he. So far
from him leaving it behind, it has taken up its position
in front, and lies waiting him there when he goes into
the unknown. His conscience re-echoes what the word
of God declares, that a sure retribution awaits sin when
this fleeting life is over.

Thus there are dangers and enemies *behind* and
before. These dangers and enemies exist for each man,
and the enemies behind and before are in league.

Can we wonder, then, that many have ardently wished that they could stop their career, that they could roll back the wheels of time, or that they could drop out of being. There are also *uncertain* dangers. No person here knows but there may lie before him the fiercest temptations that he has ever heard of. You sometimes read of calamities happening to men, such as make you shudder. You have no security that such may not descend upon you. You may yet be the victim of lingering and agonizing disease. You may be smitten with one calamity after another. You may be stript of everything dear to you—of friends, wealth, reputation, health, and left like a blackened trunk in the midst of the forest. Whatever trouble has been known to man may be yours. Whatever in the experience of others has made you tremble and filled your heart with compassion may yet be your experience.

II. *Now let us think of the meaning and import of God going before us and being our rearward.*

It will be at once seen that none but the Infinite One can guard behind and before. How feeble a man is against the past! How can he prevent past sins from going forward to meet him in eternity? What skill can avail to ward off possible dangers in the future? The mariner can do much to prepare for the storm, when he can forecast it, but he has no power to *prevent* the blast. He cannot free the ocean of its icebergs, or alter the current that surely sweeps down the mountainous masses from the frozen regions. So God alone can be behind and before. There is no enemy or danger in all the past too great for Him. The endless future has nothing to tax His energies. All the possible emergencies of life are under His control. O friends! what joy the thought should give. God is Master of past and future, and He is willing to guard you behind and before. How bleak and sad human life would look without this: but how radiant it becomes with this. Let us then take this best of all tidings home to our hearts: God is willing and ready to guard every man behind and before.

And there is one most important point to bear in mind—*the behind and the before are always associated.*

When God goes before a man, God is also his rearward. When God is a man's rearward, He also goes before him. Would you have God to go before you in life to clear your way, to drive off crushing evils and dire temptations? Does it seem to you a grand, sublime, inspiring idea to have the Infinite before you in life and death and eternity, your Friend and Guide? Remember that God will not be all this to you, unless He also is behind blotting out the sins of the past, breaking its power for evil over you, guarding you from the tyranny of evil habits. If you are indifferent about this—if you say, " The past is past and gone, I care not for it ; what are its sins and dangers to me, I reek not of the past ; only let me be led on safely, gloriously through the future." If this is your attitude of mind, you are entirely mistaken both as to God and yourself. You cannot be guided through the future unless you are shielded from the past—it is an impossibility ; and God cannot go before any man and conduct him to glory, except by severing the man from the evils, the condemnation and the tyranny of his past. God cannot lead a captive, a prisoner, a condemned man, who does not wish to be free from sin's tyranny. He leads men on to the glorious future who really wish and strive to be free from the chains and shackles of the past. Equally is it true that no man is shielded from the dangers of the past if he is careless of the future. Men are liberated and defended from the past that they may be led on safely to a grand triumphant future. We must then make sure that we take God as guard and shield both *behind* and *before*. Forgiveness of the past is essential to the future. The man who thinks lightly of sin in the past is incapable of being led in the ways of God in the future, and the man to whom the future is not a pressing concern cannot truly feel the weight and danger of the past.

Another thing must be clearly seen and embraced. There is a point between *Past* and *Future;* that is the *Present* in which we live ; and if we would have God behind and before, we must have Him in the present. A present God ; a God claimed as our Father through

Jesus Christ; a God trusted, looked to, leant upon, communed with *now*—that is the key to the whole. Look earnestly to a present God, and you may safely leave to Him your past and your future. He will ward off all dangers arising from past days, and lead you safely through the coming years. Our part is simple —we have not to bear the burden of either past or future ; we have to keep near to God in the present, cling to Him in the present, and all will be well. You will not cling earnestly to God, indeed, if you do not realize both past and future. But thinking of both past and future is profitable only in so far as it tightens our grasp of God in the present. A present God embraced by faith in Christ, that is everything. If we keep near Him, we shall not fear. Nothing can really harm the man who is walking with God. He will support us in every trial ; He will go before us and level mountains and fill up valleys ; He will dry up rivers and seas, or else carry us across them. He may lead us through fire and through water ; but He will be with us, and He will bring us to a wealthy place.

THY WILL BE DONE.

" Thy will be done in earth as it is in Heaven."—Matthew vi. 10.

IT may seem to some as if this were little else than a repetition of the preceding clause in the Lord's prayer. If the Kingdom of God comes, then shall the will of God be done on earth as it is in heaven. But the aim of this latter petition evidently is to guard against the thought of the Kingdom of God as something merely external, which comes apart from the attitude and spirit of men towards it. The Kingdom of God involves the manifestation of the supreme will, and the submission to it on the part of men. And there is also the important idea added of the actual doing of the will of God already in Heaven—Heaven, which has been previously introduced as the place where God is manifested and His children are gathered.

Will: there is perhaps no mental state or activity of which we have a clearer conception than *Will.* There is often a great mystery about *how we come to will* anything. Will often seems to depend on mere caprice. Sometimes it leaps out fully formed from a background of darkness and ferment, and sometimes we can point out distinctly the ground of our resolve : but whatever obscurity may be round the act of will, in any case we understand clearly enough what it is to will anything.

We perform more acts of will than of anything else; for its operation ranges from the simple raising of a hand or foot to the most determined and resolute purpose—to purpose formed after long deliberation or struggle, to purpose after the highest aims. What is it that prevents *our* will from being done in any case? Often it is want of power, or of steadfastness. Sometimes our will comes into collision with that of others. Sometimes it beats in vain against hard facts. Sometimes it is thwarted by unforeseen and apparently trivial circumstances. We are so ignorant; we are surrounded by so many obstructions, and have so many within ourselves, that there is nothing with which we are more familiar than the fact that our will is often utterly powerless to accomplish its resolves. The child soon begins to learn this. It is to him a hard lesson. He wishes the unattainable, he wills the impossible; and it ends in tears. Some remain children long. They, indeed, never reconcile themselves to the fact that their will cannot in many cases be done; and this often leads either to wild and fierce endeavours to break down all obstacles, or to sullen deep despondency.

Has the will of *God* difficulties to contend with? It has none in the material sphere. The will of God is done perfectly in all the facts and operations of Nature. And the will of God is done perfectly by the multitudes in Heaven. In Nature there is no freedom, and never was: and in Heaven freedom has become fixed and glorified. The will of all there has definitely, certainly, and unalterably decided for God's will, and has found its freedom in that. But between the fixedness of Nature and the resolute, free, unalterable fixedness of Heaven, there is the uncertain, wayward, capricious, perverse freedom of man on earth. Sin is opposition to the Divine will. It is the opposing of our own desires to the will of God concerning us. And the great object of religion, of revelation, of Christ, is the removal of this opposition to the will of God, and the bringing of our whole nature into conformity with that will. The will of God is to attain a triumph, a victory in us. It is to add to God's domains by the gaining over of our perverse wills to the side of God.

We shall make this matter stand out with greater clearness and emphasis by proposing the question,— Why God's will should be done, and why we should pray for the doing of God's will. There are many that have never considered the reasons why God's will should be done. They have a grudge that they should be called upon to subject their will to the will of God. "Why do we possess will at all," they ask, "if we are to surrender it to God? Are we not rather to become great and true and good by developing and strengthening our own will, instead of always subjugating it?"

Why, then, is God's will to be done, and not ours?

.I. *Because it is the Will of the Author of our Being, and the Fountain of all Existence.*

This mysterious being of ours we did not produce. We and all things must be referred back to a great, intelligent, almighty Cause, who adapted us to the world and the world to us, and who endowed us with a will and thought like His own. Can anything, then, be more clearly matter of right than that we should submit to the will of God? Has He not an overwhelming claim on our obedience? If any man persists,—"I am my own master, I shall control myself by my own will," the answer to such a man is, —"Then cease to depend on God altogether. Cease to walk on His earth, or see by the light of His sun. Cease to enjoy the society of His creatures. Divest yourself of all that is His; retain only what has its origin in yourself. You will require to strip yourself of existence, and cease to be. Your very will of which you boast,—He gave it; and He gave it for the very purpose of its being given back to Himself. He gave you will that you might become great by self-surrender, by giving your will up to God. . This is the great and only way to blessedness, and this God has most wisely and righteously ordained."

What a rebuke self-will gets in various forms continually. We call will *self-will* when it rests not on reasons and facts, but on mere inclination, desire, and blind obstinacy. A man resolves that he will sail on a certain day at a certain hour. The time comes. The elements forbid his sailing. They say plainly,— " Thou shalt not sail." If his will is self-will he replies,—" I have vowed to sail, and sail I will." He sails, and he suffers. If his will had been founded on reason and on the truth of things, he would have submitted and waited. All through life there is the same necessity for will yielding to that which is stronger and wiser than itself. A wise man recognizes the logic of facts, and bows to it. That is what we are required to do in relation to the Infinite Will. We are required to do no more to God than we are doing every day to circumstances, to men, or facts of Nature, —*submit our will.* Shall a man bend his will to facts, or men, or reason, and reckon it a hard thing to bend it to the infinite God ?

There are things which we never truly possess till we give them away. We see this pictured in the material world. The thriving tree is covered with blossom, which is splendour and glory—a living diadem of beauty. But this crown of blossoms is the effort of the tree to give itself away. The effort reaches its end in fruit, which is for man, not for itself. The tree only reaches its crown when it gives itself away.

Take the noblest feeling in the compass of our being,—*love*. We never possess love either to God or man till we give it. Till love throws itself out on an object, it is only a possibility, not a fact. It is like the gold that is spread through a quartz rock. It is gold, and yet it is not gold. Of what avail is gold which exists only as streaks and spots in a rock ? It must be taken out of the rock in order to be truly gold. So love locked up in the nature is merely a possibility : when it gives itself out and away, it becomes itself. It is so also with will, which only becomes free, and strong and pure by resigning itself to the Infinite Will. What a strength the will must gain from the bare thought that it is in harmony with the will of the Fountain of Being,—that it is no longer a separate, dark, imperfect, variable thing, but bound up with the Infinite. When your will sides with God, throws itself into the grand current of the divine, what a deep humility it gets, and yet what a calm grandeur, what a repose, and strength, and blessedness.

II. *God's will should be done by us because it is supported by the whole constitution of things.*

When anyone sets up his will against God's, he has the whole material universe against him ; he has his own being against him, and the entire structure of life. The stars in their courses fought against Sisera ; and so they still fight against self-will, testifying as they do of Almighty Power that supports them, of perfect wisdom, of unchangeable order and grandeur. A man may fight against God's will and exalt his own; but he cannot fight against the law by which obedience brings peace and harmony and joy to the soul, and disobedience brings unrest, pain, and deadness. When a man is reconciled to the will of God and chooses God's will, he feels that he is in harmony with all obedient things. Sun and moon are his kin; the farthest stars are relations of his; the brook, the trees, and all the waves of the sea are in league with him. The bird sings comfort to him, and utters his heart. All things in God's wide universe proclaim the folly of the man who thinks to oppose his will to the Infinite. He may, to a certain extent, succeed in thwarting the Divine will; but he cannot prosper, his very success will turn into shame and ruin.

III. *God's will is to be done by us, because it is perfect will, righteous and loving will—the will of a Father.*

The will of God is not self-will. It rests on righteousness, and is animated by love. God often expressly declares this. When He reasons and expostulates with men, it is to show that He requires things which are right. "Are not My ways equal?" He asks. And His servant Paul declares that the will of God embraces whatsoever things are true and honourable and righteous and pure and lovely.

In saying that God claims for His will perfect obedience because it is pure and loving, we are not guilty of the folly of saying that God recognizes in right something superior to Himself, to which He conforms. No; the reason of all things is in God's nature. God's nature is the eternal standard of the universe, and it is declared in two grand sayings of the Apostle John—"God is Light"—"God is Love." The nature of God is perfect purity and reasonableness, infinite mercy, compassion, bounty, and helpfulness. The will of God is never arbitrary ; because He is love. His sovereignty does not mean self-seeking, but the good— the highest good—of all His creatures. "He willeth not that any should perish, but that all should come to repentance." "He will have all men to be saved, and to come to the knowledge of the truth." It is when we see this, that we can with all our heart and soul pray that God's will may be done on earth as it is in Heaven. Unless you have perfect, boundless confidence in God—that He is Love in the full true meaning of the word, Absolute Goodness and Absolute Reasonableness, with nothing arbitrary—you cannot say with fulness of meaning, "Thy will be done." There will always be some reserve, some holding back, some coldness, if in any corner of your heart there lingers a suspicion of something arbitrary, unrighteous, unloving in God.

IV. *God's will is to be done, because it rests on perfect knowledge and the widest survey of things.*

There may be things which a man would think to be good and right, if he knew only the concerns of a village, but which he would see to be quite the contrary, if he embraced in his horizon the affairs of an empire. Things might seem arbitrary and needless, if you looked at the affairs of one kingdom alone, which would appear necessary and resplendent, if you could take the survey of a world. God has all space and all time and eternity under His eye; He has the interests of all times and all creatures at heart; and, therefore, there may be things in His government of which we cannot judge aright, because our vision can embrace only a little part. When a circle is very large—miles in circumference—and you see only a few inches of it, you may not be sure from what you see that these few inches form part of a perfect circle. Sometimes in the sky you see only, as it were, about a span of a rainbow : it is only from its colours, not from its inclination, that you judge it a portion of the triumphal arch. So there may be portions of the Divine will of the direction of which we cannot judge. We only see that there is a something divine and glorious in their colour. They harmonize in some grand way with what we know of God, though we cannot see their place and bearing. We require to think of God's eternal years, His vast empire, His boundless re-

D

sources, before we can say earnestly and sincerely, "Thy will be done."

We should *pray*, then, that the will of God may be done, because that will can only be done by our wills being moulded into harmony with His. The will of God can only be done in the moral world by the subjugation of souls through truth and love. God does not apply force to souls; but He has many kinds and degrees of influence that He brings to bear upon them. He can so surround and ply men, so pursue and urge them, so unite outward circumstances with internal reasons and impressions; He can so appeal to all that is highest and tenderest in them, so work upon all their dreads and loves, and so meet all the moods and tides of their souls, that they, while knowing themselves free, are constrained and obliged—are made to feel that there is no alternative—that they ought to, and that they must, submit to God.

We pray, then, that God's will may be done in us *perfectly*. We must beware lest, through indolence and sloth of ours, the will of God may be unable to realize itself within us. Let us not be content with a half-submission to the Most High, with a faint resemblance to that which He would have us be. Let us strenuously lend our hearts to full co-operation with the glorious will of God. Let us constantly pray that He may touch and vivify, strengthen and ennoble our wills. For will is the controlling and deciding element in our being, and not until it is submitted to God are we in any sense religious, whatever our creed may be. The whole struggle and discipline, as well as the strength and freedom of our life, lie in the bringing of our wills into line with God's—in the crucifying of the *self-will* and the substituting for it reason, right, truth, love, the will of God.

TO LIVE, CHRIST ; TO DIE, GAIN.

"To me to live is Christ, and to die is gain."—Philippians i. 21.

WE must beware of thinking that the apostle's desire
to depart and be with Christ is a necessary element in
Christian experience. It is the desire to *live* with
Christ and to serve Him and be like Him which is
all-important ; whether we desire to live with Him
here or *there* is a very little matter. We must remember that Paul had few ties to bind him to earth and
much to make him weary of it. But if it had been
otherwise with him, if there had been such personal
ties to hold him to this world, would it have been
right for him to reduce these to the slenderest—to
pare down his human affection in order to make the
attractions of Heaven stronger? Surely not. The true
heavenly spirit on earth is the desire to fill in the best
possible way your present sphere, to import the air of
heaven into earthly relationships and duties, to be in
your present position the best possible man in every
respect. The same temper which leads you to neglect

or undervalue any earthly duty in order that you may cherish a heavenly spirit, would lead you in heaven to undervalue *its* actual duties ; for in the onward progress of eternal ages there would be ever higher functions to discharge.   The very essence of heaven is to be perfect in every duty as it comes.

You may be entirely convinced that it would be gain for you to die—what Christian is there who is not in heart convinced of this?—and yet the attraction of the present, with all its strait and struggle, may be greater than that of the future, which is not fully realized, and which can only be reached through the bitterness of death.   To say that a man does not really desire the future life, because, surrounded and related as he is, he clings to the present, is most unfair.   His inmost convictions are simply outweighed by the urgency of present feelings.   It is of great importance, at the outset, to put emphasis on this, for the idea that it pertains to the true Christian character to long to depart and to be with Christ leads to much secret pain in earnest souls who are, above all, sincere.   They inwardly sigh for that which cannot be realized, and which, if it were, might be a serious flaw rather than an excellence ; while some, on the other hand, who are not so absolutely genuine, work themselves into a state of self-deception, and please themselves with shadowy emotions, thinking that they occupy a region of peculiar heavenliness.   Such is the grievous harm that

comes from mistaking what is accidental for that which
is essential, from taking that which sprang out of
Paul's isolation in suffering to be of the same substance
as his inner life.

To me to live is Christ, is one of those strong condensed expressions which scarcely admit of being
broken up into separate propositions. We may say
it is to live *on* Christ, to live *in* Christ, to live *with*
Christ, to live *for* Christ, and all this is true; but
somehow we feel that in looking at each of these by
itself we are losing the fulness and unity of the saying. The grand peculiarity of the words, their boldness and tenderness, seems to disappear. One thing
we feel, that while the words are plain and simple they
are yet wide and unfathomable. They are therefore
words that suit every stage and mood of the soul.
You may be in a state when definite notions on religion
seem vain and shallow, when you feel difficulties in all
ways of putting doctrines, and can commit yourself
to none, when words seem only to limit and confuse
the truth. This is a state of mind not uncommon in
the present day. Many feel painfully the cramping
influence of definitions, distinctions, and logical
divisions. These things have all an artificial look.
They look like an attempt to put bands on the tide,
like measuring and weighing the glorious sunlight.
The cry of many is to have no more of this. They
want to feel the air of truth blowing freely about

them; the widest terms are the only ones that seem at all adapted to heaven's infinite realities. To such a mood, I say, the text is exactly suited. Here are two words which sum up everything—all theology and all practical life are here. This is what Paul, the great theologian, inspired logician, mystic philosopher, enthusiast and philanthropist and toiler—this is what he brought everything down to. All his theology and all his experience and all his labour were centred here—to me to live is Christ. The springs of his life were here—his thought was fed here, and his heart. If there are any, then, who want to be devout and religious, but wish to be chained to nothing—who distrust and dislike definitions, as a kind of affront to the majesty of truth and the boundlessness of religion—this grand utterance of Paul with its daring, its abandon, its breadth, its enthusiasm, ought to satisfy them. I commend this saying to all who feel the spirit of the age drawing them away from distinctions and definitions, and yet demanding of them an earnest and decided religion as the only thing to live and die for. "To me to live is Christ." Oh! take this up. You will never find anything to suit you so well as this. Take it up earnestly. Do not break it down, let it remain in its noble simplicity and breadth. Let it be as a lofty strain of music to you. And if you are in deep earnest there is no fear but that the words will shape themselves into all needful definiteness. Living

Christ will bring everything to all the point that is needful.

There may be some, on the other hand, who feel the need of something simple and practical. It is not freedom from forms of doctrine that they want; it is brevity, clearness, practicalness. What so well suited for them as this? For me to live is Christ—surely this is plain. I cannot be in doubt, with this, what is to be the foundation, the hope and trust of my life. And if I make Christ the *hope* and *trust* of my life, the *purpose* and *rule* of my life stands out equally clear. It is an intensely practical rule—for me to live is Christ—and yet the following of it out will bring you deep into principles. Man cannot go on in any course earnestly without finding the need to satisfy his reason. So soon as he begins to ask what it is in Christ that is a foundation, what is meant by living *in* Christ, what is meant by living *with* Christ—so soon does he begin to have an idea of the depth that lies beneath these simple words. And the true way of getting into the depths is to reach them through the earnest pressure of practical life. I must live Christ, therefore I want to know what is involved in it, and *all* that is involved in it, and what it rests upon. And yet the glory of living a person, rather than living a principle or a truth, is that even when you discern but a little of the person you have the essence of him. The whole of Christ is contained in every true experience of Him.

A man may dislike all searching into principles, and yet if he has a real practical experience of Christ as his Saviour, if he has known what it is to yield himself to Christ and take Him as his all, that man has truly got a deep hold of principle: he knows in essence all the depths of theology. He who trusts his soul wholly to Christ has all the depths of theology lying beneath him.

Hence the words "For me to live is Christ" are such as breed enthusiasm. Principles in order to dominate and suffuse the life need to have the power of awakening enthusiasm: truth needs to be aglow to work to any purpose. And what but the thought of a great personality can awaken enthusiasm. It is the ring of a name, summing up in itself all truth and goodness, which puts heart and soul and eyes into principles: it is this which makes men aware what the word enthusiasm means. "For me to live is Christ"—that is something to stir the blood, that is something to make the nerves tingle and the heart throb. "For me to live is Christ"—that speaks of Gethsemane and Calvary, of days and nights devoted to the highest good of man—that speaks the noblest thoughts that have ever been uttered, revelations of God and searchings of the human heart—that breathes the tenderest wooings to the sinful soul. It is the bugle call to the sad and despondent. "For me to live is Christ"—with that there is light in the darkest hour and hope in the

most desperate day.   Christ Jesus—with that name
of infinite love we dare not be cast down, we dare
not yield to sloth or sin, we dare keep no terms with
distrust.   " For me to live is Christ " is a word of joy.
Rejoice ! Rejoice ! is the word that issues from Him as
the perfume from a flower.   Christ purposes to conquer the world by great, overpowering joy.   If you
have deep and abiding joy in Christ you know what it
is to be always triumphant, and yet always humble.
Your triumph is in Him.

One other thought here.   Life becomes more intri-
cate and difficult as we ascend in the scale of being.
How simple the lower forms of existence are—how
varied and complicated is the life of man, more and
more as it ascends using all things for its own development.   ·Does it not seem a contradiction to this
principle to speak of our life as summed up in one
thing, however great and august ?   No, friends, not if it
is true that this is a word which covers vast expanses
and depths.   In Christ "dwelleth all the fulness of the
Godhead bodily."   The glory of the word " For me to
live is Christ " is here.   It is most simple, and yet
it is the deepest and widest of things ; it is the most
easy and joyous of things, and yet the most arduous
and difficult.   " My yoke is easy and My burden is
light," "Strive to enter in at ,the strait gate "—these
are both sayings of Christ.   " One thing I do," said the
apostle : and yet his letters are full of things to be

done.   There is no mystery in these contradictions to those who *try* them.   There are many things to be done, and the way to do the many and difficult things and to find them easy and simple is to do the *one* thing in them all—to do everything in Christ and for Christ. Life grows complex as you ascend, and yet it also becomes more simple.   Just as science seems always to be getting more complex, and yet is ever reducing things to fewer principles and seeing more unity in all, so when you take " For me to live is Christ " as your guide, you get a wider, more varied range of thoughts and sympathies.   You feel a connection with all things, and yet this *one* thing you do, you seek to win Christ—for you to live is Christ.

While life is thus made full and rich, joyous and enthusiastic, yet the deepest conviction of the heart may be, yea *will* be, that it would be *gain* to die. Though you may not with Paul wish to depart, yet all the same you may be truly of his mind that it would certainly be gain for you to leave this world.   Indeed, unless a man has this persuasion, how can he even enjoy this world?   The secret fear that I am going on to a state undesirable will throw a gloom over the present ; but if I have lying in my soul, in dark days and bright days, the conviction that whenever death may come it will be gain to me, a quiet radiance is shed over life. Sometimes you have seen at mid-day, or even in the morning, clouds overspreading all the sky except a small portion of the west. Though the sun had not reached that part of the sky, yet the only brightness issued from that unclouded region. The radiance darted all round from there. So a brightness breaks all round from the settled belief that death will be the portal to a glorious world. It is impossible for a man to cherish the faintest hope of that without having some twilight of gladness and satisfaction from it. The combined light of all the stars in the sky may seem to us but little; their extreme distance dwindles their brightness down to a glimmer: yet night would be dense darkness without them; with them it is jewelled in glory, it burns with splendour. So does the darkness of the soul glow and flash with a secret hope. It is written in fire across the soul's firmament —" *To die is gain.*"

It is vain for us to ask particularly in what the gain lies. We could not understand the answer though we had it. Yet this we can understand, the gain will be the extension of what forms our highest life here. Of our present existence this is true—

"We live in deeds, not years ; in thoughts, not breaths ;
　In feelings, not in figures on a dial.
　We should count time by heart-throbs. He most lives
　Who thinks most, feels the noblest, acts the best."

And this must be true of the eternal future. Our happiness now is to be with Christ ; it will be far greater there, for we shall see Him face to face. We shall know then the joy of doing good, the joy of perfect love, the joy of the sight of perfect beauty, the joy of honour and rest, unwearied service, and endless progress.

But I like to come back to this word *gain*. Whatever your joy, whatever your work, whatever your society here—it will be gain to die. Rest in that. What a joy, what an exultation, you may have had in the company of kindred souls' here—it is the very height of being—still it will be gain to die. What a delight you may have in work, in thought, in prayer, in praise—still it will be gain to die. Let your imagination soar to the highest point of bliss and glory conceivable—still, even in view of that, it would be gain to die. If for you to live is Christ, there can be nothing but gain anywhere—especially in dying. It is only when you are faithful to God and man that there can be gain in death. Live to Christ, and that will ensure everything ; that is the safe, sweet, and high way of life. Live to Christ, then as to life and death you shall be at ease—

"Like the bird which on frail branches balanced
   A moment sits and sings ;
He feels them tremble, but he sings unshaken,
   Knowing that he has wings."

THE THREE CONTRADICTIONS OF THE LIFE IN CHRIST.

"I am crucified with Christ: nevertheless I live; yet not I, but Christ liveth in me: and the life which I now live in the flesh I live by the faith of the Son of God, who loved me, and gave Himself for me."—Galatians ii. 20.

WE are conscious of a certain tone of remoteness and extreme intensity in these words that seems to make them little suitable to us. It might be real to Paul, with his peculiar history, with his struggles and persecutions, his fierce anguish of spirit, his imperious convictions, his absolute identification of his experience with Christ's, thus to speak of being crucified with Christ; but to supply such burning impassioned words to our every-day history, our tame experience and feeble aspirations, seems like comparing the lava stream, that has just issued from the volcano, to the quiet brook that flows in feeble shallow windings within its grassy banks. To speak of our being crucified with Christ, is like comparing the easy work of common life to the grim wrestling of a warrior in a life and death encounter. And yet Paul seems to present his experience, not as some strange and never-to-be-paralleled career, but as indicating the path along which the divine life travels, and which we must needs all take. Remember the way in which this strong language is introduced. It is in speaking of the impossibility of being justified by the law, that he says, "I through the law am dead to the law, that I might live to God." The words that follow are a re-affirming, asserting, intensifying of the thought, "I am crucified with Christ, nevertheless I live." By faith in Christ, the apostle has died to confidence in the law. He had ceased all reliance in it, all hope from it. Faith in Christ had made him participate in His death. It was as if Paul had been there nailed to the cross along with Christ, and sharing alike in His agony, His shame, and His triumph. When we thus put ourselves in the current of the Apostle's thought, his language does not seem unreal when adopted by us; not unreal, but most genuine and deep, language that always carries depths and heights far removed from us, but which is true and living expression to the humblest faith. There may be few that can appreciate the words of a great poet, few to whom all their grandeur and pathos are an absolute reality; there may be still fewer who can sound the depths of a great philosophic thinker, or comprehend all the phrases he employs; yet the language of both poet and philosopher is the mother tongue of the most illiterate, the like powers of thought exist in greater or less volume among them, and all can have true and genuine glimpses of the meaning.

Language of extreme contrast, of apparent utter contradiction, affirmed of the self-same object, is frequent with the Apostle Paul. He delights in making assertions that are apparently incompatible. And in this he simply accentuates a habit of the Scripture writers as a whole. The more intense and wide in range any inspired writer is, the more does he abound in apparent contradictions. And the reason of this is not difficult to find by him who will remember what a known recognized bundle of contradictions man is; and how his apparent contradictions, while they lessen, also grow, the better he becomes; as he waxes at once narrower and broader, more minute and more comprehensive, severer and yet more lenient, less sanguine and yet more hopeful, more cautious and yet more daring, more certain of himself and truth and yet more diffident. Sometimes to the eye that seeks to scan things, the whole universe, as well as the nature of man, seems made up of contradictions, partly reconciled and partly offering little hope of reconciliation. Life owes its anguish and also its zest, its mystery and its glory, to these contradictions; and all literature that fascinates and rouses man moves in their sphere.

Let us look then at the three contradictions :—

I. *Crucified, and living.*

II. *I ; yet not I, but Christ.*

III. *Life in the flesh, and life by faith.*

I. *Crucified, and yet living.*

The word which the Apostle employs denotes crucifixion, not in process, but completed. He sees Christ on the cross when He has said, " It is finished. Father, into Thy hands I commend My spirit " ; and his inmost soul takes up and re-echoes the words, " It is finished." He hails in that death the finishing of transgression, making an end -of sin, and bringing in an everlasting righteousness. Paul accords with all his heart in the purpose and aim of that death, and adopts it as his own. As the ambassador is sent by his country to represent her, and as all his deeds, his words, and successes are his country's, so Christ represents and suffers and acts for all who, by faith and love, identify themselves with Him. It was not in their power to send Him, but they do what is in spirit the same, they with heart and soul approve of Him and His mission, all the aims He had in view, and all the means He took to gain the ends. To Him it seemed good to be nailed to the cross, to submit to shame and smiting, to wear the crown of thorns, to be scourged and clad in mock purple array ; and faith and love approve. The soldier fights not his own, but his country's battles ; the scars he receives, and the death he dies, are for his country. His march and fatigue, his watching and

E

struggle, danger and victory, are all his country's. Christ is our soldier. His death and victory belong to every one who truly believes in Him. Every one who grasps Christ as his representative may say, " I have been crucified with Christ. I was nailed to the cross with Him. That cry which He uttered, 'It is finished,' was mine." And do you think that he who thus identifies himself with Christ can be a stranger to the spirit of Christ ? Can there be any identification with Him in His death, without some sharing of His spirit? Must we not, as we think of Him as our representative, recognize His spirit as representing ours ? If Christ had one spirit in reference to God and righteousness, and we quite another, could we in any true sense be represented by Him ? If Christ had a spirit of love and confidence toward God, zeal for God's glory, and deep and wide compassion for men, while we are possessed of a spirit of hate and aversion, a spirit of self-seeking and pride, could he be our representative ? Could love represent hate? Could light represent darkness ? Could self-surrender and devotedness represent self-seeking ? Can the spirit that finds its centre in God represent the spirit which finds its centre in self ? Assuredly, my friends, when we take Christ as our representative we adopt His spirit, we grasp His aims, we yield ourselves to the same current which bore Him along. It cannot be that He is going in one direction and we in another, if He is our representative.

And can this necessary going in the same direction as Christ be realized by us without effort and pain? Can we adopt His spirit without now and again something even like anguish and a very tearing of our being asunder? Ah! we shall understand what it is to be crucified. Many a time we shall feel the nails driven in. Many a time we shall feel the heartache and the languor and the sinking. We have not all the same experience of crucifixion; and to one it comes earlier, to another later. To one it comes in sharp, sudden throes, to another in slow, dull, lingering pains; but it comes to all who are truly united, identified with Christ, and are seeking to maintain, make sure and increase their identification with Him. There are fanatics who have made it their glory to have the marks of the nails in the palms of their hands. The stigmata are their ambition. But the true marks of being crucified with Christ are such as Christ only can see. They are marks in the hands that work and care for others, marks in the soul of struggle, marks where tears as of fire have run down the face of the soul.

This pain is involved in the dying of sin. The old man dies, and for the most part it is through a slow and difficult death. The death blow is struck when a man identifies himself with Jesus Christ in His death, and can truly say, " I am crucified with Christ." But then only does the man begin truly to live. To feel one with Christ, to be in sympathy with Him, united to Him, is to be ushered into the life of God and all that love God. We live to God in proportion as we die to sin. It is evil that keeps our souls benumbed and powerless. Escape out of self into a life of sympathy and love, and you escape at the same time out of bondage and care into freedom and joy. What a parable is read to us in the transformation of decay, rottenness and corruption, into fresh, green, beautiful, glowing life. You see the mass of unsightly wasting material losing itself and passing away into new forms that bear no trace at all of their former state. What is it that does this? It is the mysterious chemistry of life. It is only life that can turn rottenness into beauty and power. Nothing in all the world except life can transmute the very least atom of corruption into newness, force, loveliness and growth. So it is love to Christ, faith in Christ, that makes us one with Him; that makes of moral corruption, decay and sin, the elements of a new and heavenly life. The heavenly life is the only life on earth of which a man can say, *I live.* Then only does he live in the centre of his being, and in its height and depth; for he lives a life of hope and of joy, a life in fellowship with the eternal God of Love, a life with a bright and boundless horizon.

II. *I; yet not I, but Christ.*

True religion, real spiritual religion, both intensifies the *me* in a man, and eclipses it. Who feels the reality, weight, and mystery of his personality so much as the man who knows the burden of sin, and who sees his own vileness in contrast with the Lord Jesus Christ? Then we begin to feel what a weight and burden it is to have a soul that is capable of being united with Christ in His love and death, a soul capable of bearing the very image of God, growing in brightness through eternity. If you have been awakened to the meaning of Christ's death, and felt the need of a personal relation to Christ, you feel also that your soul has a terrible distinctness, standing for ever alone and apart from all creatures. It has a history and a destiny of its own, as distinct as that of any star that is millions of miles apart from its nearest neighbour. But when you are truly alive to God, while the movements of your heart and the workings of your conscience are keenly felt by you, as you have heard the ticking of a clock sounding through the whole of a house; yet at the same time, in proportion as you have Christ in you, that excessive consciousness of self is swallowed up in the desire that Christ may rule in you, in thoughts of Christ and the love of Christ. The thought of all that Christ is, the wish that He may have His proper place in you, and that His joy may be fulfilled in you, the feeling that you cannot but trust everything to Him, and give your soul and all its cares and fears into His hand for ever —this outweighs that extreme feeling of self. You feel the extreme oppressive weight of your being, and the very pain of that forces you to give it all up to Christ, and then you are free. When Christ lives in you, your main thought is to please Christ, your highest wish and ambition is to be like Christ. So it is always *I*, and yet not *I* but *Christ*. The *Me*, the *I*, becoming more conscious, more alive, more aspiring, more sensitive and active than ever; and yet always being more and more eclipsed and lost in thoughts of Christ and joy in Christ. You may understand this *Me* and yet not *Me*, this *I* and yet not *I*, by the cloud that floats in the evening sky near the sun. There never was a cloud whose blackness and weight were more conspicuous. There it lies just where in all the sky its blackness is sure to be seen, and yet it is in the very place where if anywhere the blackness is sure to be transformed. See how the sun pours itself into it till at last it becomes all brightness, a very chariot of the sun. Have you ever observed the figure of a man walking along the ridge of a hill on the very line of the horizon? What a prominence the man gets in that position standing between you and the sky. He never was in such a position before. He is something great and striking. And yet if the sky grows brilliant behind him, if a rainbow should span the sky, resting one of its ends just where he is, or if a great effulgence from the sun breaks out in that quarter, how is the man swallowed up. The glory merges him, effaces him. His very bold prominence has secured his being wrapt up and lost in glowing brightness. He seems to be melted and transformed. That is the Me and not Me, the I, yet no longer I, but Christ.

III. *A life in the flesh, and yet a life by faith in the Son of God.*

The outward life is surrounded by the ordinary conditions. It is a life of waking and sleeping, labour and rest. The body has its imperious wants. The elements are its masters, cold and heat overcome it. Sleep wraps it in oblivion. It is subject to violence and accident. It is racked with pain, prostrated with weakness, poisoned and corrupted by disease. A moth or a pebble or the point of a needle may be its ruin. A breath of air may prostrate it. The man who is crucified with Christ and free of the universe must labour and suffer hardship as well as other men. The earth does not seem to recognize anything peculiar in him. Fire burns him, water drowns him, the earthquake engulfs him. Think of the ordinary life which Paul lived in the flesh. His bodily presence, as he himself says, was contemptible. He was an itinerant mechanic. He suffered cold and hunger. He was shipwrecked ; he was beaten and stoned ; he was

counted as the filth of the world and the offscouring
of all things.   He fought,. to use his own words, with
beasts, and was made a. spectacle to angels and to men.
And the life of many others like Paul, is a life of
languor and pain, a constant struggle of the spirit
against the weakness and dulness of the body. The life
in the flesh is, in all, a life of subjection to outward things
a life of opposition and of temptation, of friction, collision, and wearing down.   Looked at merely in itself,
who could see anything great in the most successful and
brilliant life in the flesh, subject as it is to so many
wants* and dangers, so uncertain, so limited, so encompassed with huge sorrows and temptations, so brief and
incomplete at the very longest.   But what a splendour
and vastness that faith in the Son of God, who loved
him and gave Himself for him, imparted to the inward
life of Paul.   That poor wandering Jewish mechanic
had, who can doubt, the noblest, most beautiful soul*
which then walked the earth.   Beaten and stoned, and
cast out, his was a gigantic spirit.   He carried in his
heart the sorrows of many men.   He burned with
ardour for the highest good of all.   His very difficulties and trials made his life shine out the more.   Men
might hate, but they could not quench his love for
them.   They could imprison him, but they could not
bind his spirit.   They only gave him more time to
write those letters, which are among the richest parts
of ᾿Revelation, and among the choicest gems of the

world's literature, with more depth, pathos, weight, and brilliance than Greece or Rome ever dreamt of.

And what was it that did this for Paul ? Let him answer. " The life which I now live in the flesh, I live by the faith of the Son of God, who loved me and gave Himself for me." Faith in the same Christ has power to do the very same for you and me. Let us by faith be crucified with Christ, and by faith lay hold on Him who loved us and gave Himself for us, and all things will be possible to us.

TASTING AND SEEING.

"O taste and see that the Lord is good."—Psalm xxxiv. 8.

THIS Psalm is a record of experience mixed with lessons and reflections formed on it. The writer celebrates God's deliverance of him, and calls upon all men to come and trust God as he had done.

There is much in the world to shake confidence in God. Calamity, pain, and loss seem to be in excess, and to be scattered about at random; and yet, a thorough belief in the goodness of God is essential to all true religion. If you have doubts about God's goodness, you cannot really love Him and trust Him. Worship is the expression of admiration which rises into adoration, where the perception or sense of God's perfection is so great and intense as to weigh upon the soul and produce awe. What, then, is the way out of doubt or disbelief of the goodness of God?

It is well to listen to arguments and illustrations of God's goodness. They may convince and set the mind at rest. But the great means is set forth in the text.

Taste, experience the goodness of God, and so you will be convinced that He is good. The full conviction comes from actual experience.

Let us then consider *what it is to taste, and why we should and must taste in order to be convinced.*

What, then, is it to taste, and what are we to taste? Here the answer must be:—Taste whatever in God's promises you feel a need for. It does not matter much where you make a beginning, for you will soon find that really to taste one promise you must taste others as well. - Are you in any trouble or perplexity, then take it to God: tell it all to Him. Cast your burdened spirit on Almighty Grace. If you do not feel relief at once, do not be surprised, do not go away in sorrow or anger. You cannot tell what God's reason may be for delay. Ask again and again, and still more urgently. If you are resolved and persevering in asking, you will either get the blessing you wish, or be led to see that some other blessing must be asked and obtained first.

You cannot think it unreasonable that God should observe an order in the bestowal of His blessings. May not this be needful for your own sake? Are you sure you would be able to receive or appreciate the blessing you ask, as you are at present? Are you sure it would not do you more harm than good?

Ask, then, I say, for any particular blessing on which your heart is set, though it be not really the first and fundamental blessing. Ask it, simply because your asking of it will be real and earnest. It will avail little to ask high blessings, fundamental, essential blessings, if you ask them in a cold, formal way. Ask for what you feel to be a necessity, something that makes you cry and wrestle, something that you can be in downright earnest for; and though you may not get that, you will get some glimpses of the reality and power of prayer. You will be rewarded by intensity of spirit, and by some consciousness of the spiritual world and of the mercies of God. Pause and consider what a blessing that is—to have a conviction deepened in your mind that this visible, material world is not all; that its hopes and fears, work and troubles, are surrounded by a vast, glorious, spiritual sphere; and that above all, and through all, and in all is the eternal, almighty, infinite God. Ask, then, as to whatever presses you, be it trouble or care, be it doubt or perplexity, be it calamity or loss, fear within or foes without,—ask, and you shall taste that the Lord is good, either in deliverance from that evil, or in the conviction that you need first of all deliverance from something more radical and oppressive.

But let your tasting be also guided by a reasonable survey of your position. Ask yourself if your main need is not the forgiveness of sin and the renewal of your nature. Think this subject seriously over in the quietness of the night when sleep flies from you, and when you feel eternity near. Ask yourself whether your first and deepest want is not that of a new heart. Seek forgiveness of all the past, and seek it for Christ's sake. Gather together all the arguments you can think of and use them with God. Read His own blessed character, His infinite mercy, His almighty power, His patience and forbearance. Plead with Him all that He has done in the past, and let all your pleading be mingled with the name of Christ and with His blood shed for the sins of men. If your earnestness is small, if it seems cold and dry for such weighty matters, tell that to God too, and make even that an argument. Tell Him that you are guilty and vile, and that, worst of all, you do not feel your vileness and guilt. Cry for a broken and a contrite heart. Be not weary; make it your burden night and day: and, though I cannot tell how God will answer you— whether He will first give you a broken heart, or whether He will keep you knocking yet a while, to deepen your earnestness, and lead you to an utter despair of self—I am as sure that God will answer you as I am of any promise of the Bible. God will answer, and you shall taste and see that God is good.

What a feeling a man has of the goodness of God who has been oppressed with a sense of sin, who feels himself vile, hateful, foul, when that promise of God is sealed to his soul: " I, even I, am He that blotteth out thy transgressions for Mine own sake, and will not

remember thy sins ": " I have cast all thy transgressions behind My back into the depth of the sea,
and they shall no more be remembered against thee
for ever ": " I am pacified toward thee for all that
thou hast done." What a deep, unworldly peace steals
over the soul. And then a man feels a new life
rising in his soul; feels, spite of dulness, narrowness,
and corruption, that he does love God and takes
pleasure in His will. When he feels the dawn of
heaven begin in his soul, and looks forward with
a calm trust to an eternity of joy, does he not taste
that God is good?

He tastes and sees that God is good when he leans
upon Him in trouble and care, feels how sweet it is to
leave himself and all his interests in God's hand, feels
a divine strength suffusing him in hours of pain and
weakness and sorrow. What would he exchange for
that " peace which passeth understanding," and which
keepeth his heart and mind through Christ Jesus ?

Speaking, now, in the plainest, simplest, coolest terms
that we can use—Is there anything that this fleeting
world can offer, any pleasure, any success, any honour
that it has to bestow, to be once compared with this
deep, solid reality ? An almighty Friend to lean upon :
Love that covers all the past, guides in the present,
makes sweet and bright all the future, and that
whispers in the depths of the soul—" This is the way,
walk ye in it." " I will never leave thee." " I will

never forsake thee." " Fear not, thou art Mine, I will hold thee by thy right hand." Can any mortal estimate the joy of being able to respond to this—" Thou wilt guide me with Thy counsel, and afterwards receive me to glory"?

This is to taste that God is good ; and when a man thus tastes, he feels that religion is a reality. He needs no proof to assure him that what can do so much for him is of God. Can he doubt his own deepest consciousness; can he doubt all his senses ; can he doubt memory, conscience, heart, and soul ? No ; to taste that God is good is to be assured of the reality of religion and its " from everlasting " foundation.

And remember, it does not require that a man should taste the whole round of promises. One or two promises of God tasted are enough to make a beginning of certainty. Many a man has had a beginning of such knowledge in the answer to some special prayer, and many a one has had it in the peace and joy of quiet habitual communion with God. He knows religion real in all its main elements, because he knows this to be real.

We are now prepared to ask *why we must first taste ?* Why not first be convinced on rational grounds that religion is real, and then, when we are convinced, make a trial of it ? Is it not reasonable first to see the evidence and grounds of a thing, and then gain experience of it ?   I do not deny the possibility of some such way as this.   I do not deny that men may be reasonably convinced that religion is right and necessary, and that Christianity is the best and most authenticated religion.   I am glad that this is so, and I desire that neither you nor I should ever forget it.   But this falls short of the *seeing*, the *knowing*, and *being sure*, of which the text speaks.

First, then, I answer, the great mass of men must and do gain experience of religion before they have any proof of it.   The great majority of those who are religions began to be so in infancy.   They cannot tell when religion began to take hold of them, or how they came to a crisis and decision.   W,as there ever any such crisis, was there ever any such well marked decision ?   There was some time when their face was turned towards God, but it is so hidden in mists and clouds and changing weather, that they find it vain to do more than conjecture.   One thing is certain : they *had experience* of religion ; they knew what it was to fear and love God, to trust and obey Him, before they were capable of analyzing these things or seeing the ground and reasonableness of them.   They learned to love Christ and commit their souls to Him before they ever thought of evidence for Him.   Must it not be so, for the most part, from the very nature of religion ?

Men *need* to love and trust the Infinite One ; they need to obey Him long before they can explore or weigh the reasons for this. Does religion stand alone here ? Is not morality on the same basis ? Children are required to conform to the moral law before they can understand the reason of it. They taste, and then see, that it is good. The first elements of knowledge are in the same position. We learn science in outline, and afterwards the proof comes. How few, indeed, are ever capable of testing the elements of geology, or the wonderful facts and laws of astronomy. We feel that the sublimities of astronomy are true, though we have never looked through the telescope. Let us come to something more elementary still. What child ever knew the laws of equilibrium and motion before he began to walk ? His walking has reference to the earth's centre of gravity and his own. There is not a star in the heavens which is not in some remote way influencing his motions and the earth's. When I lift my hand, I resist the law of gravitation ; when I let it fall, the weight of the planet helps me. But who ever thinks of all this ? We act, we experience, and the knowledge and explanation come afterwards, or may never come at all.

But any man may have ground and reason enough to induce him to be religious, though he has not experienced it. He has the testimony of those who have experience of it, the testimony of men in all ages and conditions who have tried a religious life. He has the testimony of the Scriptures, which is, to say the least, powerful, impressive and arresting. He has the testimony of his own nature. Is not he a weak, erring creature, in need of Almighty help ? Are there not sorrows in the world which the world cannot console ? Is there not death, mysterious death, to meet—-death from which his nature shrinks, and which he feels contains some dread secret ? Is it not reasonable that there should be acknowledgment of the Maker of all things ? Does not his nature in its depths, in its loneliness, burdens, and aspirations, cry out after the living God, and seek rest on the bosom of Eternal Love.

Is not all this more than enough to induce any man to make the trial, to taste what there is in religion ? Though a man may have only faith to cry, " Lord, give me faith," let him begin on that, and he will proceed to conviction and certainty. He will see and know that God is good, that religion is a reality, the solidest reality that man can know. He never can be thoroughly convinced without experience, any more than a man can be convinced and sure of the effects of light till he opens his eyes and looks, any more than he can be convinced of the reality and power of music till he comes within its range and listens.

I. *We see that religion is not of the nature of a demonstration.*

There are people who make it their boast that

whatever can be proved, demonstrated to them by irresistible evidence, they will believe. They complain that religion gives no demonstration : it does not shut a man up and oblige him to believe. Why are not the proofs of religion such as to constrain every man to believe, and leave him no choice ? Since it is a matter of such vast incalculable moment, have we not a right to expect such proof ? Is then, I ask, morality a thing of little importance—is it of less importance ? But where is the demonstration of its nature and necessity ? Where do you find the essential rules of morality written ? Ought they not, considering their importance, to be written across the sky in letters of flame, such that all nations may and must read ? Since men are every day in danger of ruining their nature, and destroying themselves and others by the want of morality, why are they left to grope and stumble, when it would be easy for God to read a lesson to all men that could neither be misunderstood nor forgotten ? Ah, God has really given a demonstration of the nature of morality, but He has not put all the demonstration in one place or one form. He has written part of the demonstration in man's own nature ; part He has written in the Bible; part he has written on the broad page of outward nature ; and part he has written on the page of history. If any man puts the whole of these together, he will assuredly find that the laws of morality are demonstrated.

In like manner there is a demonstration of religion; but it is not all found in one book. Part of it is written in experience, part in the Bible, part in the history of the world, part in the laws of human nature, part in the character and testimony of Christ. No man ever yet put all these together without feeling that it amounted to demonstration. But religion, being in its very nature a thing of experience, just as morality is, never can be demonstrated, *unless you make experience one of its terms*, and the main term. You might as well attempt to demonstrate the nature and laws of light to a man who sat in a cave, and would not come out to the sun. A man might as well expect to see the stars by looking into a powerful telescope directed to the ceiling of his room.

II. *But neither is Religion a Science or Philosophy.*

There is a science of religion in which its facts and principles are arranged in logical order; and there is a philosophy of religion in which its truths are presented in their grounds and reasons, and exhibited in their relations to the general principles of human nature and the laws of the universe. It is right that every one should know something of the science and philosophy of religion. It elevates his conceptions of it, makes him feel that religion is something great, deep, and lofty. When a man sees into the grounds of religion, sees that it is intertwined with all truth, and is the key

to man's nature and to the order of the world, he is not
disturbed by objections brought to this or that portion
of Scripture.   His belief in religion rests on something
wider than that of the kind or degree of inspiration,
or the precise meaning of isolated texts. · He sees the
spirit and drift of the whole, he sees the grand pur-
port of religion, and it does not in the least injure his
faith when men think they prove that this passage has
been wrongly interpreted, or that other teaches what is
opposed to science.   Let them prove what they like :
can they touch the great truth of the soul's relation to
God, and the adaptation of religion to the whole nature
of man?   Can they alter the fact that religion is the
deepest, most imperious want of man's nature, and that
the Christian religion is immeasurably the highest, the
sweetest, the tenderest, the most reasonable and penetrating of all ?

It is good, then, to know the science and philosophy
of religion.   It saves from many a peril, and lifts
far above puerilities and conceits—those barnacles and
weeds which fasten themselves on the great ship.   But
never let a man forget that religion is an experience, it
is a want, a need of the soul.   And a man may have a
deep and powerful religion who knows nothing of its
science or philosophy.

Just as little is religion a kind of poetry of life,
something that gives an ornamental lustre, a charm
and expansion to life.   It does all this, but it is more.

It is *an experience of God.* It is not a mere comfort to life, though it is the only comfort. It is not a utility to make human life sound and orderly. It *is* the most practical of all things, but its essence is deeper : it is communion with God. It is walking with God. It roots itself in mystery. It lives by hourly contact with the Infinite. Is *your* religion of such a kind ? Is it a tasting and a seeing ? I entreat you, be not content with a religion of morals or of routine, or of a few surface practicalities. Get into the very heart-fellowship with a reconciled God. Taste and see that God is good.

JOY IN CHRIST.

"Rejoice in the Lord alway; and again I say, Rejoice."—Philippians iv. 4.

CONSIDER for a moment in what circumstances this command was issued. It came from a prison, from one who lived in the shadow of a violent death: It came from a man who had been beaten and stoned, traduced, cast forth as the scum of the world—a man who had been deceived by many whom he trusted, who carried about with him a load of care, who was often chagrined and disappointed, who had the sentence of death in himself, who seemed to be leading a forlorn hope—a man of one idea, and that idea scouted by the foremost minds of the world, a thing for derision— a man of one idea, and that idea before his age and before every age. The burden of the message that comes from this lonely, suffering, burdened man is, *Rejoice*. And when he called others to rejoice, he was no stranger to joy himself. That Roman prison witnessed some of the highest flood-tides of joy that have ever been; he had visions of truth and beauty in the darkness of that prison which made his heart throb with high joy; he had outpourings of heart which made him feel all sorrows but a shadow; he had hope which made it scarcely possible for him at times to realize the bare prison walls; the love that glowed in his heart would not let joy go down.

But this command of his to rejoice always—the reiterated command, as if he meant to render mistake of his meaning impossible, and to hold it up as the very centre of the Gospel—this emphatic command has always been a difficulty to some. Something more moderate, guarded and balanced would approve itself to them. Rejoicing *always* is as hard a thing for some to receive, as profound mysteries are for others. Let us, therefore, look closely at the injunction.

I. And first, *we must set before ourselves that it is a command, and not a mere advice or permission.*

There are many who have never looked at the matter in this light. They would be surprised to be told that to be glad, to rejoice in the Lord, is as much a command as any one of the ten commandments—that we have no more right to be melancholy than we have to be dishonest or unloving. It is no new commandment that Paul has added to the Christian religion. The Old Testament is full of commands to be glad before the Lord, to rejoice with mirth. But in the New

Testament the matter is expressed with emphasis and clearness, and the grounds of joy pointed out. It has often seemed strange that our Lord has not included joy in the Beatitudes, when He has put such stress upon it elsewhere. Why has He said, on the contrary, "Blessed are they that mourn," thus seeming to take even a lower ground than is done in the Old Testament? In the same way it might be asked why has Jesus not said, "Blessed are they that love"? Why has he omitted love, which is the greatest of the commandments? Why has he not said, Blessed are they that hope, or, Blessed are they that believe? It will be clear to you that there must be some reason which leads Him to leave out faith, hope and love from the grand catalogue of blessedness. The reason is evident. These three—faith, hope and love—have a manifest, undeniable blessedness. There is no use saying, "Blessed are they that hope," or, "Blessed are they that love." Everybody sees that these are sources of happiness. Our Lord takes up the sides which seem not blessed. He takes up what do not seem to be jewels at all—things which the world despises, but which yet are at the root of all goodness. He flashes these in the light of heaven, and shows that they are real diamonds. And if He says, "Blessed are they that mourn," it is not because he regards sorrow as the lasting, final blessing. It is the mourning that leads to joy, not the mourning that ends in itself that is blessed. "Blessed are they that mourn, *for they shall be comforted.*" So it would have sounded strangely superfluous to have said, "Blessed are they that rejoice." And yet Jesus virtually says this many times. He reiterates the supreme importance, the absolute necessity, of being glad. And why is it that we have it laid upon us as a bounden, imperative duty to be glad? Why are we not allowed to indulge our humours and be melancholy, if it pleases us or is easier? Because we owe to God the tribute of joy; because we cannot be sad if we will but believe what God has told us about Himself; because sadness in the view of a Saviour, in sight of love like His, is unreasonable and perverse; because sadness may be consistent with a sinful state, but is inconsistent with Redemption; because sadness tends to shut us up in ourselves, and prevent the genial, sunny expansion, which is essential to a benevolent spirit. Joy, then, is a command. We are not left at liberty to enclose ourselves in gloom. We are not to think that melancholy is a self-denial which we exercise and which places us on a superior elevation. *Joy* is the superior elevation, and we have no right to say, "I am content with the lower place"; for that is equivalent to saying, "I am content to bear my own burden—I am content to take only a little from Christ." This being content with sadness, when Christ offers us joy and commands us to be glad, is in fact a subtle form of self-will and self-pleasing. It often springs from indolence, a secret shrinking from the stir which joy would produce in the soul, a clinging to self-pity and pride of endurance, an aversion to the flood, the only flood, which can swallow up self and make Christ all in all. The command is to Rejoice; let every man consider what plea he can urge for disobeying.

II. Again, *Joy comes first.*

Many are disposed to admit that Joy is a necessity, but then they say that there are things that come before it. In the very nature of things, joy is the fruit of goodness. You cannot have joy before the plants of righteousness have taken root and grown in the soul. You might as well expect the blossom and sweet perfume of the flower before the fresh life has begun to spread through the tree. Joy must have a foundation; it must be rooted in experience. Yes, joy must have a foundation. It must have nutriment. But what is its foundation—what is its nutriment? What does the text say? Rejoice *in the Lord.* Rejoice in the fulness of Christ—rejoice in His beauty and glory—rejoice in His love and tenderness—rejoice in His power to save—rejoice in all His promises which express the wealth and faithful changelessness of His heart. We are to rejoice in what Christ is. And when are we to rejoice? *Whenever we see what Christ is.* A man has no choice. Whenever Christ is seen by him, the sight makes him glad. When you go to gaze on a beautiful landscape, do you require to be told when to experience delight? Is there any particular stage when it is right to feel the joy? When you read a poem of rare beauty and sweetness, do you need to consider when the thrill shall sweep through your soul? When a man receives sure intelligence that he has become rich, or that some great honour has come to him, does he need to consider *when* he will experience joy from the intelligence? When you hear that a long-lost friend has returned, that he has reached the shore, that he is almost at the threshold, can you bid joy wait awhile because there are other things that must first be attended to? Is not joy unavoidable, necessary, inherent in the very perception—inseparable from the intelligence? And shall a man hear the glad tidings of Jesus Christ, the most joyous intelligence that ever fell on human ears, and then doubt whether it is right to rejoice and be glad so soon? It is of the nature of belief in Christ to make glad. He who is not made glad cannot have understood what Christ means, or cannot have received the truth into his heart. Christ means salvation, life, glory, honour, blessedness, to every man who will receive Him. Whosoever will receive this is under an absolute necessity of being glad. He is glad by the very fact of reception. It is not a matter of consideration, choice, or will at all.

This, then, is the answer to the objection that

joy cannot exist at the beginning—that great joy especially must be rooted in deep experience and much goodness. Great joy *must* have a deep root —a great and efficient cause—but the greatest cause of joy is Christ. To believe what Christ is, is to have an immediate fountain of joy. And this joy is used by Christ in liberating, energizing, and stimulating the whole nature. Joy in Christ's hands is not an ornament and glory that is added at the end. It is a servant that comes at the beginning to do some of the heaviest work. There is nothing like joy in Christ for doing all sorts of drudgery and menial, disagreeable work. A joyous spirit thinks nothing of heavy tasks. It is not troubled about humiliation and loss of dignity. Joy stands in the place of all this. When there is little joy, there is little enthusiasm. You never heard of enthusiasm without joy. When there is little joy, there is much proneness to fatigue, much tendency to grumbling and despondency. The joyous heart is not fault-finding. It does not grudge labour. It does not think its efforts anything great. It does not shrink from self-denial and the crucifying of the flesh. There is nothing like the warm south wind for melting the snow. When that genial wind blows the ice-bound rivers are at once aware. Away down in their channels they murmur and swell in gladness. They may seem to groan and writhe, but it means joy, and away the ice goes with a crash.

III. *Our rejoicing in Christ need not be interrupted either by sorrows or by other joys.*

The same Apostle speaks of himself as sorrowful yet always rejoicing: It seems a contradiction and an impossibility, yet whosoever will try it will find its practicability; he will even find that he cannot have continued experience of joy in Christ without sorrow, and that sorrow grows blunt and dull without joy. Who is it that has the greatest joy in any work? It is the enthusiast who enters into it heart and soul. Yes, and it is he who has the greatest sorrow when there is failure or mistake. The man who has not the joy in perfect work can have little conception of the chagrin and vexation that imperfect work causes. The friend who has the richest joy in your success, who watches your every step of well-doing with delight, is also he who is grieved with your error or sin. No one can have grief on account of you but the man who has had joy, and the more joy he has reaped, the bitterer will be his chagrin at your fall. So if you rejoice greatly in Christ Jesus, if you triumph in the thought of what Christ is, if it sends a glow through your heart just to mention His name, you will not be able to avoid pain at the thought of His name being despised. The sweeter that blessed name is to you, the bitterer will it be to think of men rejecting it, the sadder will it be to think that some misrepresent Him, conceal His glory, give the place to other things which belongs to Him, and that so many millions of the human race should still be ignorant of Him.

It is in thoughts such as these that we have an answer to the difficulties of some. They never cease to wonder at the emphasis put upon joy. To them it seems selfish and hollow to rejoice when there is so much misery in the world. When men are wrestling with pain and grinding poverty, when many are oppressed and down-trodden, when so many are the slaves of vice, so many groping in superstition—to call upon us to rejoice, and to make joy the most imperative and essential thing, seems heartless. They are disposed to say, you may rejoice—be glad if you can in the thought that you are safe; but for us, we think the words of the prophet a nobler and more fitting thing—"Oh that my head were waters, and mine eyes a fountain of tears, that I might weep day and night for the wretchedness and sin of my brother men." Does it not seem strange to men of this mood that this same Apostle, who calls upon us to rejoice, and to rejoice always, should speak of himself as having continnal heaviness and sorrow of heart, because of his brethren according to the flesh? Evidently they are mistaking what the Apostle means—they are not seeing into the depth of his thought. They do not see what was plain to the Apostle, that the more anyone rejoices in Christ, the more grief he will have at men being alienated from Christ—that the more anyone rejoices in Christ, the more he will enter into Christ's spirit. Yes; let us dwell on this: rejoicing in Christ is not simply a rejoicing in Christ's power to save—it is a rejoicing in Christ's essential character, in His self-denial, in His love of man, in His devotion to God, in His compassion and zeal, holiness and tenderness. This, and nothing less than this, is rejoicing in the Lord. And is it not plain that the more you have of this joy, the more compassion and sympathy you will have, the more true and deep sorrow you will have? • It is quite true that there is a selfish joy. It is quite true that it is a base and degrading thing to make life a round of joys, whilst he world is pining in misery and bondage. It is quite true that there may be a selfish joy in the thought of being saved, that one may nurse his heart in the thought that Christ has died for him, and that he is free from condemnation,. and that it is well with him now and for ever. It is quite true that one may rest in this and never rejoice in what Christ is—His glorious character may be nothing to him; but this is not the rejoicing that Paul meant. He recommends this narrow, selfish joy to no man. He would warn against such false, selfish joy with all his earnestness and intensity. Such narrow, heartless joy can only end in shame and ruin. But real, genuine joy in the Lord—joy in His spirit, joy in His purpose and aim, joy in His grand object—that is the great source of compassion and sympathy, that is a fountain of sorrow. Does someone say, " That joy which is always producing sorrow is not the kind of joy for me. Give me mirth, give me jollity, gaiety, constant cheerfulness. I want none of that equivocal joy which is always on the brink of sorrow. I want a merry life, and you seem to show that religion does not give this." But surely you want a mirth that will bear reflection. You do not want a mirth that flies at the touch of thought. You do not want a mirth that cannot bear the words *death, eternity, God*. You surely want a mirth that can front all facts, that can look north, south, east, and west. You surely want joy that will leave your heart human, tender, compassionate, and sympathetic. You speak of joy without sorrow. There is no such thing. The truer and keener any joy is, the closer it borders on sorrow. There is, then, no time in which joy in the Lord is impracticable. Remember that it is joy *in the Lord,* and you will see how it can be present in your hours of deepest sorrow, like a dawn rising above the darkness, like the lengthening days of spring that struggle with frost and east wind, and seem often defeated, but are marching on to sure victory.

G

WINGS.

"Oh that I had wings like a dove! for then would I fly away, and be at rest."—Psalm lv. 6.

WHO has not looked at times with a kind of envy at the flight of birds? How light and free their motion is! They range untrammelled through the fields of space. For them there are no hills to climb, no barriers to surmount. They rove free of the wide air. They sweep over mountains. They cross rivers and seas, countries and continents. Their life seems the very ideal of freedom, and presents a painful contrast to the burden and toil of human life.

Looked at in another light, birds seem to preach to us of the life of the soul. They speak of the free motion of the spirit, in the vast fields through which it roams. They invite men also to take a wide range. They speak to the soul of travelling through the vast and boundless. There is something in man that responds to this call. All the more that he is so bound and kept down bodily, he thinks of a free wide movement of the soul. Many a weary heart has gazed with a grudge after the swift bird fleeting free through the sky away to sunny shores, till he fell back on thought, and remembered that for him too there were far fields to travel, and a sure flight away from sorrow and care. Who can doubt that one great purpose of God in putting swift winged creatures into man's world, was to speak to man constantly of this higher life of his own—to whisper to man amid all his toil, his limitation, his chainedness to the ground and some little spot on it, of a wide sphere that truly belongs to him, and of freedom to be found in it.

Let me speak then of *man's desire for escape and rest, and its fulfilment—his wish for wings and his gaining of them.*

I. *The wish for escape and rest is a common one.*

There may be some who have no experience of this, and there may be others whose experience of it is something only half real, something consciously fine and sentimental, something they would like to say, something they repeat in a poetical, romantic sort of fashion, until they get to believe that they mean it. But there are many crushed spirits from whom the words of the text, or something like them, are often forced. Poetry or sentiment is far from them. The wish is wrung out from them by bitter anguish. Go to beds of pain, listen to the moanings and sighings,

look at the worn face, and the weary, restless tossings.
What is the longing of that sufferer, but that of
the text ?

Follow that man who is hurrying along the street.
Look into his face. It speaks of care that is like
to drown him. If you could read his thoughts,
you would find them wild with anxiety, now tossed
like a sea into white foam, and now again frozen into
the ice of despair. How gladly would he, if he could,
escape anywhere—anywhere from the terrible struggle.

Go into that lonely room ;—a mother is sitting there
thinking of one far away, she knows not where, on
a path of guilt and shame. Can any human words
describe the load that presses that heart, where the
very mystery of a mother's love has turned into stone.
Where can she flee from that world of grief ?

Here is a man who is in no outward difficulty. He
is sitting at his window gazing out in the sunset over
a scene of almost peerless loveliness. The mountains
are bathed in splendour, and the sky has those glorious
tints that seem too rich for this world, a silver
stream is gliding before him like the river of the water
of life, and the whole scene looks like the earnest
of heaven. Yet this man has, by this very scene, had
his memory awakened; the past is rushing over
him. He sees nothing of all this glory now. He
is forced to look at scenes which are agony to his soul.
The cold sweat is coming out on his brow, as he thinks

of those scenes of injured love, of rebellion, of treachery and ingratitude and broken hearts. Oh, if he had the wings of a dove to fly away from those terrible memories, which are making hell in his soul, while all without is like heaven.

If you could range over the earth, if you could but know the burdens, the cares, the sorrows of a minute portion of the world; if you but knew what wearing anxieties hundreds around you are familiar with; if you knew what aching heads are laid on pillows which sleep visits but little, what weary hearts there are afraid to think of the morrow, what distraction and perplexity, what wringing suspense, what benumbing disappointment, how many are marching wearily on trying to keep up a brave exterior, but with bleeding feet and hearts trickling out their very life blood, drop by drop—if you only knew a tenth or a hundredth part of these things, you would know the frequency and reality of this longing, how unutterably earnest is the force with which it bursts from the soul —" Oh, that I had wings like a dove."

And what shall we say of the longing which men often have who are engaged in the noblest struggles? Do not men who are fighting bravely for truth and right sometimes lose heart? Do not those who labour and pray for the good of men and the glory of God sometimes sink in despondency? Do not they say, " The tide is too strong, I cannot stem it "? Are not

men sometimes, like Elijah of old, ready to say, "It is
enough, let me die; what am I better than my fathers?
Let me go and be with them"? Do not earnest spirits
say, "All that I can do is like a pebble thrown into
the ocean"? The turmoil and clangour and strife of
the world, the din of dispute, the conflict of parties,
the debate and heartburnings, are like to overthrow
them, and often force out the longing to be away from
it all, to be far from turmoil and strife, and to be left
to lead a quiet life with God. Is it not this that has
drawn the hermit to his cave, and the monk to his
cell? Is it not this deep craving for room in which
the soul may realize itself, for power to live without
distraction, to breathe calmly, to look round with freedom—is it not this that has thrown a charm round the
dull, grey, leaden life of the monastery and the convent,
and made many more than content to live in soli-
tudes, among woods and fields, and by the lonely sea?
There is a good and a bad element in this. It is good
to love quiet and rest of soul, in which a man can realize
himself, and God, and eternity; but it is not well, it is
not noble, it is not good and right, to wish to escape
from the battle of life and the struggle for man and
God. It is not good or right to shirk the tasks for the
sake of quiet and repose. A man who does not feel
this longing for quiet, who never feels it, who seems as
if he could not feel it, must have some great want
about him; but he who yields to it so far as to cut

himself off from social sympathies, from active relationship to his kind, who values quiet more than truth and right and duty, is sinking into sentimental selfishness.

II. *There is a legitimate fulfilment of this longing. There are wings with which a man may flee away and be at rest, while yet he remains at his post.*

A man under the pressure of care comes out and looks away across the sea; and he cannot tell how it is, but somehow his care grows lighter. What connection there should be between the sea and his care he cannot guess, but there is a connection. The far look over the waves eases his pain. Another man looks up to the sky in a starry night, and the stars carry him away; they give him wings stronger than a dove's. He flies through worlds, and leaves his cares behind him. Another man goes out into the sunshine. It is a very bright day; it is too bright for his gloom. The sunshine goes into his soul. Another man, in his distraction, hears a band of military music coming down the street. It takes his heart by storm, routs his care, leads his sorrow captive, and makes him for a while as brave a soldier, and as dauntless and free as any one that ever braved death. Another recalls a snatch of an old melody. He heard it long ago. He does not know how it has come to him now; but it keeps sounding and ringing through his soul. He does not ask it to come or stay; but it will not go, and keeps ringing and chiming till it rings out his grief, and sets his whole mind to a different key.

Now, what all these things do in their own way for a while, faith and hope and prayer and fellowship with God do in a high and abiding way. Let the burdened soul only rise into fellowship with God, let it only grasp God and speak with Him, and it will get wings to fly.

Let me mention a few things in reference to these wings.and their flight.

We must not think that flying away from care and sorrow with these wings is any strange and wonderful thing. We expect that it will be something which will come as the result of great effort, or with some great excitement. We expect a great stretching and flapping of wings. We think it an extraordinary, marvellous thing to be able to fly away with the wings that God gives. We do not wonder that people should be carried away for a while by music, or scenery, or reverie, or memory; but we think it wonderful that they should be borne away by faith and hope. We know that men are carried away by these other things, before they know, and without effort; but we do not expect this in religion. We are wrong in this. When these wings of religion carry the soul away from care and trouble, it is generally in a quiet imperceptible way. There is no excitement or stir or tumult. A man just believes and hopes, and finds that, so doing, he cannot be downcast or forlorn. May not many lose the flight of faith and hope by not believing that it is a flight, by expecting something marvellous?

Again, *faith and hope are good wings, when they are good hands and feet.* If they are not kept in ordinary obedience, they will not be good at flying. The more faithful and hard their work of obedience is, the more sure they will be to fly away with a man from the pressure of care and sorrow. The more busy they are on the street and in the house, in the workshop and in the heart, the more rapid their flight. Keep hope busy purifying your heart, and she will be strong to carry you.

Again, *keep faith and hope well nourished with truth.* Let them be fed constantly with God's word. It is close, habitual acquaintance with the word of God that makes them strong. It is feeding on Christ that gives them energy.

Again, *we must not think that one of them will suffice to fly with.* Do not men often think that they can fly with faith alone? No doubt, faith in Christ is the main support of the soul. Everything begins with that, and rests on that, but faith was never meant to be alone. Faith must have hope along with it. We must not only trust in Christ, but nourish our hearts with the great hopes of a glorious future. We absolutely require the thought of the future; we require it to be prominent. We require to gladden and cheer ourselves with the great hope of immortality. It is for want of this, often, that faith makes a feeble flight. The more wings, the better and stronger each is.

Let us fix it, then, in our soul, let it be a settled thing with us, that there are wings by which we can fly away and be at rest. We can hasten our escape from the windy storm and tempest. We can be in the world, with its trouble, and yet out of it. We can wing our flight away to the quiet hills of God, while the din is around us. And it is not a rare and hard achievement. There are thousands and thousands of humble devout souls who do it. Ever and again, while in their place in the busy driving world, they are off to the green pastures, they are off to the sunshine; they are away from the winter that is around to the sweet summer of God. They have a chariot of fire at hand, and they go right up beyond the stars with it at once. When they are wearied and downcast, they go away home for a little. Their home is never far away. It is in their Father's bosom. When they get bewildered and disheartened, they go away to the eternal realities; they go to fellowship, and thought of eternal righteousness and love. And then they see that the things that were disquieting, vexing, oppressing them, are mere shadows—that they are only vapours; that there is no reality but the Eternal God and His truth. They see that weeping may lodge overnight, but endless joy comes in the morning. And so they go back, strong and bright, to their work and their burden, till the day break and the shadows flee away.

WATCH TOWERS.

"I will stand upon my watch, and set me upon the tower, and will watch to see what He will say unto me, and what I shall answer when I am reproved."—Habakkuk ii. 1.

THIS is not the kind of watching usually so designated in Scripture. That is a watching against evil in ourselves and the world; this is a watching for a voice from God, for comfort, direction, and reproof. It is a prophet that here speaks of so watching; but it is not exclusively a prophet's position and task, nor is it exclusively a prophet's privilege, to hear the divine voice. All God's children are taught of God. It is the high privilege of the humblest of them to wait for the voice of God, and to hear it in the chambers of the heart. What does the prophet mean by watch towers? Had he special places to which he went that are inaccessible to us? Had the land of Palestine towers of outlook for God which our country does not possess? The prophet possessed no better watch towers than we have. Our land has as many as any region of earth. A watch tower is whatever of truth or life, whatever of prayer or praise makes you feel elevated above the world, whatever lifts you above the sway of the present and visible, and makes you feel the eternal verities real. Let us indicate some of these watch towers.

Such is *Prayer*. No man can be said to set himself on a watch tower at all who does not ascend this one. But it is not every kind of prayer that can claim such a name. Generally you must have peculiar intensity of spirit. Generally you must begin at a low depth of penitence, you must struggle and wrestle with God for a blessing, you must be earnest and confident in pleading the name of Christ, you must have a deep and sore longing for the triumph of God's cause, ere you can feel yourself on a tower. But sometimes not; sometimes only to say the words, " Our Father," getting just a glimpse of what they mean, of the wealth, power and beauty there is in them, opens in a moment a wide horizon. What a view you get from the height of those words urged as prayer. From the grandeur and glories of the divine nature look around. What a radiance seems to gild the darkness of time. *Our Father.* Utter the words again, press deeper into their meaning, make them a mighty plea, feel that you are grasping the very heart of God—do you not see better than you did before ? Is not the meaning of life different from what

it ever was before ? There are words that are never
understood till you·pray them. Such a word·is *Father.*
No man · can feel what that word means till he
tries what it is as an argument with God. And when
he has thus tried it, and thoughts and hopes are
spreading before him, then let. him watch to see
what God·will say to him. Assuredly God has something special to say to him at such a time. Let him
listen. Is it not some solution of a difficulty ? Is it
not some removal of a load ? Is there not some, duty
pointed out to him in an unmistakable way ? Perhaps
you have been waiting for light upon your path in life.
Does no light come at this time ? Is there no hint
given to you as to how you should bear your cross, or
how you may help another to bear his ? Do you not,
hear some distinct and strong indication of some path
of usefulness that you are to follow ?

Sometimes it is a *Truth* that supplies a watch tower
to the soul. There is no truth regarding God or man
which may not elevate you to a height above the world
and time. The eternity of God, His unchangeableness,
His holiness, His justice, truth or mercy, what
heights are supplied by these. They are great
mountains. Only realize one of these truths and you
are away higher than any part of the Alps or Andes.
It is the easiest thing in the world to be high and to
get a wide outlook—no toiling, no flying upward, only
feel any of these truths. And you feel them, you

realize them, by praying earnestly over them, and by bringing them close to the thought of your own death and approaching eternity. Oh, the thought of death and eternity, joined to earnest prayer, will lift you up high on the summit of any grand mountainous truth, such as God's almightiness, justice or mercy. And when you are on such towers be sure to watch what He will say to you. Hear what comfort He pours out. As one whom his mother comforteth, the Lord will comfort you. Listen! Is not that a rebuke you hear? how sharp and severe it is, how overwhelming! What can you answer when you are reproved? Be assured, if you listen on these towers, you will hear comfort, rebuke, exhortation. They may come altogether, or they may come at intervals, but they will all come. You will hear, " Rejoice, Rejoice.' " Be of good cheer." "I have somewhat against thee." " Be zealous and repent." " This is the way, walk in it." You will hear on the watch tower some voice you particularly need, but it may not be at all the tone or the message that you would have expected. You would have expected consolation, you watched for that, but it did not come. Instead of consolation, a message of rebuke came to your soul, that seemed almost to sink you into the earth; or it may have been simply a reiteration, an emphasizing of some truth or precept which you knew already. You were disappointed. You listened intently, but nothing else came.　Ah! but that rebuke, or that familiar truth, was the true message of joy to your soul.　That was the beginning of consolation.

The most striking event, and also the greatest assemblage of truths, is the death of Jesus Christ.

Calvary is spiritually the highest mountain in the world, and yet it is the easiest to climb.　This is truly the mountain of the Lord.　Why do I say that it is the easiest to climb?　Because, if you look at Jesus on the cross, and think what that means, it draws you up to the summit without any climbing.　Let me think who hangs on that cross, let me tear aside the veil of custom and usage, and think who in very deed that Sufferer is.　That is the Son of Man, the Son of God; that is God in my nature, for my redemption.　What must God be: how amazing in love, how inflexible in holiness.　That is a love that knows no bounds; that is a holiness which will never change or yield.　From that cross I hear the words with a new brilliancy and depth, "God is Love," and also the words, "I the Lord your God am holy.　Be ye holy, for I am holy."　The oftener we ascend this mountain, the easier the ascent is, and the wider and more impressive the view.　And, particularly, the more we watch to hear what God will say to us, and the more we take to heart what He says to us, the more easy shall we find it to reach the watch tower which is hard by the cross of Christ, and from which the widest and truest view of all things is to be gained.

But there are watch towers of a more general and occasional kind. One of these is found in every height which gives you a wide view over sea or land. Who can tell exactly what it is, in a wide prospect of any kind, which gives a feeling of delight, sometimes of astonishment, and even of awe? It is one of the commonest of delights. Who has not felt the thrill in gazing from a lofty spire? Who does not remember the feeling approaching rapture with which, the climbing over, he looked from the brow of the hill? Often the climber has had feelings he did not expect. Somehow that wide view, the smallness of objects that were great before, the vast stretch, the smoke of cities, the faint sounds that reach from the world below, the felt near neighbourhood of the sky, altered the standard by which he measured things. He felt dissatisfied, a certain grand serenity, from the wide vision, was marred and damped by an undertone that spoke of the vanity of life, of the vanity of all things to the immortal spirit, except goodness and truth and God.

What shall we say of those great crises in the history of nations to which the mind turns with ever new interest? Have you followed the workings of men's minds through generations? Have you watched the heaving, swaying to and fro, till on some fateful day the old disappeared with a crash, and out of the swel-

H

tering chaos the new order slowly and with groans and outcries emerged? No one has read of such great crises in the history of humanity without a mingling of anxiety and enthusiasm, and without having his horizon enlarged in a way that he could never estimate. But surely there are few who have perused such scenes with intensity of interest without hearing a voice more or less distinct. What is man? What is life? What an insoluble mystery it all is! What are its tumult and fever, signs of greatness and signs of baseness! Of all marvels man is the crown. One thing amid all dust and smoke is clear—righteousness is the one permanent thing, and is working on to some grand consummation. One thing also is clear—no man in all these millions has more than a little portion of his life expressed in all those public ongoings. The true history is within, and can never be written. There, is a life beyond this. That is certain. My soul, how dost thou stand to this life to come, and to righteousness? Such times are the true mountains, the towers in the history of the world, whether they come in great struggles, like Bannockburn, or the German War, or the conflict with the Southern States, or mingled outpourings of blood and passionate conviction, as in the struggles of the Reformation and the Covenants. The thinking of them elevates and fills with thought and questioning. Is my life at all earnest as life with them was? Am I capable of struggle? Is there any

cause for which I would fight and die? Am I living
for ease and pleasure? Am I vegetating like the fat
weed that rots on Lethe's wharf? My soul, listen,
watch what He will say to thee at the great crises and
struggles, the battles and weary marches of thy race.
Were it not nobler and better to have been the poorest
soldier-peasant that carried a pike fighting for the
Covenant, for right and truth and God, than to live
without earnest interest in anything good, or any care
beyond self and its little circle? Listen, watch what
thou wilt say when thou art reproved.

There are few things equal to the history of man—it
matters little of what nation it is—for carrying you
away out of self, and setting you, a wider and deeper
man, upon a high position of observation. As you
read accounts of baseness and treachery and far-reach-
ing wrong, your heart burns with indignation, your
sympathies are roused, a moral electricity flashes from
you. And as you read of great virtues, of grand souls
that lived even above fame, and aimed at the noblest
in darkest days, who were defeated, perhaps, and
crushed, but who knew not what defeat was, whose eye
kept fixed upon the pole star of right, with a faith
which fire could not burn nor waters drown, what a
height you attain! You feel that there is a boundless
possibility in man, that he is capable of a goodness
amazing and sublime. What voice do you hear at
such times, when your soul is swelled with such

thoughts? You hear many things at that elevation, with these wide thoughts around you, that you cannot hear at any lower level. Alas, that the most of men who stand on these heights, and who, with these prospects before them, hear voices calling them to something truer and nobler, should let the voices die down and be forgotten, with the transient elevation which they had found. Taking a true, sober estimate of things, the history of almost every people, though particularly the history of Israel and of Greece and Rome, and the history of the great struggles that have been in the ages since, down to our own day, is full of watch towers on great elevations to which we may easily ascend, and where we may listen to strange, high, penetrating voices of stimulus and rebuke.

Let us leave history and come to actual life. The dullest, most monotonous life has such towers to which it may, yea at times must, ascend. You are not of an imaginative turn, you say; romance is not found in you, and you never meet with any of these watch towers in your prosaic life. Were you never at a funeral which seemed to you for once not a thing of routine? Did you never feel, as you stood there among the mourners, as if a veil were lifted from the world, and you stood away at a height above it, where all its plans and pleasures and struggles wore quite a different aspect? As you thought how earth and time were closed to this departed friend, and how they would be closed to yourself one day, did you not see something like a dream or vision of a different sort of life-plan altogether from what you had been cherishing? Or have you never felt at a dying bed, when the last farewell was uttered, or when bidding adieu to friends never again to be met on the shores of time, as if existence had been gathered up into a point, as if you were raised quite above time, and could take in at a glance the meaning of its changes, and understand what was the real drift and aim of all?

Watch towers—ah! there is no lack of them to him who will but glance at the newspapers, or note the changes that go on in life. What birds of passage we are! What an incessant pulling down and building up our life is, what a perpetual gathering and scattering! If you will but realize where you are, open your eyes and look round you on the strange melodrama of life : laughter and music in one house, the shroud and the coffin in the next ; joy and success in one, disaster and grief in another; love and sunshine here, gloom and heartbreak there : you will be raised out of the hurry and bustle, the din will not deafen you ; you will seem to occupy a position of calm, from which you survey life and take in the ocean that lies beyond. Always, when you think of the change and chaos of life, you are obliged to think of the ocean that lies beyond which we must all sail so soon. Have you not been more than once lifted up into such a watch tower, however young you may be? Did you never hear a voice something like this? "Is life all made up of change, of death and parting, of gathering and scattering? Is there not something deeper than this? Ah! yes, the heart of life, the centre, the soul and essence of it, is something above all this. How do I stand to this centre and soul, this substance and reality of things?"

Brethren, our life in this flux and reflux of things will be a poor, shallow, heartless thing, unless we get up into a watch tower and hearken what God will say to us. The heart will go out of the heart, amid the din and worry, unless we escape ever and again to a clear height and look around. Let us not be afraid that God will not speak. The fear is that we shall not be found listening; the fear is that we shall not be looking for those watch towers which every life supplies, and that we shall come from them without hearing or seeing anything.

Let us be on our guard against making up our mind beforehand what God will say to us. Let us be willing to receive the very opposite message from God. Above all, let us expect to be reproved. Whatever joy and courage and direction may come to us, it can scarcely be God's voice unless there is reproof in it. "As many as I love, I rebuke"; let us not forget that. Would it be true love that did not rebuke us, and we standing in so much need of rebuke? Oh, the blessed,

searching, bitter rebuke of God, exposing us to ourselves, and making us ashamed, how sweet it is! Do
you understand anything of this sweet bitter? If a
man listens faithfully on the watch tower of memory,
expecting and welcoming rebuke, he will get something higher and sweeter. Who is it that sees God's
face best? It is the soul that is dissatisfied with self,
that sees something faulty and wanting in its very
best. To that soul the mercy of God is very dear.
From his watch tower he looks for the mercy of God
unto eternal life. What is the sincerest and best of
men to answer when the keen voice of rebuke is heard
in his soul? He may be able to answer much that
admits the rebuke, and yet can point to something that
is genuine; his answers may justly embrace his work
and labour and patience, his consistency and blameless-
ness, the unfeigned struggles of his soul after God
through long years; but the answer that will bring
comfort and rest and joy is not found much in any or
all of these. The answer is Christ, Christ, Christ for
me, Christ mine, my hope and my all. He " loved me
and gave Himself for me." " Who shall separate us
from the love of Christ?" " I know whom I have
believed, and am persuaded that He is able to keep
that which I have committed to Him." What shall I
answer when I am reproved? I shall cry, Abba,
Father! I shall lay firmer hold on God than ever.
All voice of reproof will pass into assurance of ever-

lasting love, as one has often heard the roaring blast sink into a soft whisper of peace, and seen the black cloud first gilded along all its edges with glory, then pierced here and there with jets of effulgence, till at last it was all transformed into brightness. What shall I answer when I am reproved? I shall lay my heart before God and cry, " Search me, and lead me in the way everlasting." I shall listen to hear the other things that He says besides reproof. I am well assured that the more I look into His face, the more I shall have grand and glowing promises, words of melting love, words of tenderness beyond a mother's. I shall lie at His feet, and tell Him to do what He will with me. I shall lay my head in His bosom, and then I shall hear whispers and snatches of secrets which tongue cannot utter.

CROOKED THINGS.

"Consider the work of God: for who can make that straight which He hath made crooked?"—Ecclesiastes vii. 13.

ACCORDING to the manner of Ecclesiastes, this verse is the opposite or reverse of that which precedes it. Knowledge can do much, money can do much, wisdom can do more. It puts life into those who have it. This is the bright, cheering, sanguine side. On the other hand, there are evils that cannot be removed or remedied. God has made some things crooked, *i.e.*, wanting or adverse, which never can be made straight or favourable to man, such as defects of climate, excess of cold or heat, violent storms, volcanoes, hurricanes, droughts, and floods. There are many evils in life which man can neither avert nor remedy. On every side there are limitations—therefore do not expect too much of money or knowledge or wisdom. Human life will always be a poor, narrow, empty thing. Such is the manifest drift of the question—"Who can make that straight which God hath made crooked?" As we revolve this question, the subject opens out, and embraces the whole mystery of human life, and of the ways of God and man.   Ecclesiastes is always walking among those ultimate difficulties, and trying to lift them, or in some way adapt himself to them ; and there is none of us to whom such questions do not recur.   Every man feels more or less that he is encompassed with vast mysteries, and that a great part of these lies in the fact that there are so many things that God has made crooked or adverse, and which no power can ever make favourable.

The first thought that strikes us is that *God has manifestly made many things crooked—defective or adverse —that man may make them straight, and so raise himself.*

It would not have been good for us to have all things made straight and smooth to our hands.   It is not where Nature wears her blandest aspect that man has attained his best.   Where the earth has given him liberally and without stint, he has not developed great qualities.   It is well for him that he has had to hew the rocks, to make roads, and to cross wide and raging seas. It is well for him that he has had to fight against wild beasts, to bank up rivers from overflowing, to make walls against the sea, and to tunnel the mountains.   God has put man into a world where toil is necessary, in order that all his faculties may find exercise, and thus grow. He would have dwindled down had God made things smooth for him. Man may dislike effort, toil, danger, anxiety, planning and struggling against evils that sometimes threaten to crush him; but these are the rough friends, the blessings in disguise, that make him strong and great. Many of the noblest virtues are strengthened by these dangers and struggles, as courage, unselfishness, self-control, patience, forbearance, the power of sacrificing the present to the future. Man, therefore, can to a certain extent make things straight which God has made crooked; and this has been designed for his elevation and development in every direction—body, soul, and spirit. He crushes the rock for gold, he seeks diamonds in the mine, and gems at the bottom of the sea, he brings order out of apparent disorder, he seeks law amid apparent chance, he utilizes the wind and the waves, he harnesses the lightning; and all this God manifestly intended when he put man with his latent powers into such a world, and made it necessary for him either to fight or die.

Whoever, then, strives to make straight that which God has made crooked is simply carrying out a divine idea. It is not that there are mistakes in God's work which we may correct, but only that there are roughnesses, blanks, obstructions, which God has left for the training of men. He has left confusion, that man may find the order hidden in it, and thus enter into the

spirit and interior meaning of His work. Man does
this with the powers that God has given him, and
beyond these he cannot go. He does it, not in any
arbitrary way of his own, but only in accordance with
the divine laws. It is by strict conformity to the
nature of things which God has ordained that man
accomplishes his work of straightening. If he attempts
it in any capricious way of his own, he brings barren-
ness or disaster. Man's straightening work shows
him a supernatural being, capable of entering into the
divine ideas and carrying them out, capable of rising
above the letter into the spirit, and being a co-worker
with God.

Again, *there are crooked things which man cannot
make straight,* and which, intended for a discipline
and trial, are better to remain crooked. With
all his knowledge of the laws of nature, man cannot
avert the sweeping hurricane, he cannot extinguish the
volcano, he cannot still the earthquake. He may
come to calculate the path of the storm ; but he cannot
mitigate its violence, or change its course. He cannot
arrest the sirocco, or the simoon. In his own constitution, again, there is weakness and disease against
which he struggles in vain. He becomes bewildered
and obscured even in his mind ; a thousand changes
and chances lie in wait for him all along his career,
ready to seize him remorselessly, overturn his plans,
and wreck his fairest hopes. And death certainly

awaits him sometime, somewhere, the one dark, mysterious, crooked thing, utterly and for ever beyond his power to make straight.

But is it not good for man to have these crooked things? *It is not good* for him, if he belongs merely to this world. If this life were all, it would be difficult to show the wisdom or benevolence or fairness of so much misery inherent in the very constitution of things. A wise Creator, not to speak of a benevolent one, would surely not see it fit to expose short-lived creatures to such fierce dangers and conflicts, without any purpose to gain by it. If this little life were all to man, surely wisdom and love would make it free from such terrible calamities. But when we think of man as an immortal being in the process of education for a higher world, when we think of earth as but the vestibule to a glorious destiny for which preparation is essential, then difficulties though without remedy, then trials severe and crushing, are seen to be reasonable, wise, and benevolent. The whole aspect of calamity is changed, whenever these words are pronounced " I reckon that the sufferings of this present time are not worthy to be compared with the glory that shall be revealed in us." " Our light affliction, which is but for a moment, worketh out for us a far more exceeding, even an eternal weight of glory." Are these inevitable calamities our schooling, our correction, and chastening? Are they constraints that bring us nearer to God, and wean us from self and all created things ?—then, verily, they are transfigured ; the very mystery and darkness of time are seen to be bringers of light.

Are there, then, adverse things in the lot of any one of us that seem irremediable ? Let us not too hastily conclude that they are so. Men differ in nothing more than in the estimate they form here. It may be that there are spirits who would find the difficulties that confound you light. It may be indolence, faint-heartedness, self-indulgence, self-pity, a feeling that all things.should be made to suit you, that is fashioning your judgment as to the hopelessness of things. Are you *quite sure* that nothing more can be done to remedy things ? Have you not heard of those who have failed often, and succeeded at last ? Have you not heard some knowledge of this in those around you, or even in your own history ? Do you not feel as if. another effort were imperative ? May not yours be one of the cases where the duty is never to yield, where to maintain the struggle is to succeed, however many apparent defeats there may be? It is better far to strive in vain against crooked things, than to sit down in tame, indolent acquiescence.

But when all is done, there *are* crooked things that cannot be made straight. Yet, remember that these are not wastes. Sahara is a desert, but its burning sands are a storehouse of heat for far regions, and melt the snows and glaciers on the Alps. Your irremediable evils may be the most potent things in your lot, the most elevating, and by-and-bye the most gladdening. The struggle you have had with them before you were forced to own them irremediable has blessed you ; and now there is another source of blessing, perhaps far higher, in the very knowledge that for these crooked things there is no remedy or hope in this world. Oh, what a blessed compulsion is in that ! What a constraint to lay hold on the heavenly realities ! What a necessity for a quiet spirit lying in God's hand ! What a force to constrain you to become rich in soul, and for ever !

Again, *there are crooked things which Christ makes straight.* The fall of man is the great crooked thing, the great perplexing mystery, which has taken place under the government of God. Whatever theory you adopt of the fall of man, there the perplexing fact stares you in the face—*man is fallen.* He is a being not according to his own ideal. He feels within him a root of bitterness. The evil was born with him. It is so deep in him that he cannot throw it out. But all the same his conscience condemns the evil. Here is the difference between man and other creatures. They need simply to carry out their nature, their inclination. He, if he follows his inclination, falls into evil ; if he follows his desire, he hurts and ruins himself. He must struggle constantly against his nature. He must keep up incessant warfare. To cease the fight is to be lost. You put the question, "How can it be wrong to follow inclination, to do what your nature prompts you to do?" But your own heart knows that this is folly; conscience condemns it; the feeblest exercise of reason teaches you that human life would become a hell if men were not to curb and control inclination. Even if you say that man has not fallen, but is rising, that it is the law of heredity prevailing everywhere that entails upon him selfish and evil inclinations, you have not in the least solved the difficulty. Here is the difficulty,—How should the law of heredity involve man in strife, in self-condemnation and · loathing, when it operates smoothly elsewhere? Laws of nature do not entail agony of remorse and penitence, or the fierce battle between two tendencies; they do not draw a creature in two opposite directions. The sense of obligation, the lofty ideal of duty, the condemning conscience, the tortures of remorse and grand sense of freedom, how do these agree with a law of nature? No, you cannot explain the mystery of man by laws of nature. Nature does not comprehend him, or give the clue to his enigma.

But what nature cannot do, Christ does. What is lost, man recovers in Christ, and in the Holy Spirit of Christ. You speak of men bearing each other's sins. That seems a perplexing thing, and yet it is a fact. Men suffer every day for the sins of past generations,

and for the sins of living men. They suffer for the
sins of their parents and their children. Every man
suffers for sins not his own, unavoidably and always.
If any man rebels against this fact, I ask him how it
can be avoided in a world where men are connected as
they are? It is a crooked thing which never can be
made straight, fight against it as you will. Argue
against it, the fact remains, and is working in yourself
while you argue. But whenever you accept Christ as
the grand and crowning example of the fact, when you
believe in Him as not only suffering for our sin, but
bearing our load away, when you believe in renewal
by the Holy Spirit of Christ, in the might of God
coming to our help, you have a light on all mystery.
"If sin hath reigned, much more hath the gift of
righteousness through Jesus Christ our Lord." In the
light of the glorious truth of redemption by Christ
and renewal by the Holy Spirit, you see how the curse
has been turned into a blessing. It is an advantage
to a man, in a sense, to be born under the dread entail
of sin; it is an advantage to be included in common
calamity, for there is almighty help at hand. One
has but to hold out his hand and divine help is his.
He is included and bound up in Christ, and the effort
of struggle against evil develops a far higher, stronger,
tenderer form of goodness than would otherwise be
possible. The purity and truth and faithfulness and
love that one has gained by strife, by patience, by

weariness, by prayer, by laying hold of God, by
meditation, by a very agony of will,—are not these
something superior to goodness that has always been
possessed?   Oh, it will be found at last to have been
worth enduring all the pains, and all the sad corruption and grief, in order to rise into the great eternal
radiance clad in beauty more than that of angels, and
wielding a strength greater than theirs.   It is well for
men to have been born with a tainted nature, if that
makes them feel the poison and bitterness of evil, leads
them through divine grace into decisive rejection of it,
fortifies them for ever against it, and makes them
through eternity enthusiastic converts to righteousness
and love.   They in a triple sense are God's, by
creation, by redemption, and by the energetic struggle
and most intelligent choice of their own will in rejecting the evil and clinging to the good.

Let us learn, then, that there is no adverseness in
circumstances which may not work for good.   There
are many crooked things in the lot of men which no
ingenuity can make straight, but these may be among
the most profitable parts of experience.   The most
adverse dispositions and tendencies in a man's nature
may be made through divine strength the means of
higher blessing.   Men who feel the pressure of unruly
natures, or who have that worst of all evils, the burden
of a hard, selfish, deceitful heart, who know in themselves that they are heartless and selfish beyond con-

ception, wanting in compassion and genuine benevolence, and moved only by self-interest,—such men
are apt, when they get a glimpse of their heart, to become despondent, to think that nothing can touch or
melt them. But that very despondency which they
feel, that condemnation of self, that disgust at their
own hardness and narrowness,—what does it mean?
That is another voice within them. That is the voice
of hope. That will be the dawn of a better day. That
despondency and despair of self is really the best thing
that could be experienced. It is the virtual casting
away and disowning the old self as something of which
they are ashamed. Let them only yield themselves to
God, tell Him the plague of their hearts, and He will,
either by struggle or without struggle, either slowly or
suddenly, take away the hard and stony heart, and give
them a heart of flesh. Be assured there is no defeat to
those who struggle. It is not the man without temptations that is blessed, but the man who overcomes, who
never gives in, and who, when his strength seems
utterly gone, lays himself down on divine strength and
says—" Though He slay me, yet will I trust Him." It
is the man who never ceases praying, who, in reply to
doubt prays, in reply to fears prays, in the face of difficulties prays, in the midst of danger prays.

Do not think yourself forsaken or cast off because
crooked things beyond your remedying gather round
you. If you but cleave fast to God, not one of them

will hurt you. Look to Him, and fight on. Though trials and temptations become more than they are, look to Him and work on. The calmest and gladdest times have often been those of greatest struggle; and if you but cleave earnestly to God, it will be so with you. There are things that are crooked in time, but eternity makes them straight. There are losses and wrongs which in this world are never set right; the world is full of these things. But eternity is not far off, and that puts all things in a new light. Look on to that time of straightening. What are all the crooked things of an evil day? How we shall wonder at our magnifying of these things, when we reach that serene, triumphant radiance!

I must say a word to such, then, as feel that they are all wrong, all crooked and perverse, who feel that there is no good in them. This conviction that you have of crookedness puts you in a very responsible position. You of all men ought to welcome a Saviour. Every conviction that you have of your own crookedness is an argument for going to Christ. Whoever they may be that have self-confidence and rest in self, *you* cannot. Whoever they be that take life easy and smile complacently and dream, *you* cannot, dare not, do so. Oh, how welcome a Saviour and an Almighty Spirit ought to be to *you*.

HUMILIATION AND COMMUNION.

"So brutish was I and ignorant, I was as a beast before Thee; nevertheless I am continually with Thee."—Psalm lxxiii. 22, 23.

THE Psalmist has been sore perplexed by that great mystery in the government of the world, the prosperity of the wicked. Their abundance, their ease, their freedom from anxiety, all stood out in strong colours before him. They were in great contrast to his struggling life, always striving to direct his way aright, always tending upward and seeking the good and true. He was troubled and distressed all day long; they passed their time free from care, and everything prospered with them. Then the thought passed across his mind, and even tarried and laid hold of him, "I have cleansed my heart in vain, and washed my hands in innocency."

Well might he say in looking back on this that his "feet were almost gone, and his steps had well nigh slipped"; for thoughts of this kind are the beginning of atheism. Is it worse to question the existence of

God than to question His rectitude? What were God without righteousness? To conceive of the infinitely Holy One as favouring iniquity, is nothing less than to think of Him as destroying Himself, abdicating His throne, and resigning all things to turmoil and chaos. The most dismal of all thoughts is that goodness, righteousness, and truth are without infinite support, that they are something extraneous and foreign in the universe, and must take their chance in the general scramble. Is it any wonder that when the Psalmist awoke to the true nature of his doubts,—when he saw all that they involved, when he realized the dreadful precipice to whose brink his ·blindness and perverse stupidity had brought him,—is it any wonder he should exclaim, " I was as a beast before Thee, as foolish and ignorant " ?

The text contains these three things—

  (1) *A Great Contrast.*
  (2) *A Severe Judgment of Self.*
  (3) *The Most Elevated and Blessed Assurance.*

I. *A Great Contrast.*

What a contrast between doubting the reality of God's government of the world,—a doubt which includes in its sweep the whole range of the divine character,— and the dwelling continually with God, the being holden up by God, with the prospect of being guided by Him through all life, and received afterwards into glory! What a contrast between judging things after the outward appearance and by this brief span of existence, and seeing the grandeurs of the divine character and the horizon of eternity! What a con- trast between the mere brute-gaze upon life, which sees only so much enjoyment of the senses, and the spiritual insight which sees the deep joy in God and the rest in eternal wisdom and love! What a con- trast between the vision of disorder and chance— goodness trampled under foot, and wrong and evil triumphing—and the serene view of Almighty Love behind all this temporary chaos and transient uproar and strife! How the whole proud pageant of un- godliness, the show and clamour and display pass away like the phantoms of a dream, when placed in the view of Infinite Love and Righteousness! Think of the contrast between the sight of the walls of a prison cell for years, and the free unrestricted sight of the sky with its millions of worlds stretching out into infinity;—would this be a greater contrast than that which is implied in the text? Think of the feelings of the man who has passed years in a mine, when at last he issues into the daylight with its golden sunshine, comes in contact again with the life which is streaming through the world and glowing in its face, hears again the singing of birds, the music of the winds, the deep bass of the sea, and all the varied tones of human life and work;—do you think this would be a greater contrast than that of the text?

The universe abounds in contrasts; from the minuteness of the microscopical animalcule, to the enormous bulk far beyond that of our world or its sun; from the dismal darkness of the cave to the ethereal splendours of the evening sky. And the contrasts in human life seem as if striving to equal in extent and variety the contrasts in nature. Look at the squalid savage who can scarcely count ten, and at the brilliant mathematician who can calculate eclipses and comets for hundreds of years, can weigh worlds and suns, and even rise to the conception of the symmetry of clusters and groups of starry systems. Think of the man whose ideas are all centred on self, and who regards righteousness and love and sympathy as phantoms, and of the bright and tender souls whose one ambition has been to forget self wholly and to live for ideas, for man and for God. Think of a Nero, and a Livingstone; of the unscrupulous destroyers and corrupters of men, and of the pure devoted ones who have only lived to heal and bless, to comfort and to cheer. And think of that contrast which most impresses men in life, the contrast between the extreme of poverty and the extreme of opulence; between the man who, in rags, whines for a crust of bread, and the man who, lord of miles of land, and of many sumptuous abodes, risks thousands of pounds on a chance, and thinks it a trifle whether he wins or loses. What overwhelming contrasts these are; and yet there is none of them which in the light of sober thought can be regarded for a moment as transcending the contrast of the text.

But what is most wonderful of all is, that it is the same man who illustrates both extremes. It is the same man who both is foolish as a beast, and dwells in the constant realization of God and communion with Him.

Man makes great changes. There is no creature on earth that can surpass him here; although earth includes in its transformations that from the unsightly grub which crawls on the bottom of the pond to the brilliant creature that flashes in the summer air. Men pass from ignorance to stores of learning, from grinding poverty to opulence, from barbarism to civilization, from vice to virtue, from doubt to faith. In some cases such change has required many years, in others it has taken place so rapidly that the man has been bewildered, and unable to think it other than a dream. Of all changes is there one that can equal that implied in the text? —and yet it may require no long time to accomplish. What was it that wrought the vast change on the Psalmist? It was going into the house of God. There in the worship of God, there in the truths held up regarding God, he saw the key to the perplexing enigma. He saw that the prosperity of

the wicked was a slippery place in which God had set
them—a place of severe discipline, where temptations
to evil abounded, and where checks were few and weak.
When he looked at this brief life in the light of the
future, and as a place for the formation of permanent
character and the framing of deep and abiding relationships, his estimate of things was entirely altered.   He
saw now that the best position in the world is that
which is most fitted to nourish good principles, most
fitted to bring the soul to God, and to press it ever
nearer to Him.   He saw that true prosperity meant
prosperity of the man himself—of the inner, enduring
man—a prosperity independent of time and place, a
life in God which death itself could not touch, but
could only emancipate and heighten.   It was the truth,
the sight of the reality, which produced this grand
change.   The mightiest changes are worked by the
incoming of thought.   Let great ideas enter into the
soul and gain a true mastery, and they will bring the
soul round to an entire contradiction of its former self.

The greatest changes, then, are possible to any
person here.   You may think yourself immovable,
and the thought may bring congratulation or sorrow.
It may be with a feeling of pride and exultation that
you say, " I shall never change, I am entrenched and
fortified in my position " : and yet, perhaps, even now
there is a thought forming secretly in your soul which
may grow,—which, if nursed and fostered by a turn in

your outward life, will certainly grow. Are you not sometimes afraid that it will grow till it changes you into something the very reverse of what you now are ? If it is a thought of God and eternity, another way of looking at God, a deeper feeling of the certainty of an eternal world, take heed that it be allowed to work out its true issue. Perhaps it is in sorrow ; but you say, "I shall never change ; time was when I might have changed, but now that is past. It is impossible. I must remain as I am. I am fixed and petrified. If stone might be moved then I might." *Yes, stone may be moved.* Stone has been often moved and broken. Hearts of adamant have been softened. If only mighty thoughts gain entrance they will break the hardest stone. If you really wish to be changed, and cry to God to aid, the greatness of the change needed will be no obstacle. The greatest change may be more easily accomplished than some small one.

II. Let us look at the *severe judgment passed on self.*

" So foolish was I and ignorant, I was as a beast before Thee." It is a severe judgment—one that stamps with degradation—and if uttered with reference to another it would be outrageous. To say that a man has sunk below the level of humanity, and become as a beast, is one of the last indignities. But it is good for a man to utter such a sentence with deep indignation against himself—especially if it rises out of no passing

humour arising from disappointment and chagrin at
the poor figure he has cut, or the stupid part he has
played in allowing himself to be cajoled, outwitted, or
over-reached. Do you not think a man may sometimes come away from a scene or rehearse it in
memory, and mentally stamp and rave and tear his
hair with vexation and rage, calling himself opprobrious
epithets, such as an ass or a beast for his stupidity,
and after all be none the better, or rather all the
more a beast for his fury ? Still, on the whole, it is a
very wholesome thing for a man to be indignant at himself, and smite and buffet himself and call himself ugly
names ; most of all when there is the occasion for it
that the text supposes. When one has been so foolish
as to impeach the moral government of God ; when he
has been so stupid as to think that it can ever be in vain
for a man to be righteous ; when he has had the
blindness to envy the prosperity of the wicked, forgetting the slipperiness of their position ; or when he has
felt and acted as if there were no moral government of
the world and no judgment to come ; when he has
thought or felt or acted as if sin were a trifle, and
thrown himself out of harmony with the dreadful
denunciation of it given in the Bible and echoed by
conscience—then he ought to be indignant at himself.
There can be no error in saying that he was "as a beast,"
for the truth is he was worse than that. It is dreadful
for a man to become as a beast ; abdicating reason

which looks before and after, conscience which weighs
the moral element, the sense of the infinite and eternal,
the thoughts which wander through eternity—dreadful
to look at things merely on the outside with the gaze
of a brute—dreadful to see no moral meaning in life,
to forget that life is a school, a discipline, an arena and
battlefield.   It is dreadful; for if a man becomes as a
beast in this way he becomes infinitely lower than
a beast,—he contradicts his nature, which the beast
cannot do.   It is the awful peculiarity of man that he
can contradict his whole true self, trample on his
highest nature, pervert and ruin himself.   As the
engine-driver can reverse the engine, so man can
reverse the forces of his nature, and send it hellward
instead of heavenward.

Sometimes a man may pass such a severe judgment
on himself while he is still under the power of evil.
He goes on his way of transgression, now and again
calling himself a very beast.   Perhaps he feels a kind
of penance in the abuse he heaps upon himself.   It is
like the lash which the monk wields on his own bare
shoulders till the blood flows.   There is a feeling of
expiation both in the blood and the hard names;
one cannot tell which may have the most of the feeling.
But evidently there is some fatal want in the condemnation and abuse, however severe, when its outcome
is not a forsaking of the stupid, base, and perverse
course.   Yes, the better self in a man may pass such a

severe sentence on himself with indignation ; but it is only when he looks back on his past self from a wholly different position, that the sentence is uttered with force and with deep sorrow. It is only the man who has parted for ever with his perverse, degraded, selfish life who can fully say, " So foolish was I, and ignorant, I was as a beast before Thee."

III. *There is here the most elevated and confident assurance of nearness to God, and abiding relationship to Him.*

"Nevertheless I am continually with Thee." It is remarkable that the searching and severe judgment of himself does not prevent him from claiming God and expressing confidence in Him. At first, undoubtedly, and while a man looks mainly at himself, a thorough estimate of his sinfulness will produce hesitation and fears. But when he turns to God, when thoughts of God accompany Him all the day long, when he leans on God in all the struggle of life, when the thought of the All-seeing eye purges his soul, and the thought of eternal love upholds him ; when his last waking thought is God, and his first waking thought is God, and when sleepless nights are cheered by the thought of God,—a man must doubt his strongest and deepest consciousness if he doubts his constant dwelling with God. Yes, it is a blessed thought that the knowledge that he has been foolish and ignorant as a beast before God does not prevent the joyous assurance of His constant presence with him, nor the confident conviction of divine guidance in all the future. And what is it that gives this confident assurance ? It is simply the fact that the soul clings to God, and knows that it does so. When a soul clings to God and esteems Him the One portion in earth and heaven, do you think that anything can shake its confidence that God is ever near, and will sustain and bless for ever and ever ? No doubt there are the promises of God on which the soul may lean ; but, remember, the man whose inward history is here recorded had few promises. There were few stars of promise in the firmament at the period when the Psalms were written. The richest and grandest promises are in the Psalms themselves. It was that on which all the promises rest—the nature of God—that mainly fed the confidence of the soul. The longing of the soul for God, its yearning for nearness to Him, is the grand proof to the soul that He is with it, and will never forsake it. This is the argument that the soul uses, this the reasoning that gives it rest, whether it is conscious of reasoning or not,—Shall I long for God, cling to Him as·my all, and shall He who is infinitely better than I remain distant from me ? God's ways are higher than our ways, and His thoughts than our thoughts ; and if I cleave to Him, much more does He to me. This is the reasoning that God teaches the man who perseveres in seeking Him. He gets such sight of what God is that he cannot doubt He is with him now and always. Oh, press closer to God; closer and closer to God! Let your cry be, " Nearer, my God, to Thee, nearer to Thee!" Say, " Whom have I in heaven but Thee, and there is none in all the earth whom I desire beside Thee." And if you do this, do you imagine there will be any doubt in your mind as you say, "I am continually with Thee." " Thou holdest me by my right hand." " Thou wilt guide me by Thy counsel while I live, and afterward receive me to glory."

And what a grand, blessed thought it is, that though you justly reckon that you have been as a beast before God, your past need not prevent you, will not prevent you, from the closest and most joyful experience of God. Though you have doubted and denied, and been perverse and stupid, yet you may take God as your portion. God will not keep you far off in an outer court because you have been stupid and brutish. When once you judge and condemn yourself, and choose Him as your portion, that is all past and gone, and will be remembered no more for ever.

What is to be feared is that you will rest content in the condemnation of self,—that you will say, "I have been stupid and brutish," and not pass on to say, " nevertheless I am continually with Thee." That you may even say, with a kind of deceitful humility, " I whc have been so vile, how can I ever venture to claim nearness to God, to claim God as mine ? " Let me tell you what will cure you of that deceitful humility. Looking at God, seeing God as He is in Christ, will both lead you to condemn yourself, and give you confidence for present and future.

Let us sum up with this. He who says, " I am continually with Thee," claims the very highest position and the highest society possible for any creature ; he claims that of which he may be absolutely sure ; he claims the position which can alone be continual, unaffected by all the changes of life, untouched by death.

THE OPEN FACE.

"We all, with open face beholding as in a glass the glory of the Lord, are changed into the same image from glory to glory, even as by the Spirit of the Lord."—2 Cor. iii. 18.

THE figure here is on the whole plain, as it is certainly most expressive. We look, with an open face,—not with veil or cloud, but direct and free,—into the history of our Lord's life and death as into a mirror. It is not easy, at first, to perceive the reason why it is a *mirror* that we look at rather than a *picture*. One looks into a mirror to see oneself; but in this mirror it is not self we see, but Christ. What can be the meaning of this? Why, we ask again, is it not called a picture rather than a mirror? The reason, doubtless, is to be found in the brilliancy and reflecting power of the mirror. A mirror throws back the light on the face of the beholder; a picture does not. The Gospel is a mirror in brilliancy. It throws back a splendour and radiance on him who contemplates it. But it throws back more, it throws back a likeness;

for the Lord Jesus, though unseen, is looking into the mirror of the Gospel, and the likeness as well as the lustre of His face is reflected on every one who gazes intently.

The Glory in the Mirror, The Beholding, and *The Change effected on the Beholder,*—these are evidently the three things which a consideration of the passage involves.

I. *The Glory in the Mirror* is the greatest anywhere to be seen, for it is that of God manifest in the flesh. It is the glory of the divine, which could not be expressed in stars or flowers; it is the glory of the human—in life, in action, and suffering. The glory shown in the Gospel is both definite and indefinite; a glory of particular actions of mercy and love, and a glory as of a halo or cloud of brightness which cannot be put into words. There is this definite and indefinite glory in the universe. The glorious power and wisdom of God are manifested in particular things; the corn and the fruit trees illustrate His benevolence. But the grand lustre of the sky, the beauty that lies dreaming on the hills—who shall define it or say what it illustrates. A flower has both the definite and the indefinite glory. You can point to the harmony of the colour and the perfection of the form: but the charm of the whole—who shall define? So with the Lord Jesus Christ. We take each particular action of His, every portion of endurance, every word, and hold it aloft. It flashes like a diamond with peerless radiance. But a spirit of beauty and grandeur, a lowly heavenly spirit, a vastness of view, an elevation of aim, a tenderness of touch that cannot be defined, are everywhere.

It is a condensed but boundless picture. In order to be grasped and appreciated the picture needs to be small. The glory of God scattered across boundless space cannot be taken in by man. He loses himself in it. .But here, in the Gospel, we have a miniature of God. Your eye takes in the infinite glory at a glance. When God came into human nature he translated the vast grandeurs of eternity into human language. He uttered the unutterable. So man at his daily task can think of Jesus Christ, and have the whole breadth of God and the glories of heaven before Him. The inmost heart of God may be read in Christ, and the sufferer in his pain, the toiler in his struggle, the tempted in temptation, may read it at a glance.

In the history of Christ we have the highest and sublimest made attractive and winning. There is something in great elevation and sublimity that almost repels. It is too much for our littleness. It is like looking up to the far steep heights of a mountain,—the higher they are the fewer are they who are tempted to climb. But Christ makes elevation endearing. His heights are most winning; they are bathed in such a loving, tender, human light that we feel as if by His help we might yet reach them. They seem to be put within our reach by His tears and groans, and His asking for human sympathy in His hour of trial; by His coming down to be weak like the weak; by His need for companionship and prayer.

In the Gospel we have great variety bound together with the strictest unity. Nothing is more wonderful than the variety in such brief compass. Only three years—and what diversity, what lights and shades! At how many points He touches human life. How many different characters He comes in contact with. How many kinds of sorrow and perplexity He meets. What weakness He strengthens—what sin, rebukes. He rejoices with them that rejoice, and weeps with them that weep. He toils and is weary. He exults and groans in spirit. We overhear His prayers and communings with God. He commands and entreats. He rebukes and commends. We see Him with little children, and with men full of guile and hypocrisy. And in all these we trace the same spirit, an unbroken unity of purpose and steadfastness of aim.

And this aim in its length and breadth was concentrated in His death. Look at that Sufferer. Stand there at the foot of the Cross, and listen to His prayer. What is that He says? " Father, forgive them, for they know not what they do." Listen yet, " To-day shalt thou be with Me in Paradise." The

Crucified promises this to one crucified beside Him.
It is a thing alone, that could occur but once through
all eternity. Listen still, "My God, My God, why
hast Thou forsaken Me." What can this mean? He
who promises Paradise to the penitent robber—Himself forsaken of God. Hear Him as He looks down
from the Cross, "Woman, behold thy son—son, behold
thy mother." And then listen to the last utterance,
"Father, into Thy hands I commend My spirit."
What an impression of awe and love, of unspeakable
grandeur and tenderness, does this leave on the spirit.
It is something unmistakably divine and yet most
exquisitely human.

That Sufferer, undoubtedly, suffered not for Himself.
He bore our sins in His own body on the tree. He
was wounded for our transgressions. He poured out
His blood and soul in love, and as an offering for the
sins of men. He reconciled justice and mercy. He
summed up types and promises. He finished transgression, and made an end of sin, and brought in an
everlasting righteousness. Such is the glory we see
in the mirror of the Gospel. The glory of Christ is
that He shows the yearning of the Father's heart for
His wandering and lost children—shows that God will
do the utmost to bring men back—that God Himself
suffers in the sins and sufferings of men, that He will
maintain truth and righteousness while He exercises
mercy.

II. *The Beholding.*

There is nothing that is simpler than looking; and yet there is nothing that expresses more or receives more. Our whole soul goes out in a look. Words labour slowly to express, and after all fail to express, what the glance of a moment can do. Every man has a power of looking with his mind at objects not seen. Men pass hour after hour in looking at things which are in the past, or in the possible future, or which are the creations merely of desire and fancy. What shall we say, then, of this beholding?

First, that there is nothing more easy; and yet that it is so difficult that it cannot be done without special divine help. The natural man perceiveth not the things of the Spirit of God; and yet there is nothing more easy even for the natural man. There is a beauty and a glory in Christ that the natural man cannot see. Yet any natural man may be convinced that he needs Christ. He may be induced to look to Christ; and looking is God's ordained way of seeing. Looking in the direction of Christ clears the sight, purges the vision. It is healing to the eyes of the soul. The colour of green is refreshing and soothing to the eyes, and gazing over a large expanse strengthens the sight; but looking to Christ does more to the eyes of the soul. It takes away disease. While a man looks to Christ in obedience to God's command, a new spiritual sight comes to him from

God.   God who commanded the light to shine out of
darkness shines into his heart.   Is any one conscious
of inability to see the beauty or glory in Christ that
spiritual men see ?   Still he must look, he must look to
Christ, because he needs Him, and must perish without
Him ; and in the act of looking he will be sure to
see.   The glory of Christ will break upon him.   The
dawn of a new day will arise.   Seeing one beauty in
Christ leads to seeing more.   And he who looks thus
will cry to God while he looks.   It is not in man to
be earnest to see Christ without crying to God for
light.   And looking and crying, when together, can
never fail.   There is a mighty prayer in the look,
and the look will seek to utter and relieve itself in
words.

There is nothing easier, then, than looking to Christ.
I reiterate this ; the difficulty of it vanishes in the
earnest, supplicating look.   It is as easy to look to
Christ as to look at any unseen object.   Christ is presented in the Gospel in a way that makes Him stand
out.   He is wonderful.   He is great and glorious.   He
has great contrasts.   He is stern and awful.   He is
very sweet and winning.   His history is brief, and
painted in strong colours.   It is easy to look to Christ,
and therefore it may be habitual.   It is the most
powerful way of transforming us and making us like
Christ, and yet it is the easiest way.   If a man looks
steadily to Christ, thinks much about Him, he will not

need much wrestling. Struggle and toil may be needful now and again, but in proportion to the frequency and earnestness of our looking to Christ, they will be rare. The work of making us like Christ will go on, quiet, gradual, but deep and sure. The looking will do it all—without strain, noise or effort. It will be like photographing—only slower and deeper. Are there any of us here who are wearied with struggling with self, wearied with self culture and discipline, so constant and so barren of results? Are there any who are desponding because their efforts to rise and grow and cast out evil are so futile? Here is the true way of escape from all this. Think much, very much, always about Christ, and not much about self. Take times of thinking about the Cross of Christ. Think a long time about the Cross; often a little while does little good; it is the length of time that makes the impression. Gaze long at Him who hangs on the Cross. Be in the habit of thinking about the whole life of Christ. Go back to that always when you are alone. Do this instead of constantly fighting with yourself, and you will certainly feel a change coming over you. You will grow like Christ, and experience little effort or struggle. The victory will be gained, the battle won, without a fight. Instead of painting wearily stroke by stroke, look to the Sun of righteousness, and let Him paint Himself upon you.

III.—*The Change effected on the Beholder.*

It is a change that has glory in it from the beginning. The feeblest measure of likeness to Christ has glory in it, something of the nature of heaven. And a sure part of this glory is its desire to increase, its need to grow. This is not always a characteristic of goodness among men. It is often satisfied with itself —self-complacent and proud of itself; but the goodness that comes from looking to Christ cannot be of this sort, because Christ is always so far above it. He who . looks habitually to Christ cannot but feel how poor and low he is, and be stirred with the desire to be more like Him whom he loves.

The expression "*from glory to glory*" seems to the man who looks to Christ too strong and grand to apply to him. What earnest soul is there, conscious of sin, conscious of defect in all that he does, who would not shrink from applying that word "glory" to his poor attainments? And yet Paul, who was humble and faithful, does not scruple to say, "from glory to glory"—glory in all the stages. And it must be good for us to feel and know that it *is* glory. As long as we look to Christ, there is no danger of the thought that we have glory in us already making us proud. It makes us nobly, grandly, humble. The thought that I have that within me which is of the nature of heaven, if I but realize it, will make me very careful, very humble. This kind of honour makes one lowly.

It seems too much a mysterious and almost awful grandeur.

From glory to glory—what an inspiring word. To repeat it often is gladdening, elevating, rebuking. It is a trumpet call to great things.

We close with putting emphasis on the words, " *With open face.*" Alas, how often we look at Christ with faces veiled. Custom draws a veil over the face. False theories draw a veil. Doubt draws a veil. Every evil habit draws a veil. And there is just one way to have the face entirely open—to look always the more resolutely to Jesus.

WONDERS TO THE DEAD.

" Wilt Thou show wonders to the dead ? "—Psalms lxxxviii. 10.

THIS is the question of a doubting and yet less of
a doubting than a desponding heart—the question of a
man bewildered, confounded with calamity. The fogs
are so dense that he can neither see the sun nor stars.
In his perplexity the face of God has grown dim and
far, and his outlook on all things is dreary and uncertain. The experience is that of men in all ages. There
are times when men of the clearest spiritual vision and
firmest faith are not so confident as they once were
that God will show wonders to the dead. Human life
seems to their exhausted energies a thing played out.
They are so tired, disappointed, dispirited, that they can
soar on no wing of hope. The rainbow spanning the
sky speaks to them rather of cloud and storm than of
sunshine. It seems all a dying world, all things ending not beginning, great men disappearing, smaller ones
taking their place, the bright and true hearts becoming
fewer and fewer. Or sometimes a man's own fortunes

seem in sad contrast to the success and happiness around him. The world all so bright, but his days in the sear and yellow leaf. How cold and heartless the world seems with all its glitter. And this would be little if he could grasp firmly the hope of a glorious eternal world, but he is too prostrate and nerveless to sweep the spiritual canopy. It is all like a far-off vision which he had once seen and scarcely hopes to see again.

"Wilt Thou show wonders to the dead?" is also often the exclamation of a heart full to overflowing of the wonder and glory of this world. Human life is so rich and strange, the earth and the outlook from it so splendid, that when he thinks of dying and leaving this warm palpitating life, this crowded drama, this brilliant theatre, this grand, bright, ever new panorama of marvels, a chill comes over him. That other world, he thinks, may be real enough, but it cannot be such a glowing romantic world as this. This was the old heathen conception—and every man has the heathen element in him—that the present life is the resplendent attractive scene, the future a dull leaden grey experience, one long dim twilight. It is a feeling that creeps over the most spiritual men unless they make an effort to rise into a clearer and brighter atmosphere, and shake off the blinding, benumbing influence of earthly surroundings.

Let us then put this question, "Wilt Thou show

wonders to the dead?" in a calm, reasonable spirit,
looking at it in the light of God, and of man's nature
and history.

I. *We are encouraged to believe that God will show
wonders to the dead when we remember how many
wonders God has shown to them in this life.*

The world is a scene of wonders. There are wonders
that strike and arrest man, wonders that flash and
flame before him. And there are wonders that disclose themselves to research. There are wonders in
the stone that you strike with your foot, wonders
in the flower you tread on, and wonders in the
galaxy of worlds overhead. The clouds are full of
marvel, and the light that plays on them and pierces,
the light that fills the far spaces, is mysterious in its
brightness. Descend into the depths of the earth,
there wonders await you. Arrest the insect that flies
beside you, it is full of wonder. Lift the shell that
has been thrown up by the wave, its grace and beauty
amaze you. The sea weed astonishes you. Take the
microscope, and your wonder grows as you find the
animalcules as perfectly finished, some with coats of
mail made of flint, and rivalling the brilliant hues of
the shell. Look through the telescope at the far
heavens, and host on host of worlds overpowers you.
Your intelligence sinks beneath the weight of magnificence. Ask yourself if man, who has just had time

to look round on these wonders and examine a few of them, who has had his love for wonders awakened and stirred—if man, having been so roused up, is to have nothing more shown him. Consider that a world of wonders is a fact, a reality, the only reality of which man has experience. What other expectation then can he cherish than that of wonders? If you say that you do not expect wonders to be shown to the dead, you are going in the face of all your experience of God. Whence do you draw your belief that contradicts all experience? One would require to have a very strong ground of reason to go upon when he contradicts all that is already known. Consider, especially, that the wonders God has shown to man here render further wonders necessary. They not only increase the desire for wonders, and the expectation of them; they raise questions of a painful and perplexing kind. I look at the glory and grandeur of the world, and am thrilled; but is there not another side? Are there no wonders that make you shudder? Do not shut your eyes to the monsters of creation, to the terrible tragedy of pain, to ruin and decay and incompleteness. What a transcendent wonder man is, the greatest by far of the marvels, inasmuch as he can admire them all, explore and weigh them all, attempt at least to bring all into unity, seek the idea that underlies them all, and even rise to the conception of a beauty and perfection which is only hinted at in material things. And yet what a perplexing mystery man is. There is no creature so utter a failure, a wreck and ruin, as he often is. And shall there be no light more than this world gives on all this? Are not further wonders necessary to illuminate all this mystery? Man has produced wonders in this life which point plainly to further wonders. What a battle and confusion, what a scene of cloud and storm man has created. What crimes, black and foul, what glorious heights of devotion and excellence. Carlyle has somewhere said that a man put to death by his fellowmen in the name of justice and right and humanity is one of the saddest and greatest sights that meets the eye of the sun. And how many of these there have been in the history of the world. Think how some of the worst and some of the best of men have looked their last at the sun from a scaffold. What a vision passes before you of gibbets and blocks and burning piles. How many thousands of angelic, seraphic natures have ended their earthly career amid flames. Was that little heap of ashes that remained the only thing left of these glorious lives? Was there nothing that ascended with the flames above the smoke? Was there not something which the fire could not burn? Did the fire burn and dissipate to the winds their love, their zeal, their faithfulness to the right, to the cause of God and man? Has evil then the power of annihilating the unspeakably grandest thing on earth? Can it seize the flower of goodness with its foul hand, and crush it for ever beneath its foot? No, no, a thousand times, no. And if you feel the impossibility, the monstrous libel of the thought, if you see it to be a thought that must be rejected with utter scorn, a thought more incredible than the wildest dreams of heathenism, then what wonders await man in that world to which death introduces him, wonders of glory, and dark wonders of retribution! Shall not every mystery of iniquity be brought to shame in the light of eternity, and every hidden deed of love and every secret longing and upward struggle of the heart be irradiated with splendour? The true nature of things has been disguised, hidden, caricatured in this world; but that cannot always last. And when the truth is unveiled, the truth of all this glorious, dreadful drama of life, what wonders there will be. Every wonder of gloom or radiance in the moral history of man is the proof that greater wonders are coming. In view of this subject let us make a few brief reflections.

1. *Let us see that we are not indifferent to God's wonders now.*

You can scarcely conceive a being more out of harmony with the world in which he lives than a man whose heart is not stirred with wonder. Why was he set here in the midst of marvels, himself the greatest marvel of them all, if he is to pass through life dull,

uninterested, caring only for the material uses of
things ?   Is it nothing to him that the mountains are
sublime, that the sea is vast, stretching out in mysterious might and grandeur ?   Is the beauty of flowers
nothing to him ?   The morning light, the evening
splendour, the nocturnal magnificence, has God made
all these in vain for him ?   Is there nothing worth his
admiration ?   Has all this been lavished that he might
despise or pass it by with unthinking gaze ?   Nothing
can be plainer than the duty of every man to admire and
wonder at all the grandeur and beauty that God has made.
He is not to think that it is a pleasure that he may
forego if he likes.   It is more than pleasure.   It is
high and pure pleasure, but it is more; it is education,
it is exaltation, it is initiation into the divine treasures.
Enthusiasm lifts the soul.   Wonder opens the mind
and heart for higher disclosures.   It keeps you aware
that you belong to the infinite, that the boundless and
endless are your home.   He to whom this world is full
of wonder, who finds matter of fresh interest everywhere, whose heart often glows or is roused or surprised or borne away with emotion by sights and
sounds in nature around him—he will find it difficult
to believe that this little span of life, these few fleeting
years, have brought the whole round of wonders to an
end for ever.   He will find it hard to think that he
was ushered into such variety and depth of interest,
into such wealth and magnificence, just to cast a

hurried glance around and bid adieu evermore. If a man only makes true use of the wonder in this visible scene, if he opens his mind and heart to the wonders above, beneath, around him, if he just surrenders himself to the sublimity, the vastness, the tenderness, of sea and sky and flower, if he but lets things produce their own natural impression on him, they will so waken and stir and expand him, that he will be raised above the visible things themselves and made to think of imperishable wonders. Visible things will strike chords in his soul which no visible things can satisfy. Visible things will assuredly whisper to him that he is a pilgrim of the invisible, that they themselves are only types and tokens of things which eye hath not seen nor ear heard nor the heart of man conceived. Only be true to the wonders of earth and sky, and they will set you a-longing and a-hungering for other glories than their own. Of one thing you may be well assured, that the soul that is really roused and expanded and fired by the grandeur, vastness, and lavishness of creation will not be stumbled at the grandeurs of redemption. He who truly sees the vast scale on which God works, how much it takes to satisfy the heart of God, what floods He pours, what exhaustless treasures He lavishes, will find something congenial in God's glorious way of salvation. He will feel as if all that external wealth were a whisper and indication of a magnificence of love, of a boundless generosity in God, the eternal Father, such as is shown in the face of Jesus Christ and nowhere else. If any man looks with incredulous wonder at the amazing love shown in Jesus Christ, we say to him—go back for a little to the grand wonders of nature, try to understand what a heart is revealing itself in those millions and millions of worlds, try to fathom the tenderness in the beauty of flowers, try to gauge the glory, the deep pathos of sounds, and see if that will not help you to believe in the wonders of redemption.

2. What an elevating, cheering outlook is given by the thought that the wonders which men see now are but an introduction to God's great book.

You only see the title page now. When you leave this world another leaf will be turned. Perhaps we cannot even guess what will then be disclosed. Shall we have the liberty of roaming through space? Shall we spend the long day in visiting worlds, as we now gather flowers? Shall it be heaven to us everywhere in the boundless domains of God, heaven to feel that He is with us everywhere, and to see His glory everywhere reflected? Shall the angelic songs be mingled with the vast music of the spheres? Shall the bars be the roll of thousands and thousands of oceans, the orchestra be supplied by millions of worlds? Oh, what a thrilling prospect God sets before His children. And yet men in their faint-heartedness ask whether life is worth the living. As if God had brought creatures into existence, and was too poor to entertain them! God's entertainment of us will be magnificent beyond all conception. There are rivers of pleasure at God's right hand for evermore. Has He not begun already on this scale in the exhaustless wonders stretched around us. O man, be glad! Rejoice! You belong to a wealthy Father, a Father whose name is love. Rejoice. Rejoice evermore. There is an ocean of wonder and delight for ever and ever.

But see *that you are really entering into God's wonders now.* See that you are serving your apprenticeship to wonder here in the dawn of your existence. What things excite your wonder most? Is it some artificial painted wonders such as novelists invent? Are your favourite wonders those seen by gaslight? Do wonders need to be flavoured with some wickedness to give them zest? Do you think there can be a sign of any man much worse than this, that he has little taste for the grand exhaustless wonders of nature, but a boundless appetite for the wonders of gossip and fiction and romance? Oh the baseness of ceasing to wonder at the stars and falling into ecstasies over the sputterings of a candle and the decorations of paint and gilding. What is to become of a man in the great eternity that is before us who has never wondered at the love and all the glorious character of Christ, but has had floods of wonder for the passing marvels of the day?

HISTORICAL RELIGION.

"God, who at sundry times and in divers manners spake in time past unto the fathers by the prophets, hath in these last days spoken unto us by His Son."—Hebrews i. 1-2.

WHAT do we mean by an historical religion? We mean a religion which rests on an event or person, in contradistinction to one which rests on facts of consciousness or of space. There may be a religion which grounds itself simply on the facts of human nature and those of the external world which are supposed to correspond with them; or one which, while heartily recognizing these, does not regard them as sufficient, but bases itself, mainly and distinctively, on one or more supernatural events and divinely appointed persons. If a religion rests on an event or person, it necessarily becomes historical; the basis becomes part of the past, and, as such, belongs to the realm of history. It is here that many find objection to Christianity in our time. The objection has been made often before, no doubt, but never with the same point and urgency as now. And there are two great reasons for this. The first is that the material universe, with its laws and arrangements, occupies an undue place in human thought just now. The supremacy and universality of law. are the fundamental ideas of science ; and the horizon of science has been widening and widening so fast that men are drawn more and more to look at life and religion predominantly in the light of scientfic teaching. The other influence that operates against the belief in historical religion, though it does so to a much less degree than the former, is the attention which has been given of late years to the comparative study of religions. This study has done one great good. It has made clear that religion is an original, indestructible part of human nature ; that man is under the necessity of thinking of the infinite, and of entering into some sort of relation to it; that when he is actively religious he is in no artificial, exotic, morbid condition, but is simply yielding to the deepest, most permanent, most universal, and powerful demands of his nature. But one prejudicial influence has issued from the comparison of religions. It has strengthened, in some directions, the tendency to underrate the peculiar and historical in Christianity ; it has fixed attention upon that which is common to all religions, and ignored the absolute necessity of the supernatural and divine element in the Gospel.

So we find the current of thought in some quarters

quite set against the conceptions of an historical religion. "Let us have," it is said, "a religion which rests on the broad facts of the universe and the nature of man. Why seek anything else? A religion which carries its own evidence with it everywhere, that is independent of time or place; a religion whose few simple elements are as clear as a demonstration, and which has no artificial, elaborate, oppressive dogmas; a religion which is the sum and essence of all religions, which contains the simple residuum of truth that is in all, and rejects the superstitions which weigh upon all; this is the religion for man come to the searching light of science and to fulness of experience."

"Why," it is urged further, "should I involve myself in questions of history? How can I get any reasonable assurance about what happened 2,000 years ago? Questions of history are difficult to decide and are only for a few adepts who have leisure and learning. Is it reasonable—is it conceivable—that the religious condition of men should rest on their handling of nice historical evidence? Why not concentrate the attention of men on those simple elements which are independent of history?"

Such is the drift of the argument urged against Christianity as historical in our time; and to this must be added what is, indeed, sometimes presented as an argument, but is oftener felt as a difficulty, from the outside, by those who really desire to receive Christ. It is to this effect,—That events so far off seem dim, and that even while one is convinced of their truth, the difficulty is to feel them real and solid as we do recent things. Emerson has said, " Time dissolves into shining ether the solid angularities of fact. No effort suffices to keep a fact a fact." Every one has felt what he puts in this bold way. An event scarcely seems so real on the other side of the globe as in our own street. What took place centuries ago does not stand out so solidly as the event of yesterday. There is no denying that this is so ; but the question is, whether the difficulty in realizing the remote is of such weight as to render historical religion impracticable ; and whether, on the other hand, Christianity does not contain in itself elements specially adapted to counteract this bedimming influence of time.

It will be my endeavour in the following remarks to show, over against these objections and difficulties, that an *historical religion is a necessity*, and that the historical element is both a *help* and an *attraction*—is, in fact, *essential to the drawing and holding of men.*

But here let us first distinctly apprehend what kind of historical religion Christianity is. Is it historical only in the sense of tracing its origin to a Person who lived hundreds of years ago ? Much more than this is implied. Jesus Christ founded His religion and rested His claims upon a previous religion. He claimed to be the aim and outcome, the promise and flower, of that previous religion. He claimed both to perpetuate that religion and to abolish it—to abolish its form, to perpetuate its substance and spirit. He claimed to be the culminating point of that long history, to be that which gave it all a meaning and unity.

Christ's is thus a doubly historical religion— historical in a sense peculiar to itself. Though there were nothing else to mark Christianity off from other faiths, this would effectually distinguish it,—that it is vitally and organically connected with a previous religion. And so whatever difficulties may attend the conception of historical religion, these must be double in the case of Christianity, unless, indeed, it be that the very extent of the historical field is seen to be its strength, and the accordance of Christianity with the previous religion is seen to be the irrefragable proof of both.

When we speak, then, of Christianity as an historical religion, let us remember what is meant by this— a religion which not merely traces its origin and authority to historical events and an historical Person, but which draws its nutriment, meaning, and evidence from a previous religion, and grounds itself both on its fulfilment of that religion and its dissolution of it.

On what, then, do we rest the claims of an historical religion ?

I. *Such a religion is needed to reveal the moral character of God.*

We cannot be sure of the moral character of God. Without a revelation of Him in history, the material universe which bears such emphatic witness to God is perplexing when we seek distinct and satisfactory information as to His regard for individuals, His mercy, sympathy, patience, justice. Men who appeal with confidence to nature must shut their eyes to many things. Of goodness there is abundant proof; but will any one affirm that it is a goodness without dark clouds and heavy drawbacks? Years ago Dr. George Wilson in his *Religio Chemici* indicated the great defect in the Bridgewater Treatises—their special pleading and ignoring of the dark and terrible side of nature. Recently this side has been brought into prominence and commented upon with startling force by John Stuart Mill. Facts, well enough known but little dwelt on, or kept out of sight by a sort of tacit agreement, have been held up by him in such a way as to rouse men out of the tranquil, traditional fashion of looking at nature as a mirror of God's character. Mill speaks of the cruelty, treachery, injustice, recklessness of nature in such a way as to show that nature has not been meant as a revelation of the moral character of God, and that we must look elsewhere for this. One thing is plain : nature throws no steady or satisfying light on the character of God. She can-

not be taken as a moral teacher.   Wherever man has
got his ideas of love, right, truth, perfection, he has
certainly not got them from any wide or fair study of
nature.   How then shall we estimate the words—*just,
holy, merciful*, as applied to God ?   Can we be sure
that the interpretation which our hearts give is the
correct one, in the face of these enigmas of nature ?
And if we cannot be sure of this, what basis have we
for a religion ?   What does a religion amount to, what
does it mean, with those things unsettled—worse than
unsettled?   Here an historical religion comes to our aid
in the illustrations which it gives of God's moral dealings
with men.   We understand what God is by reading His
declarations regarding Himself in the light of the commentary afforded by His treatment of men through
centuries of history.   We become acquainted with
long-suffering, mercy, forgiveness, through the recorded
exercise of these.   How could we get a conception to
rest on in any other way ?   What God has actually
done, that is a basis on which any one can rest.   Take,
for example, the all-important question of forgiveness.
How are we to attain to any clearness on that ?   It will
not do to point us to the material universe and natural
law here.   Nature on the whole seems opposed to the
notion of forgiveness.   Beneath her most genial look lies
iron necessity, inexorable law, strife and pain ; and
her restorative processes are too limited and capricious
to give us hope.   If we say—" Then we will listen to

our own hearts. We will make our own moral nature at its best the interpreter of God. I can forgive; it is noble to forgive: and I will ascribe forgiveness to God." Does our voice in such a case carry sufficient conviction to our own heart? Seriously, can we feel quite sure in arguing from ourselves, with all our conscious corruption, to the righteous Sovereign of the universe? Can men attain, in this way, such convictions of the reality of the divine forgiveness as to found religion upon it, and rest on it entirely through all this trying life, and with the thought of worlds beyond? Has it not, rather, often seemed to man in his most earnest moods, that to decide the question of forgiveness in his own favour, in the face of nature with her stupendous legalism and her magnificent and awful order, would be only egotism and impertinence.

II. Again, a religion resting on a history is needed even *to keep alive the sense of the Personality of God.*

There exists among men a strong tendency to Pantheism. Atheism cannot long hold sway over men. It is too blank, too cold, too barren and hopeless. It is in too direct contradiction to the deepest longings of human nature. But Pantheism, which blends the universe with God, does not present such a contradiction. It does not meet the heart or the conscience, or satisfy the reason; but it has a strong attraction for the imagination. It does not cut man

off from the infinite; and yet it takes away all sense
of constraint or subjection, and perhaps even imparts a
vague elation.   When the conscience is not earnestly
cultivated, and when nature is dwelt upon either by
the poetic or the analytic faculty; when space, pheno-
mena, order, force, mutation, continuity are exclusively
contemplated, the thought of a personal Will easily drops
out of view, and the student becomes part of the All
that he studies—its reflective and conscious mode of
existence.   The very regularity of nature, and the completeness of her unity, are as a screen to hide the
personality of God.   When Will acts in a uniform
manner that can be certainly calculated and forecast,
it is in danger of not being recognized as Will at all,
but rather as the necessary flow of existence, or course
of development.   Hence arises the need of a sphere where
the divine Personality may reveal itself fully, a sphere
found only in the realm of freedom, which is that of
spirit.   In the history of God's dealings with men, His
personality stands out;   God is shown in inspired
history not to be a force or tendency or current, but
an actual living Person.   No one can read the Old
Testament without feeling how intensely the personality of God is brought out.   You might be surprised
and even shocked at times by the way in which feelings and changes are attributed to God, unless you
remembered the steady purpose running through all, to
hold up the personality of God and keep men from

lapsing into Pantheism, and thinking of God as the vague background of things. No one can read of the divine grief, repentance, indignation, jealousy, entreaty, yearning, compassion, remembrance, striving, wrestling, without learning that God is not the mere Spirit of the Universe, but a genuine personality, a real mind, will, and heart. God's wrestling with Jacob stands in the grey dawn of human history to mark the reality and separateness of the divine Will and the human, and to prefigure the Divine as striving with man down the ages. This sense of God's personality is of supreme importance ; and there is no period of the world in which it does not need to be held up and emphasized to men. Certainly it needs to be held up in our time. It is in danger of slipping out of the view of many. A certain Pantheistic tinge has got into literature. It colours much poetry and speculative science, and there is nothing that can meet this and expel it from the hearts of men but the vivid presentation of God's personality in His historical dealings with men. This appeals to the deep wants of men ; and keeps alive the sense of the need and the glory of a God who is a personal Friend and a living Father.

III. Again, the historical element is needed *to give clearness, fixity, and authority to religion.* But we are often told that religion does not require, or even admit of, any definiteness or fixity—that it is a sentiment, a feeling, a purpose and tendency, an atmosphere in life, and does not require anything definite in doctrine. A single question must suffice for this. Why is religion to be the exception in human life? Why does man everywhere else seek certainty and definiteness, feel the imperative need of something fixed and stable; and yet think such certainty needless in his most important relations? The demand for definiteness and fixity is far more imperious in the religious sphere than any-where else. Dimness and uncertainty here tantalize and oppress man, provided he is in earnest. He cannot bear the suspense, and listens greedily to any announcement that promises decisively to break it, even though it substitutes hard and terrible things. Where, then, can man get any plain, decisive affirma-tions except in an historical religion? Have the over-whelming majority of mankind ever possessed any abiding or effective light on religious matters, beyond what was given by a professed revelation? How many of the handful of men who have grasped elementary religious truths without the authority of revelation have been really without its light—direct or indirect, immediate or remote? And as to the minute residuum, who may be supposed to have attained to the possession of religious truth simply by their own efforts, can it be affirmed that they encourage the hope that the race in general is capable of such an achievement? Is there any calm thinker who would not, looking at the position of a fraction of exceptional men, be driven to despair of the religious future of the race ?

And if it be granted that God does reveal Himself in facts and arrangements, why should it be thought strange that He should reveal Himself in words ? If there is a purpose of self manifestation, why should it not attain to clearness and definiteness in speech, one of the highest facts in human nature ? Speech is man's instrument of self-evolution, and his means of defining and solidifying his ideas ; by it he raises and intensifies, unburdens and expands himself. How incredible, then, that the Highest should have nothing to *say* to man ; should not meet him on his loftiest level, but restrict Himself to lower ones ; should not utter a word, though there is so much for which nothing but words will suffice. How strange that God should reveal Himself to man in other ways, and not in the way which is man's peculiar means of revelation—language.

We have spoken of the need of *authority* in religion. Is this need, then, a reality ? Or is authority, as we are often told, hurtful to religion—interfering with its spontaneity, freedom, and genuineness ? Not more, surely, than the authoritative enforcement of morality on a child interferes with moral freedom. Does it not seem beyond dispute that an authoritative declaration of religion is necessary to overcome all the difficulties with which religion has to contend from the levity and

M

perversity of man and from the might of his present
environment ?

IV. Again, *the historical is needed in religion if the
personal element is to enter into its construction.* And
has not this element inspired more enthusiasm, raised
more armies, gained more victories, accomplished more
tasks than all others put together ? Abstract truths,
however elevated, have little power over men till they
find an embodiment. A Person is felt to be in a sense
greater than the greatest abstraction. He is something
which the greatest truth is not—life and feeling.
Hence, all religions that have ever exerted much influence on the world have been very strong in the personal element. Buddhism, for instance, which has in
some form fascinated, say, a third of the human race,
would have been nothing without Buddha. The figure
of Sakya-Muni has been the eye in the otherwise
empty socket and phantom face of the system. While
declaring, in a reaction against the million gods of
Brahmanism, that there is no God, it has made Buddha
God, and realized all ideals in him. Buddhism means
the triumph of personal will. It is the converse of
incarnation. God does not become man ; man makes
himself God. Buddhism protests against the chaos of
divinities in which man and the moral world are swallowed up; it sweeps the horizon clear of them; it
leaves not one. But, having done this, it begins immediately to repeople the void with human figures in

all stages of ascension to the Infinite and Formless. What a striking declaration this is, that man, awake to the Infinite, cannot leave it unfilled. Abstractions will not fill it; only Personality can.

But what are we to say of the difficulty said to belong to the very nature of historical religion—the difficulty of proof. How can men ever become reasonably certified of the truth of the history? Does it not require a kind of investigation for which few men are fitted? Now, this objection implies that the evidence for what is historical must also itself be historical—a statement which only requires to be made to have its unsoundness exposed.

The historical Revelation contains within itself elements of proof wholly independent of historical research. The proof lies in the contents. When one reads this historical record he is impressed with its high moral and spiritual tone; its obvious candour; the profound spiritual truths which are taught, and often only suggested by the stream of the narrative. He feels that the moral and spiritual elements are not things affixed to the record and dexterously inwoven, but that they are the soul of it all. He feels the truth appealing to the deep wants of his soul. He feels that to receive it is to be brought near to God, to be calmed and purified and lifted up. A voice tells him, as he reads, that conformity to this book would be the perfection of his nature. He feels a unity pervad-

ing it amid all its variety, made all the more conspicuous by its variety. He feels that there is one purpose and plan running through the whole. If it were a
brief, isolated history the case would be very different;
but it is long and varied. It is composed by many
different hands; and yet it is all pervaded by subtle
harmonies, references, and coincidences. Above all,
the perception that Jesus Christ is what He declares
Himself to be, the fulfilment of the Old Testament, and
also the manifestation of God, lays hold of the soul.
How convincingly bold is the conception of Christ as
the substance and meaning of the sacrifice, priesthood,
ceremonial of the Old Testament. How came it that
this most marvellous idea of a man being the meaning
and end of the temple and its sacrifices was raised into
prominence just when these were about to cease?
How came it that the death of Jesus Christ by human
violence received this vast significance, and shed a unifying light over all the past? How came it that the
defeat was transformed into such a victory as men
could not have dreamed of? How came this to be so
timed, so exactly placed, that a few years sooner
would have been too early and a few years after too
late for any such interpretation to have been possible?
Questions such as these admit of but one answer. The
testimony of Jesus is the spirit of prophecy. Christ
is the end of the law—the centre of the Revelation;
and the seeing Him to be the centre is also the

seeing of the whole field and circumference to be real.

We recognize, thus, how the very extent of the historical field is its evidence. The founding of the latter historical religion, not merely upon the former, but upon the whole history of the former; and the making the latter the flower and consummation of the former—its transformation, but yet its truest, inmost self. All this opens out a wide field of research and investigation, and puts every man into the position of an investigator and even discoverer. A freshness is thus imparted to our relations to the truth.

This is specially the case in view of the great number and variety of persons embraced in the record. God revealed His moral character by His dealings with persons, as we have seen; and this involved all varieties of character, position and circumstances. To make the history truly a revelation to us —an account of how God actually stands to the varieties of human life and character—it was needful that it should include not only the extremes of human experience, but peculiar angles, even rare and almost incredible types. And all this variety of human life speaks to the soul and heart of man in the way of proof; and it is a kind of proof that is not laborious to men, but often intensely interesting.

They who speak about the difficulty of historic proof, and the impossibility of the mass of men attain-

ing certainty, are very forgetful of human nature.
The great bulk of men are partial to the historical.
Tell them the facts of human life, give them a
little bit of genuine humanity from the olden time, and
they are delighted. For one man that finds interest
in the researches of science there are ten that turn
with quiet relish or eager enthusiasm, to the history of
men. It seems to raise the spirits of men, it redeems
their plain, everyday world to be brought face to face
with those who lived long centuries ago. And all this
long line of sacred history is full of points that appeal
to men's sense of reality, and come home to the soul
with evidential force. Every one finds a particular
nutriment or medicine for his languishing faith in
the variety of the historical revelation. One man
is revived, in his dulness, by reading a glowing
prophecy, in which a seer of that time tells of the
coming of the reign of truth and right over all the
world. It strikes him with new force as nothing less
than a divine voice that could at such a time give
so grand and cheering an utterance. Another is
brought back to more than his old faith by reading again one of the Psalms, and being subdued by its
tenderness, intensity, soaring spirituality.

Another finds it enough to ponder the Beatitudes;
and another has his unbelief changed into penitent
and longing faith whenever he turns to the account of
that scene on Calvary; while another is ever afresh

impressed with correspondences, adaptations and fulfil-
ments.   An historical religion, then—that is Christianity,   the   only   distinctly   historical   religion—is
peculiarly adapted to reach the soul with evidential
force.   It supplies the kind, and the variety of
evidence best adapted for the mass of mankind—a
warm, living, expansive, penetrative, effective evidence;
an evidence appealing to the whole nature of man, but
specially to that which is most human—conscience and
heart and soul.   The Bible is an intensely human
book ; it is overflowing with humanity.   By this it
keeps its hold on men and appeals to them, even when
they have little spirituality.   It insinuates the divine
view of things, through the pathos, mystery, struggle
and charm of human life.

We can now speak of *the difficulty of realization*,
connected with historical religion.   There is something
to many minds chilling in the thought of 2000 years.
It is not that they disbelieve, or even doubt.   It is
rather that the centuries make a misty distance
between Christ and them.   If they could but bridge
these centuries, all would be well.   The centuries
cannot be bridged, but something better may be done.
A man may be brought into a region where the centuries
are as nothing.   It is a fact that many have lived in
such an atmosphere, finding Christ as real as if they
had lived in the early ages.   It may be said, " These
are peculiarly gifted natures who have special powers

of vivid mental portraiture." No doubt there is something in this, but not much. For in Christianity there
is special provision made for the clear realization of
Christ, not only for firm belief in Him, but for clear
realization, and that in a way patent to all sorts of
minds. That way is *fellowship with Christ*. Fellowship, communion with Jesus Christ belongs to the
very heart of Christianity. A man is to live with a
present Christ; he has been called into the fellowship
of God's Son. This is part of religion as planned by
God; and we have no right to ignore this part, and
then ground objection and difficulty on that ignoring.

Christ never intended to leave His Church; on the
contrary, He promised always to be with it. And
that was doubtless the reason why He left many things
vague. He arranged matters precisely in the way of
one who intended never to go away. We do religion
great wrong, then, if we conceive of it as the endeavour
to realize an absent Christ. That is an altogether false
conception. Christianity is the constant realizing and
dwelling with a present Christ. When one leans on
Christ, speaks to Him, hearkens to catch His voice in
the soul—then it becomes a very different thing to
realize Him in the Scriptures and in religion, while,
on the other hand, this inward fellowship is rendered
clear and bright by the peculiar distinctness with
which the life of Christ is portrayed in the Gospels.
The two things act and react on each other:

Christ is thus the means of our realizing the whole field of religion. He so enters into the actual, living human world that He becomes as a part of visible things. He was visible once, and He lives on the page of Gospel history visible yet. He thus bridges for us the gulf between the seen and the unseen. He is both the visible and the invisible, and in realizing Him we learn to realize all that is within the veil. He carries all the reality connected with visibility into the invisible state.

Looked at from the outside, then, there is a difficulty in the realization of the historical in religion, but only when it is regarded in a fragmentary and unjust way. He has the key to the whole difficulty who remembers that fellowship with Christ is an essential part of Christianity. To the man who lives with a present Christ, the centuries that have rolled since He walked the Sea of Galilee seem to contract into narrow space.

CHRISTIANITY AND LITERATURE.

"I am the Light of the World."—John viii. 12.

LITERATURE, in its widest and at the same time specific sense, may be said to be Man written. Books on science or art or any special study are not properly literature. It is so far as any book has the universal element in it, so far as it portrays human life, or brings the special into broad universal relations, that it can lay claim to the name. It will thus be seen that there is a peculiar difficulty in distinguishing books connected with Christianity into the two classes of the special and the general, the technical and that which belongs to the broad realm of literature. Christianity is, properly speaking, all about man, and about man in his widest relations. The most theological books, therefore, enter deep into human life, and have no full or proper meaning except in view of man and his whole position. Still we shall keep the line of demarcation in view, and confine ourselves as much as possible to literature in the strict sense.

The question of the connection between Christianity and literature cannot but suggest itself, for the *fact* is so outstanding. Christianity has for many centuries absorbed the literature of the world. Where is there any literature to mention, except among Christian nations ? Since Christian literature began, all other voices have been hushed. Intellectual force and productiveness seem to have forsaken all other creeds. Heathenism is dumb, though it once poured forth its Vedas and its Iliad, and was represented by an Æschylus and a Sophocles. No Virgil rises anywhere beside idols now, nor does Mohammedanism or Buddhism produce science or philosophy. The poet uses no more the language of Hafiz ; and if there are bards roaming the Arabian desert or the Steppes of Tartary, their song has no power to make itself heard in the world more than the lay of the Negro in the wilds of Africa, or of the Eskimo amid his snows. China finds all her classics in the far past before the dawn of Christianity. Her look is constantly reverted. She finds no food for thought in all modern times. Except where Christianity has touched, there has scarcely been science, philosophy or poetry for a thousand years. It has been as a great river running through the centuries, drawing all the tributaries into itself, allowing scarcely a rivulet or mountain torrent to flow anywhere else. This is a remarkable fact which nobody can afford to overlook.

It is a singular thing, viewed in the light of this its subsequent history, that the early ages of Christianity and the Mediæval period should present such a barren aspect. It must be admitted that the early writers of the Christian church, from the close of the apostolic period, are as a whole jejune, without force or literary grace. With the exception perhaps of Augustine, there is no man of real genius or transcendent power among them. Certainly, after we have mentioned Boetius, it would be difficult to point to any one till the period of Dante whose works would prove attractive to any student of literature, or would greatly interest any beyond a theological and antiquarian circle. We cannot account for this by saying that literature was on the decline when Christianity had begun to make itself felt in the world. For the question will press, Why did not this new force in the world show itself by quickening the intellectual powers of men? The old ideas were losing their power to stimulate men—all things were going down because men had lost their conviction of any hold on reality. The ground beneath them could not put life into them; it could barely keep them from dying. There no atmosphere of hope. The sense of freshness was gone. It was an old world, and felt itself old. But why did not the new life, which made all things new to so many thousands of hearts in all lands, which brought hope and joy and courage and purity and love and zeal everywhere—why did not this revive also the intellects of men ? How was it possible to quicken the heart and enlarge the horizon, without touching the productive faculties and giving boldness and thoroughness to intellectual research ? How was it that the human mind, set free and illuminated, . surrounded with a boundless horizon and thrilled with the grandest themes, did not at . once blossom out ?

This is certainly a difficult question, deserving much consideration. And the first thing that occurs to us in answering it is, that the earliest shape which the Gospel assumed was an intensely practical one —and of necessity so. It proposed to emancipate men from bonds of vice and corruption. It had a battle to fight with Pagan superstition and all the pollution and wrong that issued from it. Christianity had to manifest its new spirit of truth and love. It busied itself in works of compassion and mercy. It comforted and soothed. It fed and healed. It opened the eyes of the spiritually blind. It touched dead souls into life. It had a heavy task to do ; no wonder that it forgot tasks that were being remembered a little by others—that it left the Pagan philosopher, in some cases, to his learning, and went after the slave, the captive, the prisoner, the oppressed, the sufferer, for whom no man cared.

And then remember that during the early centuries

Christianity was engaged, with little intermission, in a struggle for existence. It sought to abolish the idols; and the idolater tortured and slew the Christians, crucified them, threw them to wild beasts, and strove desperately to exterminate them. Such a life and death struggle is not favourable to intellectual pursuits. It develops zeal. It raises fervour to enthusiasm. It makes heroes and martyrs and saints ; but not many scholars, philosophers or poets. When history is being made with such intensity, and at such expense, it is scarcely yet possible to write it. When such materials of heroic elevation and beauty are being accumulated, poetry may weave them into her imperishable web,— but not yet.

There is another explanation still which reaches, perhaps, more into the heart of the matter. The old masterpieces of literature which had fired the souls of successive generations, and kept alive the ideas of literary perfection and grace, were all more or less allied with the heathenism which was the great object of dread and aversion to the early Christians. Some of the greatest literary monuments of antiquity are wholly permeated with the spirit of idolatry. There is scarcely one of them in which allusions to heathen conceptions do not occur—allusions which could not fail to be painful, or even revolting, to minds sensitive in this direction. Jupiter and Juno, Venus, Minerva, and Saturn, were not dim poetic images to them ; they were not playthings of fancy, the broken toys of the world's childhood ; they were cruel, foul usurpers of the place of the one God and Father, and His only Son, Christ Jesus the Lord, the Redeemer from sin and death. The names of the heathen mythology, which to us suggest but wild, and sometimes ludicrous, figures of fairy tales, were, to men who had but escaped from their fascination and tyranny, hideous, full of contagion and all wicked associations. Were not the blessed martyrs, who had bled for the name of the Lord Jesus, sacrificed as victims at the shrine of those impostors ? Was it not because they had refused to offer incense at the altars of those so-called gods, that they were thrown to the lions ? And were they, the children of these martyrs, to pore over and admire dramatists and poets who lauded those monsters as divinities, and associated their names with all that was august and great ? The whole literature of the past was to the awakened conscience, to the devout and joyous Christian striving to walk in pure loyalty to his Lord, little else than corruption, delusion and snare. Hence, many men of decided intellectual power saw no way of cutting off the dreadful entail of idolatry, with all its pollutions, but that of severing the entire literary connection with the past. Men who felt all the charm of the ancient literature abjured, sadly and reluctantly, orator, philosopher, poet, and historian, with all their glamour and witchery, believing that they were compelled to do so by the injunction of Christ—"If thine eye cause thee to stumble, pluck it out and cast it from thee." They were like men who had been living in palaces of finest architecture, full of statuary, gilding and painting, but where all was replete with references to idolatry. It seemed like living in a heathen temple with all its orgies and abominations. Their whole moral and spiritual nature was repelled and confounded; so they quitted the palaces, and took to living in huts, or camping out beneath the sky. So long did this tendency last, and so deeply did it lay hold of many of the devoutest minds, that Pope Gregory I. regarded it as a crime for a priest to teach grammar. The teaching grammar meant giving the key to the old classic heathen literature, with all its pollutions and seductive beauties. This may have been fanaticism; but let us not hastily or over-much condemn it, for they were not imaginary dangers which were dreaded. This was shown by what took place long after, on the revival of classical learning in the fourteenth and fifteenth centuries. The exclusive study of the ancient authors, the enthusiasm and veneration with which these were regarded, revived the old heathen spirit, though it could not restore the gods. The cultured looked back with boundless regret and longing to the old times portrayed with such overawing splendour and inimitable grace. A flood of corruption and of hard mocking unbelief swept over society. If ever Christianity was near being extinguished it was then, when the heathen spirit came back with its supreme worldliness, and without the restraints and elevation which even heathen belief and worship carried with them. Unquestionably if the old literature, saturated with heathen ideas and allusions, had continued to occupy the place it did, the battle of Christianity would have been far more difficult. The legends of heathenism might have speedily become as fairy tales, utterly incredible and effete ; but the subtle spirit of the whole, its ignoring of sin, its poor conception of man and life, its exaltation of earth and earthly pleasures, would have operated powerfully against Christian influences. So we cannot wonder at the recoil from the old literature which the early church experienced.

But it is difficult for us to estimate the effect which so thorough a withdrawal of the great literary models produced. The Greek thinkers and poets, historians and dramatists, had attained a pitch of perfection which is still the wonder of the world. It was but a brief period of excellence. Certainly, if we exclude Homer, it did not extend over more than half a century. Herodotus and Thucydides in history ; Plato and Aristotle in philosophy ; Pindar in lyric poetry ; Æschylus, Sophocles, and Euripides in the drama—what a constellation gathered round one age! It is surely impossible to gaze on this constellation, clustered round

N

such a brief period, exhibiting such perfection of form with such depth and thoroughness, such a maturity and fulness of execution, such a profusion of rich and striking thoughts expressed with such grace—it is impossible to ponder this period and its wealth of power, and to compare it with other periods of the world's history, without feeling that this age had a peculiar meaning and purpose, that it was meant to occupy a position in the intellectual world similar to that which Israel holds in the religious world. Then there was the Latin literature, not of equal splendour, and in a large measure imitative, but embracing such great names as Virgil and Horace, Lucretius and Ovid, Terence and Cicero. To have the horizon at once swept of those great lights of the intellect and imagination could not but have a bewildering effect, even though it was accompanied with a purifying of the moral atmosphere.

The masters of style were gone ; the professors of the art of the sublime and beautiful, the devotees and experts of subtle, comprehensive thinking were almost forgotten. Then began the labour of moulding thought again—began in troubled, anxious times—began when a strong practical tendency prevailed, when the old order of things was passing away with outcries and convulsions, and when a new order was coming in, full of antagonism to the spirit of the past, pressing on through tears and blood, dungeons and scaffolds. Was it any wonder that the work of expression that devolved on this new, struggling time, which had hidden and forgotten the old masterpieces and models—was it any wonder that it lacked the old finish, the old grandeur and symmetry of form? Men had unlearned the architecture of the palaces which they had forsaken. It was a secret not to be speedily regained. Perhaps in their intentness on converting and renewing the world, the most earnest and powerful spirits even despised the secret. It was a fault; but can we so greatly blame them?

The Church had a literature in those times of struggle; but it was a literature of defence and debate. Treatises were written in vindication of Christianity, and many controversial works were produced of great power and subtlety. It is true that these could scarcely be called literature in the strict sense, but they were the necessary and inevitable outcome of such a time. Christianity needed to find its place in the thought and speculation of men, as it had formed a place for itself in their conscience and heart. It had asserted and proved its claim to satisfy the soul of man; it had met his wants as a sinner, and a pilgrim to eternity; but still it had to put itself into shape for his intellect. It had not been originally put into such a form. It was needful that the mind of man should fashion the heavenly material for itself in order that it might be a thing of living interest to him, and be always in some

sense clothed with the charm of research and discovery.   The great facts and realities of the Gospel
were meant to be appropriated by the whole nature of
man, to become a vital and vitalizing part of his whole
being ;—not to lie untouched by his reason, as something foreign and incapable of being assimilated, but to
be put into genuine human guise, to be grafted into
the intellect of man, and there to produce, as the nature
of a graft is, not fruit of the solitary intellect, but the
true, genuine, heavenly fruit of the graft itself.   But
this process of grafting the heavenly vine into the
intellect or reason of man is a laborious and often
painful process, needing always to be renewed, and
never approaching perfection.   It should not therefore
surprise us that Christian literature took, in the early
period, a controversial and rather abstract direction.
Its subtle disputes about the Godhead, and about grace
and freewill, were unavoidable.   Men simply could not
pass these questions by.   Till these matters of absorbing, practical interest had attained some degree of ad-
justment to the human understanding and conscience
there was no room for other things.   It is easy to say
that huge discussions were made to turn upon an *iota*,
the smallest letter in the alphabet; but what if that
iota involved the question whether God had really
been incarnate in Christ; whether the Redeemer was
of *like* nature with God, or of the *same* nature, with all
that lies back of this, and all that flows from it ?   It

would have been sheer blindness or crass perversity that would have dismissed a question because it happened to turn upon an *iota*. It may make a decisive difference to a business calculation whether a man puts a single stroke in front of his figures, or adds a nothing after them.

But this protracted, though inevitable, fermenting of thought over the great problems left little energy meanwhile for other manifestations of intellectual life. There has been more than one such period in the history of the Church, when high abstruse questions passed quite away beyond the lines of the usual theological arena, and filled all the haunts of men, the exchange, the workshop, and the social gathering. There were times in the early centuries when the most abstract and, as we should say, curious and speculative questions, were regularly discussed in the pulpit before intent audiences, and were debated by men everywhere: just as there have been times in our own country, when the shepherd on the moor, and the weaver at his loom dealt in recondite topics, and men could meet neither at funeral nor wedding without falling into theological dispute. Such have scarcely been times for general literature, though they have ploughed deep the human soil, and prepared eras of fertility.

Literature had another obstacle to contend with in the early centuries and the middle ages, which it requires little consideration to appreciate. The Roman Empire slowly declined, and at last fell to pieces. The northern nations seized upon the provinces and overran Italy itself. A period of universal chaos supervened. The Latin language, which contained the literature and formed the bond of the empire, disappeared. A strange and constantly shifting jargon was the only medium of intercourse—language, undefined, unwritten, without grammar, becoming unintelligible every hundred miles at the utmost. It was several centuries before this seething chaos subsided and precipitated itself into distinct shapes; and obviously there was no possibility of literature in this dreary sweltering period.

Latin was the language of the church—indeed, what other was possible in that time? Theologians went on with discussions in Latin, wrote treatises in Latin, built great schemes of theology in Latin. But this dead language that had a second life in great stretches of systematizing and hair-splitting, this language of a learned class, could carry no living literature. It had no contact with the ordinary life of man. Children did not lisp it at their mother's knee; it was not shouted by boys in their sports; lovers did not whisper it; songs were not sung in it; passions and sorrows and eager debate and the tones of joy and triumph were not heard in it. Latin sufficed for the great scholastic theology—that gigantic attempt to parcel out the infinite, that vast elaborate prisonhouse of minds—but it rendered a real, living literature impossible. This can only come from the great heart of humanity, and the heart can only utter itself in its mother tongue.

It was not till the modern languages slowly emerged that literature became possible. The confusion of tongues, the universal babel that reigned over the old Roman Empire for centuries, the absolute want of any definite written speech in which men could utter themselves—was the great cause of the dark ages. No sooner did the actual speech of men begin to shape itself afresh than the darkness showed signs of dispersing.

One of the first results of the rise of the modern tongues was Dante. Some of his writings are in Latin. He, indeed, hesitated whether his great work by which he is known to the world and the ages should not also be written in Latin. He did not quite trust that sweet modern tongue of which he is such a master. It seemed to him rather a frail and precarious vehicle of thought, compared with Latin.

The first dawn of modern literature, indeed, was the Romance. This had life and blood, heart and soul, in it. The stories had come down from old heathen times in the vernacular; but they became imbued with the Christian spirit. The chivalry, the self-denial, the self-sacrifice, the purity, the lofty aim, the grand ideal,

the sense of the worth of man—these were no new
things—these were Christian ideas, which had been
working themselves into the heart and imagination of
men during the dark ages, and came out in beautiful
and touching, though sometimes fantastic shapes,
wherever the modern languages took form and a
place in literature. The very first productions of the
popular mind revealed what a great stride had been
made from the spirit of heathen antiquity. Amid all
their rudeness in form they reveal an elevation, a wideness of horizon, a serenity and trust, a tenderness, a sen-
sitiveness, and, above all, a burdenedness of conscience
and a hunger after righteousness, which are foreign to
the ancient literature. You feel that you have passed
into a period where the minds of men have been
familiarized with the great mystery of suffering for sin,
overawed, yet widened and emancipated, by the thought
of God manifest in the flesh for human redemption.
The world has evidently been unable to get beyond the
sweep of these ideas. It is a world which, at least, has
learned somewhat of the bitterness of penitence, and
the joy of immortal hope, and the meaning of sympathy
and compassion.

But the first great distinctively Christian writer is
Dante. He stands out towards the close of the middle
ages, summing up the theology and learning of that
period, concentrating it as only imagination can concentrate, breathing the life into it which only genius can

breathe, shedding over it that light "which never was on sea or shore." He is especially great as a painter of human nature; and the picture of man that he gives has the unmistakable, searching light of Christianity on it., He gives the mediæval conception of Hell, Purgatory, and Heaven in a series of portraits, passing through all the grades of vice, crime, pollution, and all the outstanding virtues. The humanity which he paints is one loftier, wider, and tenderer than the ancient world knew. It is blacker, brighter, intenser, realizing itself more—a humanity that has come into contact with vaster conceptions of mystery and love, and either been repelled or won and remoulded by them.

Yet Dante, with all his genius, is very far from presenting the spirit of Christianity. He is a fierce, political partisan, with narrow, local antipathies. He sees far into human nature, but it is often through an atmosphere of Italian revenge and rivalry. The coarse materialistic punishments he portrays revolt every human feeling, and turn the sympathy to the sufferer, however vile. The personal animus he breathes disgusts us. Yet he is one of the greatest searchers of the human heart; one of the most thrilling delineators of the terrible reality and mystery of the moral element. All through there are strange touches of tenderness and beauty. He seems the most artless, as he is the most condensed and brief, of all great poets, presenting in a few plain words pictures and ideas which others would elaborate into fine, polished, sounding sentences. Dante was certainly the first writer who brought out the moral intensity of Christianity, who flashed the lights of Christian truth across the dark wastes and into the black recesses of human nature, who portrayed the awfulness of the strife between good and evil ; and this work is not the less real that it is saturated with the crude fantastic subtleties of the scholastic philosophy. There are those who think that all these horrid pictures of torture were unreal to Dante, that they were but pictures, that the whole is an allegory, and that he himself had really other hopes for lost men. I cannot undertake to decide that question.

If we are asked for the next great representative of the Christian spirit in literature, can there be any doubt that it is Shakespeare ? Shakespeare, though he has glaring moral faults, is yet in his inmost spirit an exponent of the essence of Christianity. His height and depth and breadth rise out of Christianity. The greater part of his finest and most original thought, that which is specially Shakespearian,—the pathos, the etherealness, the far glimpses, the sense of the unutterable tragedy of life, of a secret in things that can never be told, of the intricacy and yet plainness of human life,—these are things that could not have been but for Christianity. He paints evil, often, it seems, with unnecessary coarseness, and too much as if the work were rather pleasing to him ; but, remember, he has this grand distinction from the realistic painters of evil, he gives the other side, the other side heightened all the more by his picture of the evil. He gives the other side, whether you understand by this the contrast to the evil in beautiful, loving souls, or the outcome and upshot of the evil. I need only remind you of Lady Macbeth's remorse, and of the deathbed of Sir John Falstaff. It is this giving of the other side, this presenting of human life all round, this refusing to dwell on vice and make a study of it, which makes Shakespeare a true artist. What is Art but the endeavour to present life in its wholeness and mean- ing. The real needs the ideal in order to be real. Nothing is itself apart from the whole. Therefore there can be no true art which is not religious. All conceptions of life but the religious one are fragmentary. Religion is the looking at man's life, the world, as a whole—looking at them in connection and in their meaning, and therefore it is implied in all true art and all poetry, as well as all philosophy. That is why I call Shakespeare, with all his defects and coarseness, a pre-eminent Christian artist, and an expounder of the essence of Christianity. The substance of him pro- duces on the mind an effect in the same line as the Bible.

Christianity, then, in proportion as it has rooted

itself and spread in the world, has created literature. Whenever it was freed from the impediments of its early history, whenever it found the indispensable avenue of living language, it showed its inherent productiveness. Christianity demands a literature in its very nature. The Bible requires comment and illustration, and thus an immense literature has been gathered round it. Christianity, again, has stirred the minds of men on the most momentous topics, and thus produced another vast array of books. It has translated the Bible into hundreds of languages. To the most of these it has given not only a grammar, but an alphabet. No other religion has translated its sacred books, except Buddhism, which has translated a few of its books into one or two Eastern languages. Were we to count only the books which Christianity has called into existence in that direct way for its exposition, defence, and propagation, the number would far exceed the whole literature of the world, outside the pale of Christianity, on all subjects whatsoever.

But this gives only a small idea of its productiveness. The overwhelming majority of books on science have been produced by Christian nations. Indeed, no religion but Christianity has hitherto had anything like science within its circle. In all directions in which the human mind works, the religion of Christ has outstripped all others put together. Poetry, novels, metaphysics, philology, history, natural history—all have occupied it. Mental activity has found work in all directions, and written laboriously and unceasingly.

Evidently the Gospel has an extraordinary quickening power on the mind. Even where it has not its peculiar renewing influence, it stimulates and elevates men, and incites their mental powers. Can we give any explanation of this? Can we trace the fact home to anything in the nature of Christianity? We trace it, first and mainly, to its effect on the conscience, and its emancipating influence on the heart. It is because it combines these two that it stimulates. The sense of duty and obligation is incalculably increased—while this is kept from oppressing by the great hopes, the exceeding comfort and consolation which it gives. Other religions have failed in one or other of these directions. Christianity alone has known how to unite the sense of obligation, in its greatest weight, with the sense of freedom and an abounding joy. What a conception Christianity gives of the worth of humanity! Its doctrine of redemption puts man and life in a wholly new light. Its revelation of the worth of man is only second in importance to its revelation of God as love. When man knows himself unspeakably dear to God, a radiance spreads over all things, and a grand impulse propels his faculties. God is above in His glory: eternity is to come with its grandeurs: the horizon opens all round.

Yes, the power of Christianity to vitalize the intellect and rouse the imagination must be traced ultimately to its conception of God, to its transcendent wonder of redemption, to its clear view of eternity, to its declaration of the present indwelling of God in man, and the present realization of eternal life. It is evidently in the very nature of these doctrines to expand and stimulate. What can ever take the place of these? Is it Materialism? Is it Atheism? Is it Agnosticism? What hope or stimulus is in any of these? Do they make human life great or interesting, stripping it as they do of a perfect and a future? What poetry is left to a poor weak being, creeping to the grave? What a mockery of all human aspiration the thought of annihilation is. How poor and shadowy all relations in life become, with the grave an eternal trap and pitfall in which all some day soon are to be snared like wild beasts. If this is our position, let us —poor fools of destiny—give up all talk of perfect and beautiful and sublime, of undying love and boundless aspiration. All these words are ridiculously out of place. So are imagination and poetry and philosophy. Any cheap toy is good enough to amuse poor things like us. It would not be long before the world felt the reasonableness and necessity of coming down to this, if once the religious view of man and life had disappeared.

It takes a long time for Christianity to reproduce

its inmost spirit in literature. The task, indeed, will never be accomplished while the world lasts. The spirit of Christianity is at once simple and vast and deep—genial and quiet, and yet restless and revolutionary. And this spirit has to go down into human hearts and leaven the nature before it can come out in books. Hence its very reproduction in literature is fragmentary and partial. Cowper had the earnest, pathetic, doctrinal and experimental side in his day: Wordsworth the broad philosophic aspect opening on the spirit of nature: Faber, Wesley, and the great hymn-writers, have other and quite different aspects: Browning, Tennyson, Buchanan, Longfellow, Whittier, have still other sides: while Dickens and Thackeray, Walter Scott, George Macdonald, are all varied representations of the Christian ideas. And I believe that if you place all these together, you have a nearer approach by far to the spirit of Christianity than is to be found elsewhere. The depth and richness of human nature in these writers—their pathos and beauty, intensity and hopefulness, are such as you will find nowhere else. They all show, each in his own way, how dear man is to God—that truth and righteousness and love are the soul and the secret of things, that life is discipline and education, that the measure of things is not an external one, that the great may be hidden in the lowly and the sublime in rags and wretchedness. They present man and nature together, and both in the light of the infinite. Nothing but Christianity could have inspired them ; and they in their turn repay the inspiration by giving a fresh interpretation of Christianity and deeper insight into its spirit. The general literature which Christianity produces turns out the most effective exponent of it, and helps to mould its unchanging essence·anew. The religion of Christ is always in advance of the world's literature, and will always be its grandest inspiration.

Does not, then, a religion which has shown such a vast power of creating literature in all directions bear with it a proof of its origin ? May we not say, this work is greater than a miracle ? Do we not see in it one fulfilment of that great promise of Christ, " He that believeth in Me, the works that I do shall he do also; and greater works than these shall he do; because I go unto My Father."

BLESSED ARE THE POOR IN SPIRIT.

"Blessed are the poor in spirit, for theirs is the kingdom of heaven."—Matthew v. 3.

OUR Lord begins His reckoning of blessedness with poverty in spirit. And this is evidently just, for if blessedness depends upon attainments, then the first step is to be conscious of poverty. He who thinks himself already rich, why should he desire increase? Poverty in spirit leads to mourning, and to hunger and thirst for righteousness. It thus needs only the consideration of the place which poverty of spirit occupies here to determine exactly what it is, and to distinguish it from things which may be mistaken for it.

Poverty of spirit does not mean lack of energy, deficiency of daring, purpose, or determination, though such a pusillanimous, feeble spirit may readily be mistaken for it. The two spirits may be alike in some of their manifestations. They may both convey a certain outward lowliness of demeanour, a certain willingness to yield, a certain dislike to strife, a certain

o

shrinking from prominence.   They are alike in their
contrast to ostentation and egotism, to all assumption
and vanity, but they issue from very different sources.
A "poor spirited" man, in the ordinary use of the
word, is often one who has an extraordinary measure
of self-consciousness, and a very peculiar regard for
self ; whereas, the poverty of spirit which our Lord
places at the foundation of all blessedness is rather the
losing sight of self in the grandeurs and urgencies of
truth and righteousness.   It is to be understood by
keeping in mind the use of the word spirit in the
Scriptures.   The spirit, as distinguished from the soul,
is the side of man's mental being which lies open to
the eternal and infinite.   It embraces those faculties
which discern God and the eternal, and crave perfection.   It is not something different from the soul, but
embraces the higher wants and possibilities of the soul.
There is a higher side to memory, a higher side to
imagination, a higher side to reason and judgment and
conscience ; and that is the spirit—the spirit which is
not content with anything less than the perfect and
eternal.   The poor in spirit is the man who is conscious
of his deep want.   He sees and feels his deficiency in
all the greatest matters.   He may know that in many
of the ordinary affairs of life he is not deficient, but in
reference to all the grand, searching, decisive things he
knows himself utterly wanting.   He feels that as
regards God and man, as regards his duty to himself,

to the present and the future, he is utterly impoverished. He sees a great weight of obligation which he
does not meet, and cannot meet. He sees duty stretching afar which he has scarcely touched. He sees that
everything he does is defective and incapable of being
offered to a holy and righteous God. Just as the man
who is impoverished in worldly goods is unable to
meet obligations, occupy positions, undertake duties
which require money, so the man who is poor in spirit
feels that there is a lack of virtue and goodness in
him, a lack of principle and force in him, adequate to
the demands of duty. Other men have *glimpses* of
their poverty ; they see clearly enough at times the
true state of matters, but they refuse to look steadily
at it. They turn away from it. They will not believe.
They determine not to realize it, or think about it.
The poor in spirit looks steadily at the fact of his
poverty. He tries to remember it. It is a painful
truth which he does not forget, which he is afraid of
forgetting. One of the great temptations of men is to
turn away from the painful, from that which lowers
them in their own eyes. They will resort to all kinds
of subterfuge ; they will turn to books, to pleasure, to
companions, in order to escape from the disparaging
estimate of self. Anything but lose their high opinion
of self. Anything but make full inward confession
that the self is poor and empty and defective in
reference to all the best, the deepest, the highest. But

the poor in spirit faces the sad truth about himself. He is not content to live and walk in a delusion and lie. What he cannot bear is unreality; so he looks at his motives and finds that none of them is altogether pure, that many of them are hollow or rotten, that his best feelings are cold and dull or mixed with base material, that his best resolutions are weak and fluctuating or altogether evanescent.

How strange it looks that to this poverty of spirit Jesus should assign the kingdom of heaven. For, obviously, it is the very last to think that the kingdom of heaven belongs to it. "The kingdom of heaven belong to me?" the poor in spirit says. "I am at the very farthest remove from it! I am unworthy even to touch its threshold, or to lift my eyes to it! How should that glorious kingdom of light and truth comport with my impurity and darkness?" Yet it is to this very depth of conscious poverty, to this utter impoverishment, that Jesus assigns the kingdom of heaven, and that not as a future inheritance but as a present possession. The kingdom of heaven belongs, in fact, to the poor in spirit all the while that they judge themselves unworthy of it, while they are oppressed with a sense of their poverty, while the sense of unworthiness mingles with all that they do. Strange this is; and yet if we think for a little, we shall see the reason of it, and that it is not at all the contradiction that it seems.

Ask yourself how a man comes to be so poor in spirit—how does he attain to such a sense of his poverty and insufficiency? Plainly he cannot attain to it without a wide horizon, without clear insight into himself, without a high ideal. It is because he sees the grand horizon of goodness that he has such a low idea of his own attainments. That painful sense of deficiency—surely that cannot exist without a keen sense of the beauty and excellence of goodness. If a man feels himself so far from the heavenly kingdom, this at least implies a great perception of the glory of that kingdom. And when a man sees the glory and worth of a thing, is it not in reality already his? All the glory and beauty of the summer are yours by your appreciation of them. It is no nominal ownership of a prospect which makes a man its possessor. He possesses it in the true sense who has its meaning and spirit. So he who sees the true grandeur and glory of the kingdom of heaven, who sees the nobility of worth, of goodness, even though the sight makes him feel his own utter poverty, already possesses the kingdom. It is in him. How else should he see its grandeur and glory? *It is his just because he feels his utter unworthiness of it.* The germs of all goodness are included in that painful estimate of one's self.

And here we have indicated the way to attain to this poverty of spirit which lies at the foundation of all blessedness. Take an earnest survey of the kingdom of heaven, which is righteousness and peace and joy in the Holy Ghost. Think of the glory of being like God. Think of the splendour of these three—faith, hope and love; and dwell upon the glories of love, as delineated by Paul in the thirteenth chapter of First Corinthians. Think of the richness of the fruit of the Spirit as portrayed by the same Apostle in Galatians—love, joy, peace, long suffering, kindness, goodness, faithfulness, meekness, temperance. Think over the glorious life of Jesus, and the lives of many who have caught His spirit. Think over these, in the remembrance that you are but a pilgrim here, that there may be but a step between you and death. Remember these solemn words, " Be ye holy for I am holy." " Without sanctification no man shall see the Lord." Remember how hollow, fleeting and fading all other things are. Think what the things are that give pleasure in the retrospect. Think that the fruits of the spirit are the glory of heaven and its very essence, and that no spiritual creature of God anywhere can have any worth without them. And then look in upon yourself and behold your poverty. Let not the painful sight repel you, but press the thought upon you, "I am poor, I am poor," and that will be the beginning of true blessedness. It is quite true that men sometimes recognize the utter absence of all these great qualities in themselves, and are not moved or stimulated by the recognition. They know themselves spiritually poor, but the

knowledge gives them no concern.   But in what sense
do such men know their poverty?   Only as in a
dream.   They are asleep to the whole spiritual realm of
things.   They may use the words, SOUL, SPIRIT, DIVINE,
ETERNAL, PERFECT, SIN, SALVATION; but it is as men use
words in sleep.   Or perchance, with some sense of the
glory and necessity of these things, and with a feeling
that everything without them is but delusion, they are
hopeless as to the *possibility* of spiritual wealth.
Having no faith in God's help, spiritual wealth seems
but a splendid dream to them.   They doubt whether
men have not all been, even the best of them, nearly as
poor as they are, cheating themselves and others with
fine words about goodness, elevation, perfection.   Men
who have reached this state are the most wretched of
all.   They believe in poverty, but not in wealth; and
the glory passes away from the universe.   The crown
falls from the head, not only of man, but of God.
Brethren, there is no such folly as this.   What is the
meaning of poverty unless there is wealth somewhere?
How can you say a man is spiritually poor unless you
have an ideal standard of wealth?   Where does this
idea of goodness and perfection come from?   It can
only come from the grand, ultimate reality, God—GOD,
whose infinite perfection at once shows my poverty,
and convinces me that wealth is possible for me and
for all; God, with whom all things are possible.

Is there any one depressed, then, desponding,

burdened because he is so destitute of all worth, all goodness and earnestness ? There is good news for him. He is of the poor in spirit, and the kingdom of heaven is his. The kingdom belongs to those who think themselves most unworthy of it.

It looks then, does it not, as if the influence of poverty of spirit landed us in a strange dilemma ? If the poor in spirit, always of necessity, thinks himself unworthy of the heavenly kingdom, and cannot believe himself a possessor of it, then he seems quite shut out from attaining to a knowledge of the fact of his blessedness. He has the inheritance, but the very poverty of spirit that makes it his keeps him from believing that he has it. Yes, this is quite true, if you lose sight of God. If the man looks only at himself, he will be always desponding; but let him look to God. The hope he cannot find in himself he finds in God. To the poor in spirit the mercy of God is very precious, the promises of God are very dear. Christ, the Redeemer, is unspeakably bright and gracious and mighty.

BLESSED ARE THEY THAT MOURN.

"Blessed are they that mourn: for they shall be comforted."—
Matthew v. 4.

How remarkable that Jesus should pronounce the mourners blessed, when He so much exalted joy in the tenor of His ministry. Jesus stands out among all teachers that ever were for the emphasis He put on joy. How then should He at the beginning, in laying the foundations of His kingdom, contradict all this and exalt sorrow? The explanation is not to be found in the notion that it is the fuller Gospel, which came later, that exalts joy—that the earlier stages made sorrow the prominent thing. This, though in a sense true, cannot be the explanation; for Jesus inculcates joy in the early stages, and does not forbid, but even enjoins, sorrow at a later time. The real clue to the difficulty seems to lie partly in the position of this Beatitude, following immediately after poverty of spirit. What can succeed poverty of spirit but sorrow? If a man realizes himself to be unspeakably poor, and wanting in all the main matters, what *must* follow ? Sorrow, sorrow, sorrow. It is not in the nature of things that any other emotion should result. Other feelings may come by and by, but sorrow will be first. If sorrow does *not* come after poverty of spirit, then there is some grievous lack. It is a poverty owned without the perception of wealth, a poverty acknowledged without the sense of what it truly is. If we fix our mind on this plain fact, we shall both understand why sorrow stands here, and what the very kind of sorrow is—the sort of sorrow or mourning that springs from poverty of spirit. That is the mourning which is mainly intended here.

But let us at this point, with a view to the proper understanding of this Beatitude, briefly consider the excellencies and the defects of sorrow and joy relatively to each other. Sorrow has its good points and its bad, and so has joy. What are the excellencies of sorrow ? What are its defects and evils ? One great excellence of sorrow is that it calms down the fever and excitement of the world, and makes a man long for reality, it may be for the first time in his life. Joy keeps men often in a perpetual whirl in which they scarcely know where they are, or what the meaning of things is. When the night of sorrow descends, a man sees the stars in the great firmament overhead. He becomes aware that there are vast realities which he had been forgetting. Sorrow is a telescope, though it seems to make men short-sighted. *Men see distant*

things best through tears.   In sorrow, again, the persistent conceit and pride that beset men in joy are
broken—not removed or uprooted, but *broken.*   In
sorrow a man no longer thinks that he can do everything or anything, and that there is nothing too good
for him.'   These salutary effects flow from any kind of
sorrow almost, though mainly from sorrow for sin.   Let
a man be prostrated under sore calamity.   Let him
groan under bereavement, let him writhe in anguish
under some keen strokes of adversity, let the biting
winds of unwonted poverty blow over him, let him behold his fairest prospects vanish, and taste the bitterness of disappointment; and, whatever other effect it
may have, it will at least sober and chasten him—
make him open to many things to which he was formerly shut, and lead him to recognize a brotherhood
where before he felt only contempt or indifference.
Sorrow often braces purpose, gives new intensity of
will, and an absorbing sincerity and oneness of aim.
On the other hand, sorrow has its dangers and drawbacks.   It often takes away the spring and elasticity
of life, and makes men sullen, sour, and envious.   Men
made desperate by sorrow are prepared for any plunge.
The Dead Sea of sorrow is a water that no man can
drink.   You know that there are plenty of living
things in the Jordan, but none in all the expanse of
that sea into which it flows; nothing can live in these
bitter waters.   So there is a sorrow that worketh death.

The dangers of joy are obvious.   Men by prosperity
and happiness, by the satisfaction of every want and
the success of every enterprise, become proud and
overweening. , They become insolent and isolated, are
more than content with the present, and live as if
there were neither past nor future.   But joy has excellencies which are as frequently overlooked.   Joy
expands the nature.   Every faculty reaches its height
in the sunshine.   Often benevolence expands for the
first time in joy, and love thrives there as in its
native place.   It is clear that man is made for joy—his
heart longs after it, his whole nature needs it.   A
permanent sorrow lowers the life and weakens the
force of a man in body and soul ; while joy makes all
labour easy, and takes away half the burden of care.

This comparative estimate helps us to see how and
in what sense sorrow is blessed.   Sorrow is blessed
when it is the result of seeing the reality of a man's
own state.   Blessed is the man who has got his
feet on reality, although the position may make him
wretched.   Blessed is he who has got away from false
estimates, from dreams and delusions !   Who would
live in a lie for all the paltry comfort it brings ?   Who
is there that does not experience a certain satisfaction
in the midst of his sorrow over his spirit's poverty and
sin, in the very thought that at least he is not blinded
and hoodwinked, not utterly dull and dead ?   Oh, there
are thousands of souls who would not give the tears,

the anguish, the heartbreak, the agonies of contrition which they feel, for all the false joy, the hollow elation they used to have. They may not be conscious of any hope in the bitterness of their grief, but they would rather have it a thousand times than the falsity, hardness and wrong in which they used to live, calling it happiness. Sorrow is blessed when it is not the mere regret for what might have been, but withal the yearning for something better in the future. The sorrow with which a man mourns over the ruins which cover his past, the unspeakable regret with which he thinks on what might have been, on the garden of fertility and beauty that might have spread over all the vanished years, when he thinks what he might have made of life, and when he considers what others have made of it who had less vantage than he,—this sorrow may be only so much waste, a vain expenditure of that which his sins have left; yet, surely, when compared with callousness, there is something noble in this waste. There is something at least to be admired in the feeling that men sometimes have, that they with all their sin and wrong have no right to be glad. They will not lay hold of a happiness to which they have no claim, and thus add one more and worse vileness, as it seems to them, to all the wretched guilt, hollowness and mockery of their life. Yes, the melancholy of men is often the best thing about them; it is their one monument to justice, truth and love—a monument, not of marble, but of lava thrown up hot out of the depths of their being and that scarcely grows cold through all the years. This sad monument to truth and right may remain a barren thing, but this is most unlikely. For the weirdest, blackest, ruggedest monument of lava touched at the top by the sunshine of hope is transformed into the finest marble. Look, you can see the streak of sunlight as it tinges the summit, and as it creeps down the grim pile, transforming it all and making it to flash with radiance. There is fulfilled that .promise of God, " O thou afflicted, tossed with tempest and not comforted, behold I will set thy stones in fair colours and lay thy foundations with sapphires. And I will make thy pinnacles of rubies, and thy gates of carbuncles, and all thy border of pleasant stones." And what prevents any sorrow, however dark and heavy, from yielding to the influence of hope ? It is ignorance of God, want of faith in his mercy or power. This is the peculiar temptation of sorrow, that the deeper it is the more difficulty it has in yielding itself to the influence of hope. And yet, in very truth, the deeper and heavier a sorrow is, the nearer it lies to hope and consolation. Its very weight drives it to the necessity of hope and of God. Its sense of God's holiness lies very near to the sense of His love and mercy. When I look up to the sky, black clouds may oppress and terrify me ; but in that same sky, where the clouds are the radiance is to be seen. Surely a man who looks aloft, and sees only clouds, will by looking a little longer see more than clouds. Happy is the man who looks to God, though at first the look may bring only gloom. Clouds do not last always. We think them enduring, but they are not lasting like the sky, the sun, and the stars. The mourning soul that looks intently above will find it so. " Weeping may lodge for a night, but joy cometh in the morning." Blessed are they that mourn, and that see and feel that; while a true mourning is incomparably better than a false joy, yet a true joy, however slight, is better than the heaviest mourning. A joy in righteousness is better than sorrow for the want of it. To be glad in the love of God is a far greater tribute to it than sorrow, because it is not seen aright. A sorrow that hugs itself, and nurses itself, and is secretly proud of itself, as all lasting sorrow is prone to be, has already become a heavy curse. A sorrow may be so proud of itself as to look with scorn and injustice upon all joy as something shallow and blind. It forgets that, while there is a blind joy, the true joy in God sees far more than sorrow does. Sorrow sees only His hand or His arm, joy sees His face. He who has once seen the face of God cannot be sad.

Blessed are they that mourn, then, for comfort is theirs, and theirs alone. Blessed is the springtime because it has advanced from winter; blessed still more is the springtime because it will not last, but

lose itself in summer. A perpetual springtime would
not be blessed. It is sweet to see the snowdrop and
the crocus; but what would this sweetness be, if they
were not the sure promise of something better than
themselves ?

Blessed are they that mourn, when the mourning
leads them, drives them, forces them out of self to
Christ; when it shows them that there is no salvation,
no healing power, in the bitter discipline of pain; that
Christ alone has the true medicine, an open and yet
secret medicine, of the soul. There is no power in the
world which can teach this lesson so well as sorrow
—and therefore, "Blessed are they that mourn."

BLESSED ARE THE MEEK.

"Blessed are the meek: for they shall inherit the earth."—
Matthew v. 5.

THERE is none of the Beatitudes which seems such an open contradiction and paradox as this; and yet it is taken entire from the thirty-seventh Psalm, and has many echoes throughout the Old Testament. The originality of Jesus here does not lie in this separate Beatitude by itself, but in the position in which it is placed. It stands here in the very order which explains it, accounts for it, justifies it. The originality of an architect is not in the materials he employs, nor is it in the shapes, the curves, angles, pillars he introduces; every one of these may have been employed frequently by others. His originality is in the new position he assigns to material and to form. The originality of a composer is not in the sounds he evokes, but solely in the order and succession. So Jesus is wholly original. The order contains the great secret, and sets forth the worth and glory. True meekness comes from poverty of spirit and mourning for sin. In any other position meekness is not understood—indeed, it is not itself. A man may seem to be very meek, who in reality is only dull, and does not perceive or feel the affront or injury. There is a meekness of self-interest. Men every day submit to much that is trying to temper and patience, purely because their interests are involved. From the highest to the lowest, this is matter of daily experience. When a shopman submits with a smile to the unreasonableness, the insolence, the ignorance, and all manner of offensiveness of customers, betraying never by a single movement of the muscles, or a glance of the eye, what he suffers or what the amount of his amusement is, nobody supposes that he has a claim to any superior meekness. He takes it all as a matter of business. He would reckon himself a fool, if he were to lose the chance of making a sale for the sake of giving vent to his vexation or his mirth. The frequenter of high society, where all is bland and smiling, and every strong expression is banished, disguises chagrin at slight or inuendo, because to appear to see or acknowledge such a thing would be degradation, and would in fact be altogether out of the question. · He would not make himself absurd by any manifestation of feeling. You may have seen among boys that, when one meets with an affront, or any injury from another boy, which it would be dangerous to resent in any way, he frequently takes the earliest opportunity of relieving his feelings by being cross, offensive, or injurious to some smaller boy. So it goes on all through life ; the subordinate who is snubbed, compensates himself by snubbing some inferior, and often carries his vexation to his own home. Wife and children inherit the last reversion of resentment and wounded feeling. Instead of coming home to bless their fireside with sunshine and joy, men frequently bear with them the accumulated suppressed grudges, the slights, hard hits, friction and disappointment of the day. They whom in their hearts they love best are those who have to bear their spleen and ill-humour. Their meekness is all expended in the world. If it were genuine meekness, do you think it could be so expended ? Would it not shine out conspicuously in spheres where there is usually so little to obstruct and cloud it ? Meekness is the mildness, gentleness, patience which men display under provocation or wrong, not because they *must*, out of regard to self or from fear of consequences, but because they have a lowly opinion of self, a great regard for God, and a true good-will and compassion toward men. Sometimes they have little else than compassion toward those who injure them. The violent, insolent, injurious seem so poor and miserable, so utterly mistaken as to the ends of life, that pity for them swallows up the sense of personal wrong. These seem more to be pitied than the blind, or the deaf, or those labouring under some heavy delusion,—all the more to be pitied that their blindness is self-chosen, and comes from an evil heart of malice and wickedness. Surely the most to be pitied is he who labours under the worst disease, a disease which infects his soul, poisons and embitters his whole nature, and makes him an heir of wrath and perdition. You can feel little else than compassion for a man who is making his own existence sour, hollow, and wretched in order to serve a grudge; especially when you think of him as a frail, dying man who, in spite of all his pride and violence and passion, must shortly pass into eternity, and appear before a holy, heart-searching, and just God.

It is from thoughts like these that true meekness springs. The *appearance* of meekness may be assumed by pride which scorns to betray any sign of pain, which dreads above all giving the offender the satisfaction of thinking that he is capable of inflicting a wound. Cowardice may wear the garb of meekness. But true meekness is brave. It does not shrink from right or truth. It endures bravely work or suffering for God and man and eternal right. True meekness believes in God and eternity, and therefore cleaves to right, and will not diverge from the path which has been chosen in the light of reason and conscience. False meekness is soft, can be made to deflect by threatening or overbearing. Hence men who are naturally meek may have the greatest difficulty in attaining genuine spiritual meekness. Their native yieldingness leads them to acquiesce too easily. They do not need to bend their will, to subdue their temper, to teach themselves patience by the higher considerations. They submit, and are accommodating without reflection, by a kind of necessary impulse. No need for them to bring thoughts of God and of love, duty and compassion to bear upon their hardness and stubbornness, for that has already given way and disappeared under the action of far lower influences. And, brethren, is not this only one instance of natural good qualities proving obstacles in the way of the acquisition of the higher and spiritual? A man is naturally joyous, and that often prevents him from feeling the need of higher joy. He is naturally amiable, obliging, compassionate, and it may be that very excellence that prevents him from feeling the need of true spiritual love. He knows himself more genial, sociable, compassionate than many men who appear to be more religious than he, and so he concludes that he is really a better man than they with all their religion, and needs no change. Another man is possessed of a firm will, and does not feel the need of divine help so much as a man of a weaker will may. Another man has great prudence and circumspection from his very temperament, and is very prone to forget that these are only surface qualities, proceeding, it may be, purely from caution and regard to self, and that they have no moral value without the deep and wide qualities of love for God and man.

The meekness, then, which is blessed is not dulness, inertness, cowardice, policy or caution; but true patience and forbearance from higher motives, calm submission to God's will, when adverse, and placid acceptance of the opposition of men, without being turned aside by it from one's own conviction of right. The truly meek man has such a sense of his own sins and shortcomings that God's hardest dealings with him seem not more than his due; and the slights, obstruction, opposition, reproaches, and scorn of men seem to him in some sense or other his due, though not at all in the sense that others deem. Men who are conscious to themselves of blameless integrity, utter sincerity and habitual walking with God, may be, and will be, so pained and humbled by their imperfections and failures, by their deadness, dulness and deficiency in all the higher elements, that neither friend nor foe can blame or judge them so severely as they do themselves. This has been the secret of many men who have filled prominent places in the world. Of Paul, of Augustine, of Luther, Calvin, Cromwell, of Wesley and Whitfield, and many others of recent times. Looking up to God in confidence and great joy, their cry was that of the old Psalm, "O God, let them curse, but bless Thou."

But how can the meek be said to inherit the earth? Heaven they may inherit; but earth,—that is the portion that falls to the strong and wise and politic. The meek are pushed aside. It is the self-assertive, the confident, the ambitious who do not wait for good fortune, but conquer it and constrain it to come. For an answer to such questioning we must look to the course of the Psalm in which this Beatitude is found. The Psalmist saw the wicked flourishing, but he saw also that their prosperity did not last; he saw that it was the meek, who held on by right and truth, that ultimately triumphed. Their meekness was not their only quality; they had energy, perseverance, industry, integrity, but it was by meekness that they held on to all these. Meekness was the guard and preservative and atmosphere of all the rest. Meekness showed them possessed of that strength and wholeness of character which wins. What happened in the days of the Psalmist repeats itself in all history. It is the meek, the meek from great qualities, not the meek from expediency, who rise in the long run,—and often it is not a very long run. On the surface, history seems to show that it is violence that conquers; beneath the surface, it shows that it is steady, patient persistence in right that gives the aseendeney. Through the ages there is a clamour, a shouting, a shrieking, an uproar, and victory seems to follow in the train : ah, but look deeper,—the world passeth away and the lust thereof, but he that doeth the will of God abideth for ever. After the fire and the tumult have vanished, hark ! that is the still small voice again. Many waters could not quench it, nor the floods drown it. What is it that is rising to the top to-day, that is leavening all institutions, shaking all tyrannies, bidding the oppressed go free ? What is it that is hastening to assuage the pains and sorrows of men everywhere, and casting the idols down ? What is it but the glad tidings of Him who was meek and lowly, the King who came riding upon an ass, the Conqueror who died upon the Cross ? He did not cry, nor lift up, nor cause His voice to be heard in the street. And yet His sound has gone through all the earth and His words to the end of the world. No cause has come through battle and suffering like His. Beginning at Calvary, its path has been marked with blood and tears all through the centuries. It is meekness that has secured the triumph for all the truth and blessing which the Gospel carries. Without meekness the very first century would have seen the extinction of the Church. Endurance in truth and right conquered all the legions of the Roman empire. And if the Church had been only more faithful to the meekness and endurance of Christ, and always stood aloof from craft and policy and force, its triumph would have been more complete to-day. What is true, my friends, on a large scale, is true on a small. The meek inherit the earth ; not the peevish, querulous, fitful, ambitious, restless inherit the earth, but the men who have their centre and quiet home in God. They inherit the earth, though they may own not an acre, and though a lowly roof may shelter them. The men who have ceased from self and from man, and are bent to the will of God,—they inherit the earth.

The following principles briefly stated lie at the foundation of the matter, and will let us see our way through all the obscurities and apparent contradictions which surround the text, and with these we must conclude.

First, *a man can only possess anything in proportion as he possesses himself.* You can only possess yourselves by meekness. Without meekness you are constantly seized upon and carried away by all sorts of friction, delay, opposition and pain. Possess yourself, *then* only can you possess the earth.

Again, *you cannot be said in truth to possess anything unless you understand it.* It is only those who are meek from great principles who have a wide enough horizon and a proper standpoint to survey the world.

Further, *you cannot be said to possess anything unless you possess something better than it.* Unless you possess something better than the world, you cannot get any true hold of it.

Still further, *if you yourself are possessed by the world, if you are its servant and slave,* you cannot possess it. It is the meek alone who are free, and are not the servants of time and chance and circumstances.

In fine, *it is only the man who possesses God who can possess himself or anything else.*   When you lay hold of God, and claim Him, and enjoy Him as your own in Christ, and walk with Him in meekness and humility, then your soul lives and is opened out and truly inherits the earth.   *Possess the greatest, and you are able to possess the smallest.*

BLESSED ARE THEY THAT HUNGER AND THIRST AFTER RIGHTEOUSNESS.

"Blessed are they that hunger and thirst after righteousness : for they shall be filled."—Matthew v. 6.

HITHERTO the progress of the Beatitudes has been from one stage of depression to another, poverty of spirit leading to mourning, the two combined producing meekness. Now the progress takes another direction. The next three speak of the three great relations of the soul to righteousness, to men, and to God. They that hunger and thirst after righteousness shall be filled. They that are merciful shall obtain mercy. The pure in heart shall see God. How finely hunger after righteousness begins the new series. How grandly it concludes in the seeing of God. How strikingly is the necessity for mercifulness shown by its being inserted between hunger for righteousness and vision of God.

There is nothing of which men can have a more vivid conception than hunger and thirst. These express the most universal, most persistent, imperious, and painful wants of man. Hunger after righteousness is a continuous, strong, and keen desire for conformity to the mind of God. Of this deep desire it is affirmed that it shall be satisfied. He who hungers for righteousness shall have it. It is a law running through the whole constitution of things that for every real want there is some supply. The eye wants light, colour, beauty, and the want is met. The ear wants sounds varied and harmonious, and its desire is satisfied in the world of nature and of man. The body wants food to sustain it, and the earth and air and sea contain ·the elements that it needs. The reason of man wants materials to gratify it, materials for research, analysis, construction, and these are given to it. It wants to find some principles outside of it that it is conscious of in itself, and finding these it rejoices and is glad, grows strong and assured ; it is fed by all nature, it pastures on the stars. So the imagination of man needs food, and finds it in clouds, in streams, in sunshine, in morning and evening.

Let us notice, then, that the desire which has the promise of satisfaction is hunger, a deep want which steadily and persistently craves for its object. Every man has some sort of desire for righteousness at some time or other, and in some of its many aspects. Often a gleam of desire rises in the bosom of those farthest from righteousness as they hear of some noble deed, of a life spent bravely and meekly in the service of others. They could wish then, sometimes even in a passionate way with tears and self-reproach, that their life was such. But this is not hunger. Hunger is a steady, painful sense of want, an abiding feeling of an imperious need that must be satisfied. Hunger of this kind has the same efficacy that it has in the natural world. Men often remark that it is hunger that moves the world. There are many other things that move the world of man, some of them of a lower kind than hunger, and some far higher ; but hunger is that force which makes sure that there shall always be some movement, and that all shall participate in the movement. Conceive, then, what would be the influence of a steady, painful desire of righteousness similar to bodily hunger—a desire, a sense of want that *must* be gratified. If one were to feel pressed by a longing for righteousness in a way that would not allow itself to be forgotten or pushed aside, that made him constantly uneasy and restless, do you not think that such an one would be on the certain road to be filled ? His painful, aching sense of want would set him on effective seeking of righteousness, and make him willing to take any means that were necessary for his satisfaction.

Looking at these facts, then, what is the answer to the question,—Why are men who know of righteousness and approve of it not more righteous—why are they so far from the ideal which Christ has given ? The answer must be,—It is because men are not hungry. They do not feel a want of righteousness like that which they feel for bread. If they had deep hunger for righteousness, it would not allow them to rest. What we all want, then, most of all, is more hunger— a persistent, deep, pressing sense of want. How shall we get that? By looking at God, and desiring the glorious qualities of God; by looking at Jesus in His life and death; by looking at eternity, and thinking what is of value there; by looking at the world of men, and thinking how much it needs the influence of righteousness; by looking each at himself, and think- ing how grievously he comes short of what God requires and conscience demands. It is a good way of awaking the hunger after righteousness to read the life of some man who has been distinguished for goodness. It is a thousand pities that so many memories of men eminent in goodness are written in such a way as to repel people of discernment. They are often flimsy and sentimental. There is something unreal and morbid in their ring. This is greatly to be deplored; for a true, simple, unvarnished account of the life of any man eminent in goodness is one of the strongest forces in awaking dissatisfaction and shame at oneself, and stirring noble longings after a higher and truer life. What a rebuke comes to the heart, what a smouldering fire is felt, how the smouldering fire bursts out into a grand flame! The high walks of goodness are made sweet and winning; they are in-vested sometimes even with a fascination.   I would say to young people especially—for they are more susceptible of the influence of example—if you would win a grand hunger for righteousness, for a noble, un-selfish life, read the memoirs of some who have lived greatly, lived above the petty aims of ordinary men. They might be in the ordinary business of life, but they filled it with a heavenly spirit.   Their ambition was to gain the grandeur of the soul, and to make their life rich in good works.   The account of these souls comes to us like a sweet song, or like a martial strain.   It is like the blast of a bugle, the shrill note of the fife, or the rattle of the drums.   We may feel this influence even from a powerful work of fiction describing an ideal life, which is yet true to the reality of things.   But all works of fiction have this great drawback, they are *fiction ;* and though they may stimulate for a while, their influence is slight and fluctuating compared with that of which you can say, *This is true.*   Carlyle has somewhere said, " The power of the simplest bit of reality may be something alto-gether incalculable !   Such a little bit of truth and solid fact may have lessons wide as the universe and long as eternity."   Because this witness of Carlyle is true, I would repeat,—Nourish a grand hunger in yourself by reading the lives of men who have lived deeply and toiled nobly, who had high aims and were true to them, often in spite of weakness and pain, and poverty and disappointment.

It is an astonishing thing, if you consider it, that the promise and assurance of being filled is not made to the possessors of righteousness, but to the hungerers for it. And yet consider this well, and you will see that it means far more. The actual realized righteousness that any man possesses must always be far short of that which he hungers for. What you truly hunger for belongs to you already. You claim it by your hunger. How could you possibly have this strong, persistent desire for it unless your soul were already attuned to it, in harmony with it? The higher in goodness any man is, the more his hunger for goodness will dwarf his actual possession, the less he will be satisfied with his attainments. How, then, is it said that they that hunger are blessed, because *they shall be filled?* My friends, we must distinguish between the satisfaction of estimate, and the satisfaction of simple possession. So far as the estimate of our goodness is concerned, we can never be satisfied. We have but to look to the Word of God to see how small our attainments are. But even small attainments in goodness give a measure of satisfaction before we are aware of it. No man can do any good deed without being there and then blessed in his deed. Even a little genuine goodness imparts a sweetness, an aroma to the soul. You have sometimes been in a room, poor and bare perhaps, and with insufficient light. What was that sense of pleasantness and satisfaction that somehow seemed to penetrate you, and carry your thought away to the fields and woods ? You did not at first think of it as odour, but on looking round you traced the delicate, subtle influence to a little flower that bloomed in the window. So even a little genuine goodness gives a fragrance and sweetness to a man's own soul. The doing of good, the being good, apart altogether from your reflection, gives satisfaction. Nay, whenever you begin to reflect on it the pleasure begins to fade. The bloom passes away from your flower. It seems a poor thing, and its odour even begins to be matter of doubt.

But Jesus meant something more than meets the ear when he spoke of hungering and thirsting for righteousness. What is the centre, kernel and foundation of righteousness ? What is its fountain and its perennial support ? It is the righteous and holy God. What is the righteousness we hunger for ? It is the being like God. There is no other righteousness than that. This at first seems discouraging. Is it the very righteousness of God I must hunger for ? Then how hopeless it seems. If it were only something less than that, there might be hope. Ah but, friends, the very thing that seems to drive you to despair is full of hope. It is a well of confidence and joy. This righteousness that I hunger for belongs to the most loving and generous being, the Being who is love, and from whom all love comes. A man who believes in God cherishes no vain chimerical desire for righteousness. It is all in God. When God is his, he feels that, however poor his present attainments in goodness are, the whole is shown to him in God. He is poor, but he has an almighty and most bountiful Friend, who will put him into possession of all things. What a satisfaction any man has who can say, God is mine! That man is truly filled. What can he want more? Your actual possession of righteousness will never fill you. But your possession of the kernel and source of righteousness, your hold of God, will satisfy and fill you.

We are never made happy by the mere reality of what we are. We are only happy as we get beyond that, and exercise boundless trust in God, and hope in His mercy and goodness and power. All true hunger for righteousness involves this. If a man truly thirsts for God, it is for Him as the righteous One, the source and centre of righteousness; and if he truly thirsts for righteousness, it is the righteousness which has an eternal and infinite foundation in God. Let no man embrace in his hunger less than God, for only as he hungers for God can he have any pledge of satisfaction.

BLESSED ARE THE MERCIFUL.

"Blessed are the merciful: for they shall obtain mercy."—Matthew v. 7.

I HAVE delayed till now reference to the correspondence between the Lord's Prayer and the Beatitudes. At this point it becomes most striking. The fifth petition in the Lord's Prayer is, "Forgive us our debts, as we also forgive our debtors;" and the fifth beatitude is, "Blessed are the merciful, for they shall obtain mercy." It is the obtaining mercy that is the object and end of both, and this *obtaining* is in each case connected with the *exercise* of mercy. Again, this beatitude of the merciful follows immediately on that of hungering and thirsting for righteousness. The petition in the Lord's prayer for forgiveness follows on that for bread. Can we fail to recognize the correspondence between the prayer for bread and the blessedness of hunger for righteousness? We are certainly led to the reflection that it is the man who has had his hunger satisfied, as Christ only can satisfy it, who is inwardly disposed and constrained to the exercise of mercy. To feel your utter need, and to have that need met, must produce a benevolent, compassionate feeling toward men. How dry and hard, on the other hand, is the compassion and sympathy of a man who has never mourned bitterly over his own sinfulness, who has never known his own utter poverty before God and in view of the true ends of life. He throws his compassion toward the suffering, the needy, the fallen, as from a high superior position. He never acknowledges himself. one of them or near them, but stands on a grand point of eminence from which he can survey them, and be thankful that he is not as they are.

You must, then, in the study of this beatitude, as of all the others, look to the order in which it stands, remembering that it is part of an organic whole and owes much of its meaning to the position in which it appears. If you remember that every beatitude supposes the existence of all that has gone before, supposes that the soul has had some real experience of every preceding part, you will not be surprised that it is said that the merciful shall obtain mercy. It will not seem to you then that the merciful deeds of a man are represented as the *cause* or *ground* of his obtaining mercy of God, for you will remember that the blessed man has been already described as mourning over sin and comforted, as poor in spirit and possessing the kingdom, as hungering for righteousness and being filled. You will see that all these previous qualities are needed to explain this compassionateness and its connection with the compassion of God. Obviously it must be in a very peculiar sense that the mercifulness of the blessed man brings upon him the mercy of God, since he is already in possession of God's comfort on account of his mourning for sin, and in possession of the kingdom on account of his poverty of spirit. If you dwell upon the fact that the merciful are said to be blessed because they shall obtain mercy, if you are stumbled at this because it seems to teach salvation by works, then you must equally take into account that this blessed man is supposed to be already in possession of the kingdom of heaven on account of his very poverty of spirit, his utter absence of anything good or meritorious. Keep in mind that poverty of spirit comes first, and makes him a possessor of the kingdom, and that will lead you to see in what sense the merciful obtain mercy. It is the merciful who are already in possession of the kingdom of heaven, the merciful who are already comforted because of their mourning for sin—it is of them that it is said, " They shall obtain mercy." It cannot be a meriting or buying of mercy in their case, seeing they are already in possession of it, in its grandest form, the kingdom of heaven. But they who are truly in possession of the kingdom are in possession of a compassionate, faithful, sympathetic spirit. This is one main part of their wealth. What would the whole inheritance be to them, if they themselves were hard, unmerciful, without compassion or sympathy. Such men are poor where-ever they are. They have no inheritance either in earth or heaven. The kingdom of heaven cannot belong to an unloving soul.

There are some that have a tacit, preliminary objection to this exaltation of mercifulness, compas-sionateness, sympathy. It actuates them none the less that they never bring it into express collision with this beatitude or any precept of Scripture. Their minds are alienated from this and every other similar precept of the Bible, by their having taken up a different stand-point. Their favourite maxim is that a man ought not to allow his life to be dominated by feeling, but by reason and the sense of right. They point to the enormous exaggerations that feeling makes—to its huge mistakes and excesses. They show how sympathy and philanthropy often injure the very persons whom they wish to benefit, and they often work themselves up into a climax of righteous indignation by declaring that philanthropy has done more harm than good, and that he is the best benefactor of his race who allows men just to inherit the results of their own conduct, their vice or folly or thoughtlessness; that it is unwise and pernicious to struggle against the work-ing of the laws of the universe which tend to weed out and destroy the vicious, the thriftless, the incompetent

and the weak. Thomas Carlyle has done a great deal
to spread this view of things. His vehement denunciation of shams, and pretence, and weak assumption
and fussiness, are to an extent healthy. The world
needed this, and our nineteenth century in particular,
with its self-conscious and over-ripe philanthropies.
But one asks with astonishment, after hearing denun-
ciations against feeling, and fervid appeals to the laws
of the universe, whether the *feeling of scorn* can be a
much finer thing than the *feeling of compassion and
sympathy,* and whether a man may not forsake reason,
as much in glowing indignation and scathing satire,
as in sympathetic helpfulness ? Are not men in error
often when they declare themselves guided solely by
reason, and not at all by feeling ? A man's reason
seems to go all right by principles. But how comes it
that the reason of one man takes one road, and another
quite the opposite ? Ah, there is something behind
reason, inspiring it, filling it. That is feeling. There
is a benevolent reason, and a reason, hard and selfish.
There is a reason full of sunshine, and a reason that
carries winter with it. Men talk grandly about their
moving only by reason and principle, and not at all by
feelings, when in reality it may be only feeling that is
using the forms of reason, finding grounds and motives
and causes for itself. One man is impelled and guided
by hard, selfish feelings, and he finds reasons to justify
and demand his course. Another man is dominated by

tender feelings, but he does not own this to himself. He, too, wishes to be regarded as guided mainly by reason.   The truth is, it is not reason that originates or sustains the best actions.   Reason has the place of a guide, controller, and critic on our life; but the best, steadiest, most beneficent movements have come from benevolent compassionate feelings.   It is these that keep alive the fire of good deeds and sweeten all ordinary relationships of life.   It is these that feed the great enthusiasms that have blessed the world.   And there is no man that can say this at times better than Carlyle, no man that can show better than he how flimsy and feeble all phrases and maxims and reasons are when cut off from the great flood-tides of beneficent feeling.   When one surveys the wide field of history and looks at the world as it is, and his own experience of it, how often do these words of *Aurora Leigh* present themselves :—

> " When all's done, all tried, all counted here,
> All great arts and all good philosophies,
> This love just puts its hand out in a dream
> And straight outstretches all things."

There is nothing more difficult for one to decide than the question whether benevolent feelings, compassion, pity, sympathy, in any particular case, are the result of mere natural good feeling, or spring from the operation of higher causes.   If one knows that his life as a whole is swayed by faith that worketh by love, he

ought not to be anxious to determine whether particular good actions are due to this or to natural tenderheartedness.   He will never be able to answer this
question.   Look at that fruit tree nailed up on the
wall ;—who could tell what amount of the excellence
of its fruit is due to the soil, what due to culture,
what due to position, and what due to the sunshine.
We know that all these elements are mixed and combined and act upon each other.   We are not to think,
because compassion is spontaneous and immediate, that
it must be simply the outcome of natural kindness,
and not at all of a spiritual order ; for that tenderness
may be the result of much previous reflection and
much looking at Christ.   The sustained habit of· being
good and doing good results in a kind of permanent
necessity of being sympathetic and helpful. We should
not then be careful to settle the question,—which, indeed, never can be settled,—whether our benevolence
and compassion are due to natural or to spiritual
forces.   A natural fountain of goodness may become
spiritual, and a spiritual helpfulness may become
utterly unconscious, spontaneous and natural. There are
two things that are of much more importance to think
about.   The first is that *natural tenderheartedness of
childhood tends to pass away, and may be completely
effaced in the next stage of youth.*   How often a morning is bright and genial, and the day that succeeds
blustering and stormy.   A child may be of a quick,

sensitive sympathy, moved to tears of compassion at once, swayed by every generous impulse, and yet the youth turn out hard, sour, querulous, overbearing. How sad to see such a change. The fine gold has become iron or dross. And yet this hard, selfish youth may continue to estimate himself by these childish manifestations. He buoys himself up on a tradition of his early years. "These," he says, "interpret what I am; I am really most generous and sympathetic, whatever I now appear." He does not seem to be aware that character may wholly change. The tender grace and beauty of early years may be succeeded by hardness, unless higher influences begin to operate upon them. The spontaneous generosity of childhood will not last, if it is trusted to spontaneous operation in later years. It must have thought and effort then, else it will die.

The other thought that requires emphasizing is this: *The compassionate or sympathetic action must often come before the feeling of compassion or sympathy.* Men who have no conscious impulse towards sympathetic deeds should yet force themselves to do them; for the right action has often a great effect in producing the right feeling. Begin to do good, even though your spirit be cold and hard, and, if you be persevering and faithful, your heart will soon begin to glow and burn, and you may attain to a very enthusiasm of service.

And let us be well assured that a compassionate,

merciful, helpful spirit belongs to the very innermost essence of religion.   It is not a thing about which a man may become careless, like some curious question of interpretation, or some corner of a creed.   In Christ Jesus *faith which worketh by love is everything*—faith which *worketh*—not faith that just thinks about itself, and tries to find out whether it is genuine or no, but faith which *worketh*, which sets a man in motion, and keeps him obeying and striving, which worketh by *love* of the loving Christ.

BLESSED ARE THE PURE IN HEART.

"Blessed are the pure in heart: for they shall see God."—Matthew v. 8.

Who has not been astonished many a time both at what men see, and at what they fail to see? Two men pass along a road, and they see quite a different class of objects. The one has seen only that there are so many houses by the way, and many or few people; the other has seen the beauty of the prospect, the kind of plants that grow by the roadside, the play of light and shade across the fields. A man versed in natural science goes through a country and sees traces of geological strata. His mind takes to theorizing on the history of the configuration of the country, and finds everywhere support or the opposite for some hypothesis. To another there seems little else than one object in the world—man. He is a student of human nature, and wherever man is there is his book. One man will go through a country, and see only signs of evil. He has a quick eye for what is base. Another seems never to notice this side of things, but if there is any hint of nobleness, goodness, or truth, he is sure to be struck with it. One man sees the comic and grotesque everywhere. The world seems to afford little but material for joke and laughter. Another sees everywhere signs of sorrow, decay, disaster, and death.

Man sees not only with his eyes, but with his reason and conscience, his memory and his whole history. The whole of a man's nature and all his past look through his eyes at every object which he earnestly contemplates. He cannot keep his acquired skill, his knowledge of the world and men, his reading of history, from influencing his sight. His taste and his distaste, his pride or humility, his sorrow and his joy, his temperament and his aspirations, are all elements in his seeing. Seeing, then, depends on one's mental state. According as a man *is*, he sees. This fact gives us the clue to the declaration that "the pure in heart shall see God." What is it to be pure in heart? What is purity in anything? When do we call any object pure? An object is pure when it is free from foreign admixture, when it contains nothing which it is not according to its nature to contain. The air is pure when it has no foul vapours in it, and has its proper constituent elements in their right proportion. Any metal is pure when it is free from alloy. We have only to consider what the true original nature of the heart is, to know what purity of heart means. Purity of heart denotes the absence of the taint of evil thoughts in any direction. A pure heart is one not centred in self, but having its centre in God, not fixed on pleasure or self-gratification of any kind, or swayed and made to swerve from right by any desire or regard to self. In other words, purity of heart is sincerity, integrity of desire and purpose. Of course there is no such thing as absolute purity of heart in this world. But in proportion as any man *is* pure in heart he sees. In proportion as his imagination is free from dreams and images of evil, in proportion as his feelings are free from malice, uncleanness, bitterness, in proportion as his will is sincerely bent upon the good and true and the pleasing of God, he sees God. He sees Him not with his bodily eyes, but with his spirit. God is a Spirit, without shape, appearance, or form, and can only be seen by spirit. Even men, who think little of God and spirit, must acknowledge that the greatest, most powerful things in the world cannot be seen. Who ever saw an idea with his bodily eyes ? And yet ideas are very real, and rule the world. Truth and reason and love are wholly invisible ; they can never be seen by the eyes. But truth can be seen by the mind ; reason sees reason ; the heart sees love. In like manner, taste sees the beautiful, and the conscience right and wrong. And the spirit of man sees God. As men discern truth and right and love, not with their eyes, but with their mind, their heart, their soul ;

even so they see God.   They see God in the wisdom,
grandeur, magnificence of the universe; in the vast
sublimities of the midnight sky, and in the glory of the
moon; in the waking hopes of the dawn, and in the
mingled gloom and glory of the evening.   They see
God in communion with Him in the depths of their
heart.   They see God in the workings of conscience, in
their aspirations after goodness and right.   They see
Him in their strivings, in the subjection of their will.
In the night of suffering they see God, and in silent,
lonely watchings in the darkness.   God becomes a
most real presence to them at three times very specially :—when they are most intent and absorbed in
prayer; when they are most in harmony with the will
of God by thwarting their own wills, and by painful
self-denial; and when in the hour of deep suffering
they cast themselves entirely upon Him. · They see.
too, God in history, and in the course of events around
them.   Above all, they see God in the Bible, and pre-
eminently in the face of Jesus Christ.   Sometimes in
looking at Jesus Christ, in gazing upon Him in Gethsemane and on Calvary, they see a glory, a brightness,
a lustre and splendour that make all other things
seem unreal.   They feel that having seen that glory,
and while it remains visible to them, they can never be
burdened, or sad, or wayworn, or doubtful.   All difficulties vanish in the glory of Christ's face.   If any
man will come, and, with an earnest and sincere heart,

not intent on selfish aims, look and gaze at Christ, listen to Him saying, "He that hath seen Me hath seen the Father," and ponder over His life and death in the light of these words, he will see God. God will be known by him as most real. He will be a felt presence, a delight and a joy, an inspiration and a hope to him wherever he goes. Life then will become for the first time truly great, rich and deep. Life is grand and sweet when you feel and see around you everywhere an infinite presence—holy, loving, kind, gracious, tender, merciful—and can say, "This is God, my God, mine in a way that nothing else is mine." And such a glorious privilege may belong to the weakest, meanest, most degraded and polluted of men. God is seen by the contrite heart that laments its sin and longs for purity. God is seen in His glory through tears shed at the foot of the Cross.

How wonderful it is to think that the invisible God became visible in Jesus Christ. God walked the earth in human form, and so long as the history of Christ remains, God is seen in human form, walking, speaking, doing, suffering. Christ is the bridge between the visible and the invisible. In the history of Christ God is still visible to bodily sight. By the seeing of the eyes we rise to the sight of the spirit, just as through the sight of the grandeur of the sky we rise to the vision of the invisible grandeur of God. If, then, you would actually see God—not merely believe that He

is, not merely be rationally convinced of His existence, but *see* Him, *know* and be as sure of Him and
what He is as you are sure of anything you see with
your eyes,—look earnestly and look long at Jesus
Christ.

Here the question naturally presents itself,—How
is it that so many men who are apparently earnest and
sincere, and anxiously desirous for the vision of God,
do not see Him in nature or science ? Do they fail in
purity of heart more than other men, more than many
who have seen and found God ? Is it want of purity
of heart that explains their failure to see ? It is not
for us to give any such explanation, or even to hint at
it. We dare not, must not, resort to any such explanation ; we have no right to do so. And happily
there is no kind of necessity that we should. We
have the explanation in the bold saying of Lalande,
the French astronomer,—" I have sought the heavens
with my telescope, and I have not seen God." It is
not with the telescope that one can see God, or any
spiritual thing. Would a man have much success who
should search for righteousness, or love, or sympathy,
with either telescope or microscope ? You might with
more reason expect telescope and microscope to enable
you to read Hebrew or German. A man must feel
that he has a spiritual nature ; he must listen to the
longings, the yearnings, aspirations, wants, hopes, and
fears of his own nature ; and if, with these clamouring

R

in his soul, he sweeps the sky, either with or without a telescope, he will not fail to see God. It is little to say that a man is sincere and earnest, if he is not awake, if he is not conscious of what he himself is. The sincerity of a soul not awake does not matter much. If a man will not believe his own soul, if he will not listen to his own heart, how shall he believe the sky? No wonder that some scientific men do not see God. They are so absorbed in weighing, and measuring, and analyzing, that whatever does not yield itself. to any of these methods seems to them non-existent. They blind their eyes with the microscope and the telescope. It is neither by mathematics nor by chemistry that one can understand his own heart, or any mental or moral subject. And if men become absorbed in material things, shut their eyes to the invisible grandeurs of the soul, no wonder that they come to the foolish and shallow conclusion that there is nothing but what can be weighed and measured. They never seriously ask themselves what is the use of all this outward complexity and grandeur, if it does not serve some abiding purpose? Is all this elaborate vastness and sublimity only drifting vapour and dust, moving on in a meaningless dance? The reason— that moral sense that I feel within me, and know to be real and greater than all the outward universe—is not this reason, this moral law supreme everywhere? The poet, listening to his own soul, weighing his soul,

and surveying the universe, sees God. Hearken to
Tennyson—

> The sun, the moon, the stars, the seas, the hills, and the plains—
> Are not these, O Soul, the Vision of Him who reigns ?
>
> Earth, these solid stars, this weight of body and limb,
> Are they not sign and symbol of thy division from Him ?
>
> Speak to Him thou for He hears, and Spirit with Spirit can
> meet—
> Closer is He than breathing, and nearer than hands and feet.

The telescope, then, through which you may see
God, is your own heart, your own soul and spirit, your
own conscience and will. Make sure use of that, and
you will find God everywhere. *Even your sense of
wrong and sin will help you to see God.* Many may
search the Bible and never get a glimpse of God, if
they do not use their own heart and soul as telescope
and microscope. And any one may understand how
purity, sincerity, integrity of purpose, make the sight
clear, who will think of such an experience as the
following. It matters little whether he owns it as his
own or thinks it true of some other. A man is visited,
haunted by thoughts of God, and of the need and
reasonableness and necessity of a devout life. But
when he comes closer to decision there is some sin,
some habit, some course that must be given up. Shall
he give this up ? There is a struggle, but he decides
not to give up the sin. He says he *cannot* give it up,
or, at least, *not yet.* Now mark what follows. He

knows that God sees his determination not to give up his sin, so he cannot pray to the all-seeing God. Then follows alienation, and suspicion of the Most High. He thinks that God is opposed to him, and then all his notions of the Divine Nature become dim, distorted, and confused; it is no longer the true God that he sees.

Do you recognize this little portrait? Is it at all true to your experience? Then you have a genuine commentary on the text; then you know how easily the 'sight of the soul is dimmed. Oh, let us be afraid of clouds coming between us and the Sun. The Sun will shine on, but we will not see Him.

BLESSED ARE THE PEACEMAKERS.

"Blessed are the peacemakers : for they shall be called the children of God."—Matthew v. 9.

THAT is, the peacemakers shall be owned and recognized as like God, bearing their Father's image. He is the great Peacemaker coming Himself to the world in the person of Christ to make peace.

In inquiring into the elements that constitute the peacemakers we find that this is the first: a love for peace. There are some men that notably have a hatred of jarring and contention. They are tranquil, and wish tranquillity and concord all round them and everywhere. There are those who carry an atmosphere of peace with them. Their look is benignant and pacific, and men often feel it difficult to come to heat and high words in their presence. These men may not be in any active or aggressive way peacemakers, but the subtle influence proceeding from them instils peace into men around them, and is really the most aggressive agent in the spreading of peace. Often if you *talk* to men about peace your words may seem a rebuke and kindle a greater fire. Natures that are given to war are for the most part peculiarly inflammable, and the slightest intimation of any desire to correct them or suggest something different from their actual procedure, is apt to be resented. But he must be an altogether abnormally quarrelsome man who is offended by a peaceful demeanour. It is a force that steals into him and captures him before he is aware. It utters no rebuke or advice, it seems altogether unconscious, and yet in a mysterious way it checks outbursts of passion, it rebukes by its very composure, it makes men think of an invisible presence though it never mentions it. There are many meek and lowly souls, therefore, who are potent peacemakers, and yet would never have what would seem to themselves the presumption to undertake the function of composing quarrels. It is perhaps only in a dim way that anybody recognizes their power, but nevertheless it is one of the greatest and most healing forces in the world. Men of this sort will be utterly surprised to find on the supreme day of the disclosure of secrets that they are credited with great works of peacemaking, that they are recognized as peculiarly like God. "What," they will say, "what did we ever do to reconcile men? Alas, we were too quiet and inert." It will then appear that the mightiest way of *doing* is *to be, to be utterly and truly what you appear.* No force or substance can be without its effect in the spiritual, any more than in the natural, world. By the law of gravitation, every material body has power of attraction in proportion to its weight and contents; so it is in the moral world. There is a force of which he cannot be deprived proceeding from every true soul in proportion to his real moral weight and intensity. And whatever special element of goodness a man may have, *that* makes him according to its measure a peacemaker. All integrity, faithfulness, purity, honour and rectitude tend to the establishment of peace. Whatever of fairness and thoroughness and downright sincerity a man may have constitutes him a peacemaker. All a man's self-denial and self-control, all his power to repress impulse and passion, and live on the higher level of reason, truth, and love, constitute him a peacemaker.

But, especially, in so far as any man's goodness rises above the sphere of conscience and moves in the sphere of love, benevolence, unselfish and cordial goodwill, is he a potential peacemaker? Somehow there is in the goodness of men who are predominantly conscientious an element that does not make for peace. It often seems rather to infringe on men's self-respect, and makes them contentious. A highly conscientious person comes into a company, and it is felt at once that an element of discord has got in. This goodness is self-conscious and hard and seems a kind of challenge to all and sundry; and before they are aware people find themselves taking up the challenge and becoming combative. Another man who is of a far higher type, but does not seem to know it, does not seem to *think* of goodness at all, but to be drawn to his fellowmen by an inward power—he is added to the company, and soon composes the incipient strifes without a word. The man of conscience frets, the man of heart and soul soothes and fuses into harmony.

But we must be on our guard against confounding this kind of peacemaking with softness, and dislike to trouble. One may be of what is called a peaceable spirit merely because he has no decided convictions, nor is very much in earnest about anything. An indolent torpid existence is of course peaceable. A shrinking from trouble, a dread of the commotion which debate raises, may lead to utter treachery to truth and righteousness. How often one sees people congratulating themselves on being men of peace, and blaming those whom they are pleased to call "fire-brands," when all the notion they have of peace is repose, neutrality, indifference to the cause of God and man. Very instructive in this view is the order in which the Beatitude comes. What immediately precedes it? Purity of heart, and the seeing of God. The true peacemaker is the man who is intent first on purity of heart and the seeing of God in all life and work. You find the same connection exhibited in the description of the wisdom that is from above as first pure, then peaceable. And in the exhortation, " Follow peace with all men and holiness, without which no man shall see the Lord." Peace can only be reached through truth and righteousness, and he who is careless of truth and righteousness is destroying peace, however desirous of tranquillity he may be. The man who in his deepest heart desires peace may often seem a disturber. He is obliged to be so in order to be the follower of that great Peacemaker who, when about to offer Himself for our peace, said, " I am not come to send peace on earth, but a sword. I am come to send fire on earth, and what will I if it be already kindled." The true peacemaker, then, is he who values truth and righteousness more than quiet, and yet who in his heart of hearts hates debate and strife, who inwardly sighs for peace while he girds on his armour. Strife is with him a hard necessity ; peace is the element in which his own soul moves amid the loudest alarms of war : he earnestly wishes peace to all men, and longs and prays for its dominion everywhere.

This leads me to give prominence to the thought that the *true peacemaker is one who is intent on making peace among the discordant elements in his own soul.* What a wild, seething, whirling, chaotic world there is within ! What an uproar the passions make ! How unruly imagination is ! What a turmoil is created by contention between reason and inclination, between the will and the conscience, between regret, despondency, fear and hope! It is all in vain for a man to try to be a true peacemaker *without*, unless he has done something effective to make peace *within*. How shall he bid the storm 'to cease? When Jesus was about to still the raging waves, how futile would any other voice have been. As futile seems any voice of ours to command peace. Let the voice of Christ be heard. Let His blood speak peace. Let thoughts of the infinite and eternal be realized. Take up the truth once for all and hold to it, that it is God's will that is to be done, that you are not to listen to any voice of passion or interest, but simply to let the will of God rule your life. Then you have peace. The voice of pardoning love throws peace over all your troubled past, and the voice of God's supreme will hushes the contentions of the present; and so the voice of hope spreads peace over all your future. Listen better and better to that voice. "Take My yoke upon you, and learn of Me; for I am meek and lowly in heart: and ye shall find rest unto your souls." The more you inherit Christ's bequest of peace in your own soul, the more you will possess the true spirit of the peacemaker; for His is a peace by truth and love, a peace by repentance and forgiveness, a peace that is His own free gift, and yet which can only be reached and maintained through labour and watching. It is by looking to Christ that we are saved, on the one hand from the error of taking indolence and timidity in the place of peacemaking, and on the other hand, from putting real love of contention and debate in the room of a reluctant contending for results which are most dear to the soul and heart.

Again, he who would be a true peacemaker *must keep in mind what are the main causes and occasions of the destruction of peace.* Unless one keeps these fully before his eyes, his best intentions will end in failure, or worse. One of the chief of these causes is the magnifying of small things in daily life and contending for them with heat. Another is the habit of positive dogmatic assertion, which many excellent conscientious people have. Their opinions on any subject are uttered in a cavalier, defiant tone, and these men are almost always impatient of contradiction. Many again seem to think that if there is anything in a man's bearing or manner not to their taste, that is a sufficient reason for being repulsive or offensive or openly cold toward him. They pass judgment on almost all men they meet, and their extempore decisions are not concealed. Now, it is impossible, of course, that men we meet should all make upon us the same impression. There is a secret judgment which we all pass upon each other every hour of the day, without trying it or being distinctly aware of it. The evil comes when this unavoidable judgment grows intentional, when a man deliberately sets himself to judge others, and even prides himself on it, and most of all when he gives *expression* of any sort to his unfavourable judgments. This is perhaps the most fruitful source of ill-feeling between man and man. Closely allied to it is the difficulty that some have of being what I might call neutral. They seem to be under an impression that they ought to be either decidedly for, or decidedly against, every person with whom they are brought into contact. And so they are at secret war with a great many people, with whom they may have scarcely spoken. If any person fails to please them he displeases them. They are in effect angry with men, because they do not conform to the hidden standard which they carry about with them. Oh, if they and others would only occupy their critical faculty upon themselves! If they *will* dissect and weigh, let it be themselves. How profitable that would be! But one of its first results would assuredly be a gentler judgment of their fellowmen, a dread of judging them at all. A knowledge of oneself, deep sorrow for one's own faults and sins, a constant endeavour to be free from them, and a true, benevolent, sympathetic feeling for men, form the sovereign remedy against this censorious spirit so utterly destructive of peace.

If a man has a true peacemaking spirit, he will find plenty of room for its exercise in this world. There is nothing, however, that requires greater tact, judgment, and genuine transparent good feeling, than the bringing of men to peace who are at variance. It is not every man who is fit for this office. Many men with good intentions only make matters worse. But though the position of a direct mediator between men is a most difficult one, yet the peacemaking spirit, the friendly, benevolent, sympathetic spirit, is within every one's reach, is incumbent on every one, and is really the most potent allayer of quarrels. It is not so much a rebuke to them as a solvent of them. It melts them like sunshine. It is like the south wind, in which ice cannot exist.

What a blessedness the peacemakers have, then! There can be no fuller blessedness than that which is theirs who, by the lovingness of their spirit, lead men to believe in the love of God, who by the power of their gentleness point to a God who does not wait to be urged to reconciliation, but sends abroad the news of His pardoning mercy in Christ. In such a world as this, so full of separations and of pain, where hearts are sundered by such little things, where there are so many who have suffered irreparable wrongs from trusted hands, and having ceased to believe in men, are losing their hold of God ;—how blessed in such a world are they who by their ministry of peace are able to make reconciliation among men and restore their faith in God.

How fittingly, then, do these seven Beatitudes culminate in the blessedness of the peacemakers. All the other graces are included in this grace of theirs, and in their blessedness all other benedictions are involved. Behind that penetrating, gentle power of

theirs, which rules the hearts of men, lie the great
depths of spiritual wealth and blessedness. The
poverty of spirit and the mourning for sin ; and the
conquering meekness which springs from these ; the
constant endeavour and longing for righteousness, the
mercy and the purity of heart, which are blessed of
God—all these are involved in the supreme grace and
benediction of the peacemakers, " For they shall be
called the children of God,"—fellow-workers with
Christ."

THOUGHTS AND ILLUSTRATIONS.

(SELECTED.)

ABOUT RELIGION.

ONLY in religion does the spirit of man realize what freedom is; here only does he range the Infinite, and feel at home in it; here alone does he abide in the Eternal.

Religion, from its nature, cannot be exclusively, or perhaps mainly, the result of an argument. After all argument there must be room for faith, which is the mind making a step forward beyond the argument or demonstration in obedience to her own wants and aspirations.

Religion is the poetry of life. Yes, and it is also the plainest prose. Religion is glorious prospect, lofty vision, sublime aspiration, transcendent experience, mysterious ineffable communion; yes, and it is also painful struggling. It is toiling and rowing. It is reaping with bent back and diligent hand. It is gleaning wearily at times a few ears of corn. It is climbing slowly in the dark. It is weeping and groaning. It is retracing the steps. It is to be disheartened and crushed. It is to feel at times as if you were forsaken. It is to march on in the rain and wind over muddy and sometimes trackless roads. It is to be lost on a stormy sea, in the dark, with neither sun nor stars appearing. It may be what is often worst of all, to tread along a flat monotonous road, where there is no adventure and no sign of progress. It is the faithful performance of small duties whether you have feeling or no feeling. It is the rigid adherence to duty and to God, though no joy seems to come out of it. When any one in the glow of romance says, " I will follow Thee whithersoever Thou goest," let him not forget that the road may lead through all these things. He will find out that all the dull drudgery of life is necessary to the romance, and will very soon discover that there is no romance or glow in religion at all, unless one can find it in the monotony and drudgery and watching of life.

ABOUT GOD.

We should fix it in our minds that nothing short of love is worthy of God, and that nothing can please Him which is not done from love. We should remember that God is the Infinite Perfection, the Eternal and Perfect Beauty. We should try to grasp the idea of God as the Almighty, Self-Existent, All-seeing Sovereign. One ; and then think that love is the very centre and crown of this Infinite. We should reflect that all the vast, incomprehensible extent of His nature is penetrated by love and by purity. We should think that all the beauty of earth, all the splendour of the sky, all the glory and tender grace of flowers, all the magnificence of sunsets, and all the mysterious grandeur of the midnight heavens, all the loveliness that ever glowed in human faces—all are but faint indications of His beauty.

Do you think that all who admit the love of God really feel persuaded and sure of it? Quite the contrary. It is a rare thing to believe that God is love.

To love God is to have no more bondage. To love God is to be free. To love God is to be in the inmost secret of things. It is to have the noblest power swaying our hearts and lives, and to breathe the very atmosphere of heaven. It is to have a searching influence going through us that will quietly but certainly expel sin.

Oh, see how in Christ God makes His love and compassion visible, makes them human, turns them into flesh and blood; looks at us with human eyes, speaks to us with human voice, comes and catches us with a human hand, and says, " Love Me, oh, My child, love Me. I love you with a love stronger than death, deeper than the sea, and as long as eternity. I am come to seek and save the lost. Oh, My wandering lost child, come back; come to Me and love Me."

HALLOWED BE THY NAME.

The sacredness of God is the best inheritance of all His creatures. If that goes, there is no sacredness, no grandeur, no worth anywhere.

SORROW OF GOD.

There cannot be a greater error or a more grossly unscriptural statement than that which represents the Infinite Father as a stranger to sorrow. Men have said that sorrow would be a proof of imperfection, and that therefore God can have no experience of sorrow. But perfection is not insensibility; it is infinite sensibility. God is infinite in feeling as He is in all else— in love, in indignation, in sorrow and joy.

JOY FROM GOD.

You have seen a sunshine that played along the ground and made the icicles flash and even glow with different colours. It gilded the snowy peaks of the mountains, it flung radiance over the frozen rivers; but when it had played for hours, it produced no change. It did not set the heart of nature a-beating; it did not waken a single song, or liberate one flower, or one blade of grass. That is a picture of many joys, and comforts, and refreshments. But not of the comfort and refreshing from God's truth and spirit, from God's fellowship and promise. *That* always leaves something permanent; it adds to the strength, the bulk, the stature of the inward man. It is like the summer's sun beating on the bark of the tree. Lay your hand on the bark; it is warm, it is glowing. That radiance is not mere gilding. It is going into the very heart of the tree. It is entering all the leaves; it is expanding the girth and shooting out branches, and even the roots in the dark earth are thrilling with it through their minutest fibres.

VICTORY IN GOD.

When we welcome God into our hearts to dwell there, then we overcome. We must not think that a God outside of us, with all His might and love, will bring about our triumph. Yonder in the heavens is the resplendent sun, the source of heat and vitality; and there down in the dark earth is a seed which just wants the sun's streaming into it to make it alive. But if the seed is too deep in the earth, the sun's rays will not reach it. It must be brought nearer the sun.

HOME WITH GOD.

It is the presence of God that makes home. He who feels at home with God is not a stranger anywhere.

REST IN STORM.

Have you seen the huge billows come breaking up against the rocky wall of the harbour? Have you watched the hungry, seething foam, the wild remorseless dash, the furious swelling of exulting waves, and seen how harmlessly it broke and fell from the immovable rock, and how calm the water was in the harbour within? No tumult there; it is all peace and rest there. So it is with a soul that is in Christ. The whole breadth of His eternal nature is between it and danger. As soon as you are beneath the wings of everlasting love, you are as safe as if you had been there a thousand years.

When keen winds blow and wither the blossoms and leaves, is there for us a great sheltered valley where summer reigns? Have we even quiet little nooks of evergreens and flowers, while frost and snow are lying thick over the most of our life? Or are we content in our sorrow and trouble to struggle heavily and drearily on, scarcely believing that anything better is possible? Do we think that dejection is a thing unavoidable, and reconcile ourselves to it? Then, truly, we are the worse of our trials. The chill is not bracing us, but creeping in to seize upon the heart. We are adopting the tone of the world. We are taking up the sad, dull, leaden tone of those who do not believe in a Father. We are losing our belief in the summer of love. We are seeing only the valleys covered with mist, and not looking up to the slopes and peaks that bask in the eternal sunshine.

FATHER.

The word *Father* puts an end to the oppression of awe, by putting love in the centre. It is but the halo around love—its guard and security.

The highest saint can say nothing more than *Father*. The soul that has been longest in heaven, and made the best use of his opportunities, can yet get at no word which shall express so much as " Father." No word which claims such relationship, no word which involves such confidence and obedience.

WORSHIP.

Worship is the festive season of the devout soul, and in this season the hallowing of God's name reaches away over territory in the heart and life that lay uureclaimed before. Often this reaching over, this claiming, this laying the hand upon new territory, may seem to end with the worship. It is but like the sound of Sabbath bells heard far in the stillness of the Sabbath morning. The chimes of God, in the elevation and joy of worship, are heard away up in regions where they never reach at any other time, and away down in cellars and dens that never echo to divine sounds at any other period ; but gradually those Sabbath sounds come to linger in these outlying regions, the echoes reverberate along the corridors and in the recesses, till the next period of worship awakens them, and so by repetition the sacred elevating music becomes permanent; it is always there. The life has been transformed into a true temple by the reverberation of worship steadily and persistently through its domains.

Spring worship is that of faith and hope. Summer, that of confidence and wondering joy. Harvest worship is especially the joy of gratitude, that wonders over the past and rests in the fulness of the present.

PRAYER.

Prayer is not a thing which is the sooner exhausted the more intense it is. The more earnest any prayer is, the more a man is inclined and constrained to pray. One earnest prayer leads to many more. When you pray for one thing, this leads you to feel your want for others.

HEART AND GOD.

Must it not be that these too shall yet find each other—the sorrow-laden heart and the compassionate God; must it not be that the heathen shall turn away from all their broken cisterns to the boundless flood of joy and comfort in the loving and eternal God? Shall not the deep and mighty sorrows of men at length do for them what nothing else could do—lead them to a Father and a home? Shall not the tenderness of God triumph over darkness and bondage?

INFINITE.

The Infinite is the ocean for souls to sail on; there

they are free and balanced. Laid up on the shore of
the finite, they go to wreck.

LAW.

The higher any creature is, the more he needs, for
the sake of all other beings, to be girt with law.
The sun and planets must obey strict law, else the
result were disaster and ruin. And the sin of a
spiritual being spreads and destroys.

Law is the expression of love.

ATONEMENT.

The atonement of Christ did not originate mercy;
mercy originated the atonement. "God so loved the
world that He gave His Son." Mercy is not bought
by Christ's death; but Christ died that mercy might
be exercised in accordance with justice.

REDEMPTION.

Redemption, with all its wonders of love, compassion and suffering, is justified by the spiritual nature
of man.

Redemption is not the extravagance of love, though
it is love going to the extreme of reason and right. It
is love doing all that love can do, without ceasing to be
love, and becoming frenzy.

WORDS OF CHRIST.

One of the most touching things in human life is
when the letters of long vanished years are taken out

of their repository, where they are carefully hidden with the choicest relics of the past,—with locks of hair, and rings, and withered leaves. Ah me! how those old letters make the past live, how solidly they bridge the gulf of time! How fondly and earnestly are those words read, and how surely they witness to affections that can never die, and ties that never can be broken! Even so in our earnest, solemn hours do we go back to the very words of Jesus—the words of our Father. We say, as we lay our finger on the expressions that suit our case, that meet our wants, or dispel our fears: "These are His words; there they are; they cannot change or deceive; they are the words of God, that cannot lie. O blessed be His name, that He has put His word into visible shape before me. .I need this; it gives me rest; it makes me rich. ' Thy word I have taken as my heritage for ever, for it is the rejoicing of my heart.' "

THE MARVELLOUSNESS OF THE SOUL.

You have seen the clouds flitting across the sky— now thick, now fleecy, now dark, now coloured with all brilliant hues. You have seen them spreading across the face of the sun, drifting over the moon and stars. Is not this spectacle of day and night like the vast soul of man? There is something unsearchable, mysterious in the soul. Though it seems shut up in a small house, it feels itself wider and deeper than the sea, as broad as the sky, and broader. Who can fathom the marvel of its union with a body formed of the earth, or tell what God had in view in thus uniting matter and spirit? What a marvel that the body should have power to burden the ethereal soul, and that the sorrows of the soul should wear away the body. Who can think that this complicated, vast, deep nature, so multifarious and unsearchable, belongs to himself, *is* himself, without a feeling of awe? If a man feels awe in looking at the sky, with its wonders and mystery, much more may he feel it in looking at the firmament of his own being, with its stars, its clouds, its glory, and its gloom. For this thought comes to give weight and intensity to the whole,—All this is myself, and must be so for ever.

MYSTERY.

There are mysteries all around and within man. The sky is mysterious in its height and vastness; earth and sea in their depth, and in the working of their forces. Realize the thought you think, and you find it stretching away into infinity. Trace the word you utter, analyze and weigh it, and you are landed in the unsearchable.

THE COMMON FAITH.

It is the glory of faith that it can touch everything, that it goes into all the hidden nooks of life, and works wherever man works. Faith in God the Father, and Jesus Christ the Saviour, will teach a man to hold the chisel and to ply the pen; will teach to plough and sow and reap; will help the schoolboy to learn his lesson, and the statesman to guide his country. Faith sustains him who crosses the sea, and cheers the lone mother in her deserted home. Faith brightens the dying eye with victory, and cheers the heart of the widow and the orphan. It is the *common* faith—the one thing that suits all men everywhere, and works everywhere the same end.

ETERNITY.

When a man will not look at eternity, all other magnitudes grow little; all wideness and vastness disappear from his thoughts.

All wideness of heart is narrow, as long as it is confined to things. The universe is not large enough; time is not long enough. There is need of God and eternity.

INTENSITY.

It is a melancholy fact that intensity seems often to be purchased at the expense of breadth and richness. In order that a man may be a good instrument for any work, it would often seem as if he needed to be nothing else—as if he must cease being a man in order to be a good working machine.

Let me see a man who knows thoroughly some one thing, who has gained his knowledge by labour and pains, by long struggle and patience, it may be even by poverty and privation. That is a man to be venerated. He is a greater help and example to his race, and a greater honour to God, than millions of superficial repeaters of platitudes about universal knowledge.

MUSIC AND SONGS.

Would you rise above the clouds? Keep in the region of song. God has given us song, that we may rise into a pure and serene atmosphere at once. Oppressed and laden souls have many a time at a bound, by song, soared away beyond the stars. In song we anticipate heaven. Heaven is the land of rest, and in song we rest. Heaven is the place of triumph, and in song we triumph.

Each of us is a violin, which only needs to be played upon by a divine hand.

Mozart, Beethoven, and Handel seemed but to write down what they heard played by an invisible hand; thus, their labour seemed to be, not to invent, but simply to reproduce fully what they had heard.

Man by song throws an atmosphere of dignity and intensity around his life; he idealizes the common; he sets forth the grandeur and mystery of existence; he links laughter and tears, all the comedy and tragedy and routine of life, to something vague, unspeakable,

incomprehensible. For, is not music something unfathomable ? Who can analyze or tell where its power
lies ? To the simplest minds it is a testimony, a felt
proof of something inscrutable, impalpable, ethereal,
surrounding human life—something that no man can
grasp, or weigh, or measure, and yet possessed of untold power.

How many touching human songs, powerful channels
of feeling, are like the rivers of Damascus. These flow
from Lebanon, strong and clear, and make the plain of
Damascus a marvel of fertility ; but they flow eastward
into the desert, and are lost in sand and morass. Such
are many plaintive songs that speak to the heart; they
are lost in the sand of time, they do not flow into the
infinite. But all the Bible songs, be they of sorrow
or joy, of hope or fear, however diversified their
channels, flow toward God.

Music puts religious truth in its true atmosphere.
There is something infinite in the suggestion of music.
It bursts all the barriers of space and time, and rouses
great longings in the soul. It never meets with anything in human life that comes up to its own dignity.
There seems, as a rule, in fine music to be something
greater and deeper than the words it is allied to. But
music allied to the vast thoughts of religion finds it
has met its equal and superior. The highest music of
the greatest masters labours in vain to give adequate
utterance to the thought of redeeming love, the beauty

of goodness, the majesty and tenderness of God, and the thought of a glorious eternity.

The same melodies of joy and sorrow are played over and over again in our existence; but they are played on different instruments, they are sung in different keys. Sometimes they are played with the tones of a trumpet, and sometimes with those of the harp or the flute. Sometimes the music is but the sighing of the wind through the long grass, and sometimes it is the rush of the blast through the forest, or the roar and crash of the billows on the shore.

" CUP OF ASTONISHMENT."

Have those who have had so much of surprise in their life, to whom the " cup of astonishment " has been given, more than once or twice, have they been more to be pitied than those whose life was more calculable? On a calm survey of things, is it not worth the trouble to have had life so thoroughly roused up and set on a new track? It is like having several lives, compared with the tameness of many an existence. It is to be made rich in varied experience in spite of yourself. It is to know something of the breadth of human possibilities—to look at the world several times with new eyes —and every time to have new experience of the truth of God's promise; every time to have found out afresh that no word of His, however wonderful, fails. What a shaking is implied in these unexpected things; and surely incrustations and fetters must fall from the spirit with every such shaking.

GRIEF.

Great sorrow may be manifested by many who seem great in nothing else. Their greatness is shown, not by their talents, or their shining virtues, but by the intensity of their grief.

SORROW.

Many a one has had to trace the beginning of better things to some sorrow that made a pause in the flow of his gaiety. Sorrow threw him in upon himself. Amidst mirth and genial company, at home with everybody by geniality and overflowing humour, he was never at home with himself. The hearth of his inner life was cold and forsaken. He always knew it, but would not think about it. But now, in sadness, he is at home with himself, he realizes what he is, he looks out upon all things with seriousness; and that is the beginning of better things.

BURDEN OF CHRISTIAN LIFE.

When you take God as your salvation your work is not ended. It is only begun. You only begin to see what a great work you have to do. You look round the whole of life: you look within, you look up, and you are overwhelmed with the magnitude of your task.

You see vast heights to climb and great depths to fathom. You discern a wide sea of endeavour, and you recognize the immense work and toil there may be about some little thing. The problem of life stands out more awful than ever. The more you see of the love of God, the more you are afraid of its terrible earnestness. The more you drink into the life of Christ, the more you feel its unapproachable grandeur and beauty.

DEFEAT.

Viewed in the light of eternal truth, a man may never achieve such a victory as when he is utterly defeated in his plans and work. The patient, loving, trustful, courageous spirit in which he accepts defeat is the highest victory.

The languor that comes of despondency and baffled effort is one of the greatest perils of life. It leaves a man the prey of terrible evils. The only chance that such an one has is to *strike for that which is higher.* There is strength and joy in high aims. They put courage into a timid soul. A wide horizon draws out and ennobles a man.

FAILURE.

The heroes and benefactors of the world are seldom the invincibles who have never been defeated, but rather those whom failure, again and again, has wakened up; who have been driven to their wit's end and made inventive by necessity.

Let us see that our failures and reverses are not losses. They need not be. Our mistaken energy, our fruitless endeavours are not waste, unless we *will* it to be so, and go down to a lower level. The impetus may all be gathered up, increased by the direction being changed. The terrible energy and determination that men often gain from defeat, the rousing up of every particle of force that is in them, the triumph that issues from grim desperation—let these things never be forgotten in our battle of life.

If your service of others has failed, is it not because you served them in too poor and narrow a way—forgetting their highest good? Perhaps your service was too formal and mechanical. Perhaps it was of a nature rather to increase selfishness in others than to cure it. Do not cease to serve others, but try to serve more wisely. Try to serve more and not fewer, and to serve in a higher and more permanent way. Do not shrink back into self; that would be perdition. Be more resolved to serve than ever, and you cannot fail.

WEARINESS.

It is for want of Christ, for want of a sense of God's love, for want of rest in God and delight in Him, that men grow weary. They are like mariners who try to accomplish their voyage by plying the oar, while they allow their sails to remain furled in the midst of the winds of heaven. Poor weary toilers—what a dismal life they are leading with their oars. It is honest work —it is patient persevering—every foot of progress over the waves is purchased with straining and heaving. But why do they not look up ? Do they not hear the breeze singing through the rigging ? Let them change the direction of their labour. A voyage with oars would weary any man. Men were not meant to cross the ocean with oars. Sails that catch the winds, that gather to themselves the might of the breeze—these make a voyage something else than a toil. And it is thus, and not otherwise, that the voyage to heaven must be accomplished. Men will grow weary if they do not spread their sails for the winds of God.

MONOTONY.

The efforts of the spirit of man to escape from the wearisomeness of monotony are not anything to laugh at, however mistaken or exaggerated they may be. There is a great truth lying at the bottom of them, which it were well for all to keep in mind. These protests of the heart and soul against monotony—these cravings for stir and commotion, are far nearer the truth, even when they are in their grotesquest shape, than the flat, stale decorum of self-satisfied religionists, who take for granted that religion is only a respectable garment—a staid and orderly conduct of life, quite free from sighing and crying.

DISAPPOINTMENT.

It is good to be crossed and thrown down and disappointed. It is good to be made small and little in one's own estimation. It is good to be emptied out, and to have your fine schemes turned into nothing. Then when you have no schemes, when your beautiful dream is a wreck, when you are brought just to wish to please God, you have reached a point at which a real beginning can be made.

DESERTS.

How sad to think that we ourselves may mar and frustrate a divine promise, and make it necessary for the loving God to put us on a far lower level than He designed us for; to confine us to deserts and mountains, when the desire of the heart is to bring us into full and glad possession.

Men sometimes get perplexed and puzzled, and need to go away back to the desert, to learn what solitary watching beside the mountain and stern discipline of themselves can do. They ought to be in the promised land of religion, but with their confusion and half belief nothing better than the desert is possible.

JOY IN SORROW.

There is a wintry lustre of the sunshine that plays about the snow and ice, and makes it sparkle and flash with various colours, and only softens the surface to prepare it for a deeper hardness, when night returns. But there is a sunshine, or even only a warm wind in the dark, which melts the whole mass. So there comes upon the soul in sorrow—often suddenly and mysteriously—a warmth and a glow that overwhelm the sorrow.

Everywhere there is a beauty not required by utility. The tints of the shell were not needed by its inmate. Fruits could have been produced, without all the splendour of flowers. A world could have existed, without the glory of the rainbow, or the heavenly grandeur of sunset and sunrise. And is it a wonder that God should be willing to give His sorrowing children a very exuberance of joy?

Sometimes those who have had the fiercest pain, or most crushing sorrow, are visited by flood on flood of joy—a deep, fervid joy such as they can scarcely contain. This passes away, but its effects do not. The heat of a summer day passes, but it writes its history on plant and tree, on grass and shrub. It has left strength and beauty as its witness. So do these high times of joy, when they pass away, leave the heart and soul strong and tender and brave.

FAITH AND PATIENCE.

Faith is the upward look, the gaze that sees beyond the clouds; it is the staff on which the pilgrim leans. Patience is the back that bears the burden of life. Faith is the expanding leaf and blossom of the tree that absorbs the sunshine. Patience the branches that

bear the load of fruit.   Faith is the side that is turned
to God.   Patience the side that is turned to the toil
and trouble of earth.   Faith has regard to that which
is glorious and eternal.   Patience has regard to that
which is hard and bitter, but brief.

FRUITFULNESS.

In the early summer, when the blossom is on the
tree, how bright and gay it looks.   How cheerily the
branches nod and wave in the passing breeze.   But if
those blossoms pass into fruit, what a great change
takes place.   As the fruit enlarges, the branches bend
lower and lower, sometimes they press the ground and
are like to break.   You have seen them often supported with stakes to keep them from giving way
under their load.   That is a picture of the dissatisfaction of a fruitful soul—bent to the earth when most
productive.

PILGRIM SPIRIT.

It is the pilgrim spirit that sees the pillar of fire.

PROMISES.

The promises are like the flowers that cover the earth
in early summer.   There are delicate little primroses, like
the snowdrop on the edge of winter.   There are times
when promises, like snowdrops, suit men best.   There
are great stretches of fresh, bright promises, like the belt
of the blue gentian flowers far up the Alps.   There are

promises almost hidden by some precept or doctrine or fact, like flowers hidden by their own leaves or by grass. And there are promises that flash and glow like the blossom of the apple tree. The promises are sublime as the stars, though near as the flowers. The promises cover the whole of life and reach on through eternity.

Just as a man can go nowhere on earth, but the sky will be overhead, by day filled with sunlight, and by night thronged with stars, so he can be in no position in which the firmament of divine promise does not stretch over him.

HOPE.

There is a kind of hope which is generally asleep, but wakens up now and again, and says to itself, " I think I am going to heaven "; and then goes off to sleep again, like a man travelling during the night by train.

DESIRE AND HOPE.

Desire and hope do not by any means always keep pace. There may be vehement desires for results, where the hopes are but feeble. And some of the greatest sorrows of men rise from the desire of blessed results, with but little of hope to illumine. Vehemently to desire the right and good, and yet to have a sinking of heart as to its achievement, is a noble, bnt it may be a crushing sorrow.

ENERGY AND HOPE.

When God is dimly seen by us, when divine realities grow pale and thin, when we are cold and hard, and seem to know of no heavenly sunshine or dew falling on our own souls, then the hope of the world's conversion recedes into the far background. But when we know the power of God to enkindle love in our own souls, when principles of right and truth strike deep in us in answer to prayer, when the ice of self is broken up, when in our sorrow a great consolation rushes on our spirits, when a vast gladness rises and surges through us in spite of trial, disaster and death, when the thought of God fills us with a peace that passeth understanding, when evil thoughts are driven out of us, when our spirits rise on wings of confidence and desire toward God, when fellowship with God is so close and deep as to keep off all low and corrupt influences,—then we possess an unshaken confidence that all the world shall yet turn to God. We laugh at impossibilities. We know that God reigns and works. We find nothing else credible than the triumphs of truth and love, and in the clear atmosphere of our spirits the far-off can almost be touched.

NATURAL GOODNESS.

Some people will allow no good in anything that is done just from a generous impulse, from native compassion and generosity. That is a mere weed, they think.   And the evil is, that while they depreciate what is done from mere generous impulse, they may forget to do the like from the higher motive which they applaud.   It is a mere weed, you say.   Ay, but there are weeds that are healing medicines; there are weeds that breathe a sweet perfume, while cherished' garden herbs may fail, rotting at the root.

DISOBEDIENCE.

In nature there is no possibility of disobedience. The planets never disobey, nor the suns.   Nor does the pebble, the wave, or the leaf.   The mere fact of disobedience proves that you are more than a part of nature.

POSSIBILITY.

A man can do all that he can get God to do for him; and God has promised to give all strength to him who strives for a new heart.

PRESENT AND FUTURE.

We cannot breathe in the present without the future.   We need the music of coming years, as well as the melody of the past, to stir us,—only over all and through all we must hear the grand, sweet notes of eternity breaking.

THINGS HUMAN AND DIVINE.

Of all things in the world, the heart of man is the best key to the heart of God.   And it is of vast importance for us to learn to see in all human life, in its plain trivialities and common details, figures and reminders of the eternal realities.

SECRET WORK.

Has not God Himself taught us the glory of secret work in the way He finishes *His* secret work,—His crystals away in crevices, His painting of shells, His exquisite touch on untold millions of little creatures? And so He is saying to us, " Work on in the realm of the hidden, where no eye but mine can pierce. Cultivate beauty there."

DAYS AND YEARS.

If we do not measure our time by days, and live from day to day, we shall not be able to number our years to any purpose.

USEFULNESS—CONSCIOUS AND UNCONSCIOUS.

No man can work well for himself without benefiting others. The most recondite thinking even of the lonely student turns out sooner or later to be for the good of the whole world. But surely it is to be expected of a man that he intend and purpose to be of use, that he should not be content to be useful in a blind, unconscious, mechanical way, as the wind, and trees, and the mill-wheel. He ought to elevate his work, and put life and meaning into it, by the thought and aspiration to be useful.

ONE AND ALL.

Any wrong done to one recoils upon all. When men were slaughtered to make a Roman holiday, benevolence was slaughtered in all hearts.

PURPOSE.

Often a man thinks a purpose to be in his heart, when it is only in his imagination. He imagines himself doing great things ; he sees himself a hero striving a noble strife ; he fights battles, he suffers, he bears, he achieves, and his soul glows with the feeling of it all. It is all fine as a picture ; and if it could be carried out, as a picture, he would be glad to see it done ; but there is no purpose in his heart that would really go through all this.

LITTLE THINGS.

Only think of it. What may be the most precious thing to God that you ever did in all your life ? Perhaps some little matter that you soon forgot, some mere trifle, as men would call it ; and yet, in the motive and spirit of that, you came nearer to the mind of Christ than you ever did, even in affairs that cost you labour and pains.

FOLLY.

No folly is so dangerous as that which looks uncommonly wise and austere and melancholy.

THINGS THAT MAKE ASHAMED.

All great and high things, all beautiful and rich things, all that have the power of stirring the soul to its depths, have also the power of making ashamed.

DEVELOPMENT.

Time is needed to grow into true effectiveness. You may often see in the hedgerows, while the leaves are falling, not a few flowers on the bramble bushes, possibly in some sheltered nook you may see them even in November. How beautiful they are, with their delicate fresh white, among brown and falling leaves. But what purpose can they serve now ? They attest the vitality of the plant, and lend a pathetic loveliness, but they can never come to fruit.

DRIFTING.

The drifting boat goes downwards, and so it is with man. He that has no aim drifts, and he that drifts goes downwards.

THE WEAVING OF LIFE.

Time takes up and weaves into its web all things good and bad—dreams and reveries and idleness. Half-formed thoughts, shadowy desires, fully shaped resolutions and endeavours, broken words and full sentences, sighs, groans, laughter and tears, random deeds and regular work, silence and noise, music and discord—all pass into threads, and are woven in.

THOUGHTS OF DEATH.

Men look at the sun through smoked glass; so the dark thought of death helps us to realize the Infinite One.

Thoughts of death may be taken as a bitter draught, after which a man goes with new zest to the sweets of the world.

SELF.

You can only cultivate self by getting out of self and touching the Infinite.

DOWN AND UP.

God lifts up the man who goes down. Let our care be to sink. God's care will be that we shall mount on high.

CAREFUL OVERMUCH.

There are those who are so tormented by scruples that they can venture nothing great or magnanimous. Propose the noblest undertaking, the most devoted self-denying of enterprises,—they cannot move till they have carefully anatomized it. They puzzle and probe till they take the heart out of it. So anxious are they to be perfectly, certainly, evidently right, that they drift into great wrong.

COMPROMISE.

Oh, it is a miserable, tantalizing, superficial, distracting thing—this trying to go through life avoiding extremes, wishing merely to be safe and successful and respectable, not caring for right, having no enthusiasm for truth, not thinking anything worth suffering for, or being in earnest about, anxious only not to have so much wickedness as will bring loss or damage of any kind.

SIMPLICITY.

A simple life is the freest and best—a life in which men are neither slaves of appetite, nor living in the bondage of hard discipline.

INTIMACY.

Intimacy is a matter of affinities which can scarcely be explained; it may depend on a thousand things that make up a certain subtle atmosphere. This atmosphere may be dissipated without any distinct fault on either side; men grow away from each other, merely in the process of being true to their own individuality, to their own sphere and surroundings. In such cases there may be no room for either granting or receiving forgiveness. Intimacy is matter of taste and opportunity, and can only be shared by a few. Benevolence and forgiveness are of universal and unchangeable obligation.

TEMPTATION IN GOOD THINGS.

The temptation in things known to be bad can seldom be great to a person of any principle, but the temptation that lurks in good things, in the very best. things—who can be sufficiently on his guard against that ?

THINGS WRONG BY THEMSELVES.

There are some things that are always wrong, when they are alone. Faith is wrong, when it is alone. Obedience is wrong, when it is alone. Knowledge is wrong, when it is alone. Each of these by itself is like the rowing with one oar. Row as faithfully as you will, you make no progress. Your motion is a delusion—it all turns upon itself.

BEFORE HIS TIME.

We are familiar with the phrase, "a man before his time." But perhaps no one ever fully realizes what that means. Think of a tree tempted by a delusive bit of genial weather into expanding its blossoms in December or January, aud you will have at once a conception of the man before his time—and his troubles.

TROUBLES OF PREACHERS.

If a man has the spirit of his own time, if he preaches the everlasting Gospel, in the language of the present day, and discards time-worn phrases, he is denounced as unsafe. There are those who cannot understand why, if he has the same spirit, he should not employ the same words as others, and they express aloud their doubts of one who does not seem to know that certain phrases are hallowed by time. If, on the other hand, a preacher delights in the old phraseology, he is called a man behind his day whom no thoughtful person could listen to. If he is of a metaphysical turn, and cannot help going into the grounds and reasons of things, this, instead of being welcomed as a source of wealth, is denounced as a preaching of philosophy. If a man has no metaphysical tendency, and never tries to sound the depths, but confines himself to the obvious truths, he is quickly put down as shallow and superficial. If a man is speculative, he is called abstract and dangerous; if he is practical, he is called commonplace. If he is a simple Gospel preacher, it is said of him that he has nothing new, that it is always the old story; and if he embraces a wide range and takes the whole Bible for his text, it is said that he does not preach the Gospel. If he preaches the necessity of a new birth, he is said to be driving men to despair; and if he dwells more on obvious matters, he is said not to be spiritual. If God has given him a touch of humour, and he thinks it quite unnecessary to leave this at home when he goes to preach, he is accused of levity and of forgetting the solemnity of the house of God; and if he is very solemn, he is called heavy and unnatural. If he deals in generalities, and never comes near actual life, he is called vague and pointless; and if he has a pointed realistic way of preaching, speaking from life as it really exists among men, he is accused of personalities, and excites enmity. If a preacher of the Gospel were to think of all these things, he would be afraid to open his mouth. But if a man has really a message, if the word of God is burning in him, he will make his face as a flint, and utter the word fearlessly, whether men will hear or forbear.

QUESTIONS.

They who really wish to learn must both listen and question. There are some that listen and do not question; and there are others that question and do not listen. Let us not stop to inquire which is the worse. They are both bad. A man or child who listens, and has never a question to put, never a difficulty to remove, never a doubt to dispel, can scarcely be taking a very earnest hold. He can scarcely be realizing and taking home what he hears. Perhaps he is allowing difficulties that could easily be removed to block up the way. It is quite likely that questions may be troublesome, and therefore may be discouraged. There are those who bristle all over with questions. They are nothing but questions. They are so full of their questions that they do not listen to an answer. They have no patience with answers. Questions, questions, that is what interests them. They would be disappointed to think that their questions could be answered. They require to be reminded and to lay it seriously to heart, that man lives by truth, by reality, not by questions about it; that life is not a debating club; that man has a need to act, and needs principles on which to act; a need to live, and needs principles on which to live; a need to be, and needs principles on which to be—principles without which moral or spiritual being is impossible.

IRREVERENCE.

See a character flippant, irreverent, holding nothing as high and solemn, turning all things into jest, sneering at greatness, ashamed of being thought to have reverence or awe of anything; you may see a clever, dexterous, even astute man, but you do not see a profound or truly wise man. The want of reverence betrays the want of insight, and gives warning of something radically unreliable. The really solid and genuine man, faithful and thorough, may be generally known by even an extreme of reverence. He sees much to reverence, much material for awe and solemnity, when other minds see only material of contempt. Of all things it seems to him that the mocking, depreciating spirit, that turns all things into jest, is the most sadly foolish and inane in a universe inhabited by moral, spiritual, immortal beings, and where all things heave with spiritual and unutterable meanings.

SPOKEN AND UNSPOKEN.

The inexpressible, the unutterable, is always greater in every true earnest spirit than the expressed.

FATHER AND MOTHER.

There are those whose memory of father and mother becomes more vivid the older they grow, whose sense of loss is at times as bitter as ever it was. I tell you, the oldest man or woman is a little child again, when thinking tenderly of father and mother.

"JESUS SAITH UNTO HER, 'MARY.'"

There is a way of pronouncing a name that no art can imitate, because it is the full unconscious leaping out of the soul. The soul in that one word reveals itself, and reveals you. The tones of the voice express the relation of the soul to you, and its conception of you. Two histories, indeed, are given in the utterance of the one name—that of the one who utters, and that of the one to whom the name belongs.

ANTIQUITY.

Tenderest feelings enshrine antiquity, and make it sacred. To think lightly of the past, to trample upon it, or turn the back upon it, is regarded by the great human heart as a sign of shallowness, coldness, frivolity. Thus error becomes fortified by some of the deepest and best feelings of the soul. It is entwined with thoughts of men that have toiled and suffered

U

—men that have fought the battle of life, and left the earth to their children. How can a man, with any loyalty to the past, with any regard to those who once trod the same ground as he does, now say calmly—"Our fathers inherited lies, vanity, and things wherein is no profit." Some spirits, rather than say this, shut their ears to all that can be said. Their one principle is to adhere to whatever their fathers honoured.

MATTER AND SPIRIT.

All material things come within the spiritual range, through their connection with spirit.

PASSERS BY.

There are always those who go to gaze on misfortune and calamity. If there is anything wrong, anything sensational or tragic, it has a fascination for them. There they are staring, questioning, whispering, pointing, shaking their heads, bemoaning, perhaps even shedding tears. They seem to find a satisfaction in it. They are pleased that they are so sympathetic. But they nevertheless pass by on the other side.

PRIDE.

Pride will subsist on very lowly fare. It will glory over the plainest things, as if they were a sumptuous feast. As children sometimes wear a chaplet of daisies or buttercups, so pride will carry quite ordinary attainments and fancy them sparkling diamonds.

RECEPTIVENESS.

Great receiving is great doing. When a man receives greatly it forces on action. The amount of life within him obliges him to work. The abundance of love constrains him to run, and makes running easy.

PROFUNDITY.

There are different kinds of profundity. There is a kind which is like the old folios, and seems to be all written in Latin or German, or something quite as difficult to understand. It is a crabbed, sour profundity, which never lets you forget how deep it is. There is another kind of profundity which sparkles and effervesces. If it takes you down a pit, it is a pit lighted up with diamonds. You do not grudge going deep, if there are such lights all the way, and if the deeper you go the flashes are more abundant.

DESIRE THE MEASURE OF POSSIBILITY.

The greatness of man's desire is the measure of the latent energy of his nature. His hunger is the sign of the possibilities that are in him.

NO LOSS.

Nothing good ever dies. Every sigh, every secret prayer, every groan and struggle and secret act of good adds in some way to the imperishable wealth of the world.

THE WORLD PASSES AWAY.

We are reminded of the passing of the world by the withering and falling of the leaf. The autumn wind whirls along the ground the sere foliage which a few weeks ago was the charm of the landscape. How brilliantly it shone in the sunshine. How sweet for the eye to rest upon was the expanse of fresh varied verdure. It seemed as if in its multitudinous leaves— so finely cut, so symmetrical, so delicate and graceful, and yet so strong and active—it had rushed up to draw abiding life for the sombre earth from the sunshine and vital air. It was like an immense grasp of earth upon the elements of life, the earth holding out its hands, in prevailing entreaty, for more life and strength. Now it is all fast vanishing. Earth's grasp is relaxed, and the tide of death is once more surging over the world.

Every year the leaves return. But every year there are eyes that see the budding and the falling leaf for the last time. The same leaves never come back, nor do the same men. The world passeth away.

It is the human element that makes the world to us. Trees and mountains and streams are but the framework of the picture. We live in the hearts that love us. The familiar faces are our joy and strength. While they are with us, we do not notice change. Leaves fall, snow covers the ground, spring rushes up in freshness and bloom, but the same faces are near us, and we discern little change in them. But some day, when we think not, a familiar face disappears— goes perhaps beyond the seas, or crosses the sea of time—and with that face truly the world passes away !

How startling, bewildering it is when one that seemed almost a part of ourselves, sharing our thoughts, responding to our feelings, entering even into our guesses and dreams and speculations, goes away never to return. And such experiences are among the common things of life. The youngest are often familiar with them, and every stage in life has its memories of farewells uttered with a bursting heart. How, then, can we forget that the world passeth away ?

PERMANENCE.

It is a delusion we practise on ourselves when we think of things as less real and weighty, because they are brief in manifestation. The thoughts that under-lie them may be permanent, yea, everlasting, though the outcome was but a momentary flash.

What is filled up and energized by the thoughts, the aspirations, the deeds, the joys and sorrows of spiritual and moral beings, is the solidest of all things, however brief its appearance may be.

Long before history began, before the Romans came,

our wandering ancestors, looking out from their huts
and caves and tents of skin, saw Ailsa and Goatfell
and Ben Nevis as we do; and they had kindred feelings of awe and wonder stirred in them. They felt, as
we do, their littleness and frailty beside these immense
structures. Doubtless the mountains were to them
also, even in their darkness, steps to some sense of the
Infinite and the Eternal.

THE UNITING POWER OF GOODNESS.

Wickedness isolates; righteousness and love and self-
denial alone unite men, and form a foundation for
human life.

UPWARD.

You have seen a tree, prevented by surroundings
from stretching its branches out on all sides, throw its
whole vigour in an upward direction. How straight
and tall it shot up right toward the sky. So men,
when hemmed in on all sides, can at least shoot up—
nothing can come between them and God. They can
be like mountain peaks to draw down God's rain upon
the earth.

THE RIVER.

Men have all along felt the solemnity of the gliding
river, flowing on and on through the years and centuries,
a picture of constant change, and yet of abidingness.
How many a pilgrim through the world, footsore and

weary, has gazed on the gliding stream ever changing, never ceasing, and thought of his life fleeting fast away. Yes, the rolling river is one of the most impressive teachers of men. It sends its solemn lessons gently into the soul. It woos men to earnest and high thought. " O man," it seems to say, " thou canst not flow without care as I do,—but thou fleetest as fast. Thy course is changeful like mine, and like me thou rushest toward a great sea. Thou too hast banks which confine and yet preserve. Thy liberty like mine is in flowing on within thy banks. Thou reflectest on thy bosom a grander sun and more brilliant stars than I. And there is a higher guidance than any that I can know."

SUNSET.

Sunset grandeur is prophetical. It proclaims in a tongue that all men can understand that the last of earth is meant to be the best ; that farewell to earth is not a sad thing ; that it means—Hail, endless day ! Hail, eternal brightness and glory !

FAREWELL.

It is a suggestive thing, is it not, that the most southerly point of Greenland is called Cape Farewell. That means farewell to ice and snow, farewell to obstruction and darkness and frost—now for the sunny south, now for the open sea and genial lands. " Adieu, mountains of ice," the mariner says, " I am going home."

SYMBOLISM OF THE VEGETABLE WORLD.

The vegetable world is rich in symbolism, illustration and suggestion. Standing midway between the mineral and the animal, between the stone and man, it contains facts and principles belonging to both.

I have sometimes seen a tree on a tiny islet in the midst of a river. There was little more than space for the trunk of the tree; but there it maintained its hold and grew, sending its roots away down beyond the reach of the stream, working their sure, silent way beneath the rush and tumult; and so does the mind of man often feed on truth, solid and still, while the flood of circumstance sweeps whirling by.

LENGTH OF DAYS.

The desire for completing the round of life leads the child of God to present this prayer:—" Take me not away in the midst of my days." There is a noble dislike to incompleteness in the bosom of man, more especially in the bosom of men who have been awakened to principle and to truth. This dislike to incompleteness is connected with the success of work. A desire to make things complete is one of the most useful desires that can animate men in the world. The desire to leave nothing unfinished, but to bring things to their rounded state, before we lay them aside,—this, I say, has a most important and beneficial influence upon our career in this world. And the child of God wishes that life may be complete. An ideal of human life in this world comprises certain distinct portions—youth, manhood, and age. A life is not complete without the three ; and is it not natural and right, then, for one to desire completeness in this direction, more than in any other that falls within his experience in this world ? It is right that he should wish for the full experience of this mortal life, knowing what is in it. He has had experience of youth, he has had some experience of manhood, it is right that he should wish to have experience also of what age will bring. Each has its peculiar charm and profit, and its peculiar joy ; and it is right that a man should wish not to leave life, until he has gone through the several phases of existence.

CHRIST AND SOCIETY.

Christ inculcated no doctrine of political liberty. He did not even in words prohibit slavery. But he taught the greatness of the individual soul,—its grandeur, its best possibilities, the equal nearness and dearness of souls to God, and that each man may have, and must have, immediate fellowship with God, and must obey God for himself.

NEW TESTAMENT ESCHATOLOGY.

The New Testament has not drawn aside the veil either from heaven or hell. It deals in language that is pictorial, figurative, striking,—language addressed to the imagination rather than the understanding. It has been given to no man to say exactly or certainly where the figure ends and literal reality begins. All these bright and glowing pictures of heaven, and all those horrid pictures of hell, are but vivid ways of saying, "It shall be well with him that fears God; it shall not be well with him that does not fear God."

DISTORTED TRUTHS.

Oh ! who shall tell the awful battles that have taken place in hearts when the human exaggeration or contortion of a divine truth was mistaken for the truth itself, and the tortured spirit knew not whether to hate it or to hate himself for hating it.

MYSTICISM.

If you have ever on a clear summer day gazed across the sea, and thought of God and life ; if you have ever looked at the mountains with one peak lost in the clouds and another bathed in light, till you rose to the feeling of an infinite perfection and sublimity ; if you have listened to music till you heard the music no more, but felt yourself in the limitless, and had a sense of a perfection beyond thought, you have been for the time a mystic, and have really understood more about it than a history of mysticism could give. For all such history loses itself in details, in accounts of strife and vagaries.

Man has a sense of the Infinite, call it by whatever name you like. It haunts him. It whispers to him. It speaks to him out of the far horizon. It gleams in the starlight. The sea, sleeping beneath the moon, dreams it and mutters it. The most of men are mystics away among lonely moors, and on the wide seas beneath the stars. Time and space disappear. The whole natural universe passes away like a cloud. The soul and God are left,—God the one reality, of whom all things are a transient picture.

All prayer, all devotion, has in it the essence of mysticism. It is the flight of "the alone to the Alone."

EVOLUTION.

The existence of the spiritual nature in man is not at all clouded or obscured by the evolutionary theory of origin. Theories of origin can never affect facts of consciousness ; they can never explain away the moral sense, or lessen the feeling of obligation. It is impossible for any one honestly to hide from any duty, however high, behind a theory of evolution. The very sight of the duty brings him within its sweep. The perception of the grandeur and glory of religion shows him obligated to a religious life. The fact that he can hope and fear for eternity, marks him as belonging to it, and bound to think of it. The fact that his nature needs the thought of God and of eternity to satisfy it, is the most imperative of all facts and the most convincing.

Whenever freedom began, man, framed out of nature, rose into the region of spirit. The attaining to the sense of freedom is the leaving the realm of nature. Whenever man became conscious of self, began to make himself the subject of reflection, to take up his nature, as it were, in his hands and reflect upon it, and its meaning and purpose, he passed into the spiritual realm.

THE FALL.

The Fall, though a real fall, was yet in a true sense a rise—a calamity, a real sin, and yet a stage toward a higher knowledge of God, and an enlarging of self— a thing without which the highest life could not be.

JOY OF CREATION.

What high joy some have had in watching dim imaginations passing into form—in witnessing a new thing coming above the horizon—the result of long brooding or sore agony of spirit. What an illustration it is of the goodness of God, that He has granted to His creatures such an approach to the joy that He Himself has in the exercise of His sovereign creative energy.

FORGIVENESS.

God's forgiveness is not, as some say, a receiving of

the penitent back into favour, while the penalty of his transgression still remains. This is to make divine forgiveness really less than human. Man remits penalty, much more does God.

EDEN.

Eden is not the symbol of a glory passed away never to return; but the picture of the ideal which shall be made actual in every soul that comes to God. All the plants and flowers that grew in the old Eden shall bloom in the new; ay, and there are plants in the new Eden that were not in the old—plants of deep and bitter penitence and noble struggle, of fervent gratitude, of grand exultation; plants that have a richer beauty and a rarer odour than any that Eden knew.

THE END.

PRINTED BY ROBERT MACLEHOSE, UNIVERSITY PRESS, GLASGOW.

CATALOGUE OF BOOKS

PUBLISHED BY

JAMES MACLEHOSE & SONS

𝔓ublishers to the 𝔘niversity of 𝔊lasgow.

GLASGOW: 61 St. Vincent Street.

1890.

JAMES MACLEHOSE AND SONS, GLASGOW,
Publishers to the University.

————

MACMILLAN AND CO., LONDON AND NEW YORK.

London, . . . *Simpkin, Marshall, Hamilton,*
Kent, and Co., Limited.
Cambridge, . . *Macmillan and Bowes.*
Edinburgh, . . *Douglas and Foulis.*

————

NOVEMBER MDCCCXC.

PUBLISHERS TO THE

UNIVERSITY OF GLASGOW.

Messrs. MACLEHOSE'S

Publications.

ANDERSON—LECTURES ON MEDICAL NURSING, delivered in the Royal Infirmary, Glasgow. By J. WALLACE ANDERSON, M.D., Physician to the Royal Infirmary, Glasgow. Fourth and Cheap Edition. Fcap. 8vo. 2s. 6d.

"An admirable guide. In many respects the best manual we at present possess on the subject."—*Lancet.*

"The very important subjects these lectures discuss are severally treated with clearness, precision and sound judgment."—*Spectator.*

"Dr. Anderson's admirable little book contains just such information as every nurse should possess, and this is seasoned with much wise advice and many good maxims."—*Birmingham Medical Review.*

"A valuable text book. Throughout his instructions Dr. Anderson is always practical and clear."—*Health.*

ANDERSON—THE ESSENTIALS OF PHYSICAL DIAGNOSIS : A Guide-Book for Students. By J. WALLACE ANDERSON, M.D., Physician to the Royal Infirmary, Glasgow. Fcap. 8vo. 3s.

"The work is accurate and well arranged, and ought to be popular with students."—*British Medical Journal.*

ANDERSON—On the Curability of Attacks of Tuber-
cular Peritonitis and Acute Phthisis. By T.
M'Call Anderson, M.D., Professor of Clinical Medicine
in the University of Glasgow. Crown 8vo. 2s. 6d.

ANDERSON—On Affections of the Nervous System,
their Diagnosis and Treatment. By Professor M'Call
Anderson, M.D. Demy 8vo. 5s.

ARGYLL, Duke of—What the Turks are. 8vo. 1s.

BANNATYNE—Guide to the Examinations for Pro-
motion in the Infantry. Part II. Containing
Questions and Answers on Regimental Duties. For the
Rank of Major. By Lieutenant-Colonel J. Millar
Bannatyne. Fifteenth Edition. Crown 8vo. 7s.

BARR—Manual of Diseases of the Ear, for the Use of
Practitioners and Students of Medicine. By Thomas
Barr, M.D., Lecturer on Aural Surgery, Anderson's Col-
lege, Glasgow. Crown 8vo, Illustrated. 10s. 6d.

"The best manual on the subject that has been produced for many
years."—*Medical Chronicle.*
"The book deserves to have a large circulation."—*Archives of Otology.*
"An excellent Manual."—*Liverpool Medico-Chirurgical Journal.*
"Replete with sound practical information."—*British Medical Journal.*
"Is as valuable and condensed a summary of Otological work as exists in
the English language."—*Glasgow Medical Journal.*
"For its size, we know of no work to surpass it in the information it
contains, its clearness of style and the comprehensive grasp taken of the
subject."—*Dublin Journal of Medical Science.*

BATHGATE—Progressive Religion. Sermons by the late
Rev. William Bathgate, D.D., Kilmarnock. Crown
8vo. 6s.

BEGG—THE DEVELOPMENT OF TASTE AND OTHER STUDIES
IN AESTHETICS. By W. PROUDFOOT BEGG. 8vo. 12s. 6d.

" A volume of Essays, not only thoughtful, ably written, and suggestive
in themselves, but also, as a whole, affording illustration of the modern
reaction from the old practical form of philosophy associated with Scotland."—*Glasgow Herald.*

BELL—AMONG THE ROCKS AROUND GLASGOW. A Series of
Excursion Sketches and other papers. With a Coloured
Geological Map. By DUGALD BELL. Second Edition.
Crown 8vo. 4s.

BIRRELL—TWO QUEENS : a Dramatic Poem. By C. J.
BALLINGALL BIRRELL. Crown 8vo. 3s. 6d.

" This drama is founded on the story of Lady Jane Grey and Mary Tudor.
The language throughout is flowing and imaginative, and the delineation
of character is, in some places, masterly."—*Dundee Advertiser.*
" This drama may be read with both pleasure and profit by students of
this eventful epoch in English history."—*Scottish Leader.*

BLACK—THE LAW AGENTS' ACT 1873 : ITS OPERATIONS AND
RESULTS AS AFFECTING LEGAL EDUCATION IN SCOTLAND.
By WILLIAM GEORGE BLACK. Crown 8vo. 2s. 6d.

BLACKBURN—CAW, CAW ; or, the Chronicle of the Crows :
a Tale of the Spring Time. Illustrated by J. B. (MRS.
HUGH BLACKBURN). 4to. 2s. 6d.

BLACKBURN—THE PIPITS. By the Author of " Caw
Caw," with Sixteen page Illustrations by J. B. (MRS. HUGH
BLACKBURN). 4to. 3s.

" This is a charming fable in verse, illustrated by the well-known J. B.,
whose power in delineating animals, especially birds, is scarcely inferior to
Landseer or Rosa Bonheur."—*Courant.*

BROWN—THE LIFE OF A SCOTTISH PROBATIONER. Being the Memoir of THOMAS DAVIDSON, with his POEMS and LETTERS. By the late JAMES BROWN, D.D., St. James' Church, Paisley. Third and Cheaper Edition. Crown 8vo. 5s.

"A worthy record of a man of rare genius—dead ere his prime. His poems are as beautiful as flowers or birds."—*Dr. John Brown, Author of "Rab and his Friends."*

" A very fresh and interesting little book."—*Saturday Review.*

" This life of an unknown Scotch probationer is equal in interest to any-thing of the kind we have seen since Carlyle's 'Life of Sterling' was written. Thomas Davidson, as a poet, as a humourist, as a simple, loving. honest, reticent, valiant soul, demands adequate recognition at the hands of the critic—a career kind and unostentatious, glorified, however, in its uneventful homeliness by a rare vein of poetry and a rich vein of humour."—*Black-wood's Magazine.*

" It is an unspeakable pleasure to a reviewer weary of wading through piles of commonplace to come unexpectedly on a prize such as this."—*Non-conformist.*

" A charming little biography His was one of those rare natures which fascinates all who come in contact with it. A picture of a man of high purpose, quaint humour, strong, but reticent affections, and profound Christian faith."—*Spectator.*

BROWN—LIFE OF WILLIAM B. ROBERTSON, D.D., of Irvine, with Extracts from his Letters and Poems. By the late JAMES BROWN, D.D., Author of " The Life of a Scottish Proba-tioner." Fourth and Cheaper Edition. Crown 8vo, with two Portraits. 5s.

" We trust this book will have a popularity such as few biographies enjoy. It deserves it. An interesting story, much wit, more wisdom, glimpses of men and places, poetry grave and gay, and, pervading all, the character of a most lovable man, make up a rare book."—*Liverpool Mercury.*

" A book full of refinement and charm."—*British Weekly.*

"Sufficient justice can hardly be rendered to this memoir in our limited space. It is one to have, to study, and to go to frequently."—*Cambridge Express.*

"One of the most interesting volumes of biography issued in Scotland this year."—*Scottish American.*

"A character almost more lovely than that of the sons of men,"—*Scotsman.*

CAIRD, Principal—AN INTRODUCTION TO THE PHILOSOPHY OF RELIGION. By the VERY REV. JOHN CAIRD, D.D., Principal and Vice-Chancellor of the University of Glasgow. Fourth Thousand. New and Cheaper Edition. Crown 8vo. 6s

" A book rich in the results of speculative study, broad in its intellectual grasp, and happy in its original suggestiveness. To Dr. Caird we are indebted for a subtle and masterly presentation of Hegel's philosophy in its solution of the problem of religion."—*Edinburgh Review.*

" It is the business of the reviewer to give some notion of the book which he reviews, either by a condensation of its contents or by collecting the cream in the shape of short selected passages ; but this cannot be done with a book like the one before us, of which the argument does not admit of condensation, and which is all cream.........The most valuable book of its kind that has appeared."—Mr. T. H. Green in *The Academy.*

" It is remarkable also for its marvellous power of exposition and graceful subtlety of thought. Hegelianism has never appeared so attractive as it appears in the clear and fluent pages of Principal Caird."--*Spectator.*

" Probably our British theological literature contains no nobler or more suggestive volume."—*Mind.*

CAIRD, Principal—SERMONS AND LECTURES. By the VERY REV. JOHN CAIRD, D.D., Principal and Vice-Chancellor of the University of Glasgow. 8vo. 1s. each.

1. MIND AND MATTER. A Sermon preached before the British Medical Association, August, 1888.

2. CHRISTIAN MANLINESS. A Sermon preached before the University.

3. IN MEMORIAM. A Sermon on the Death of the Very Rev. Principal THOMAS BARCLAY, D.D.

4. THE UNIVERSAL RELIGION. A Lecture delivered in Westminster Abbey, on the day of Intercession for Missions.

5. THE UNITY OF THE SCIENCES. A Lecture.

6. THE PROGRESSIVENESS OF THE SCIENCES. A Lecture.

CAIRD, Professor E. — THE CRITICAL PHILOSOPHY OF
IMMANUEL KANT. By EDWARD CAIRD, M.A., LL.D.,
Professor of Moral Philosophy in the University of Glasgow, and late Fellow and Tutor of Merton College, Oxford.
2 vols. Demy 8vo. 32s.

" It is quite the most comprehensive and maturely considered contribution
that has yet been made by an English writer to the understanding of Kant's
whole philosophical achievement.   It is every way a thorough and masterly
performance."—*Mind*.

"It is now some years since he published his 'Philosophy of Kant,' the
merit of which was at once readily recognised, and in the present work he
produces a more complete study, not limited to the Critique of Pure Reason,
but dealing with Kant's whole work—his metaphysics, ethics, teleology,
and religion, and viewing them in their mutual relations, and as a consistent
whole.   This is a great advantage, at once doing justice to the thinker, and
giving benefit to the student whose acquaintance with isolated or special
portions of Kant's writings is highly unsatisfactory."—*Scotsman*.

"Of the work, as a whole, it is difficult to speak in terms at once
sufficient and temperate.   It is, and must for long years remain, *the* English
book on Kant.   .   .   .   Remarkable, not only for the minute restatement
of the critical system, but also for the independent philosophical power by
which it is abundantly characterized ; it is to be regarded as much as an
original contribution to speculative thought as a commentary upon the
Kantian theory.   No student can afford to be without it ; every expert
must be prepared to reckon with it."—*Scottish Review*.

"At last we have in English a critical-exposition of 'The Critical
Philosophy of Kant,' which, for thoroughness and ability, can hold up its
head before any similar attempt in other languages."—*The Academy*.

"The object of this book is to give a connected view of the Critical
Philosophy, showing the relations of the three *Critiques* to each other,
and to the other works of Kant which may be regarded as illustrations or
developments of his main argument.   The first part, on the *Critique of
Pure Reason*, deals with the same subject as my former work, entitled *The
Philosophy of Kant*, but, except in a few passages, it is not a reproduction
of it."—*Extract from Preface*.

CAIRD, Professor E.—THE SOCIAL PHILOSOPHY AND RE-
LIGION OF COMTE.   By EDWARD CAIRD, M.A., LL.D.
Crown 8vo.   5s.

" No good account of Positivism in its social and religious aspects was
available for general readers or students till this volume appeared.   This
little book serves as an admirable introduction to the Hegelian treatment
of history, religion, and the state."—*Athenæum*.

CLAIRE—A SCOTCH STORY, by the Author of "Vida." Crown 8vo. 6s.

"Worth reading for the Scotch characters alone."—*Scots Observer.*

CLELAND—EVOLUTION, EXPRESSION, AND SENSATION. By JOHN CLELAND, M.D., D.SC., F.R.S., Professor of Anatomy in the University of Glasgow. Crown 8vo. 5s.

DEAS—HISTORY OF THE CLYDE TO THE PRESENT TIME. With Maps and Diagrams. By JAMES DEAS, M. Inst. C.E., Engineer of the Clyde Navigation. 8vo. 10s. 6d.

DERBY, Earl of—INAUGURAL ADDRESS on his Installation as Lord Rector of the University of Glasgow. 8vo. 1s.

DICKSON—ST. PAUL'S USE OF THE TERMS FLESH AND SPIRIT. Being the BAIRD LECTURE for 1883. By WILLIAM P. DICKSON, D.D., LL.D., Professor of Divinity in the University of Glasgow. Crown 8vo. 8s. 6d.

"An able, thorough exposition."—*Scotsman.*
"Prof. Dickson is the first to give to the subject the earnest and elaborate treatment which it deserves, and the consequence is the book will be an indispensable help to the students of the Pauline Scriptures."—*Aberdeen Free Press.*

EGGS 4D. A DOZEN, AND CHICKENS 4D. A POUND ALL THE YEAR ROUND. Containing full and complete information for successful and profitable keeping of Poultry. Small 8vo. Twentieth Thousand. 1s.

"The most complete little treatise on the rearing of poultry of all kinds, and the production of eggs, that has ever come under our notice."—*Ayr Advertiser.*
"Since the publication of 'The Henwife' no book has appeared that discusses the subject so explicitly and exhaustively; and the present volume has the merits of being much more concise and better fitted for common use."—*Daily Review.*

FORSYTH—A GRADUATED COURSE OF INSTRUCTION IN LINEAR PERSPECTIVE. By DAVID FORSYTH, M.A., D.Sc., Headmaster of the Central Higher Grade School, Leeds. Second Edition. Royal 8vo. 2s.

"We are bound to say that this latest book is one of the best. In fact, we know none that surpasses it."—*Athenæum*.

"This book is a model of clear and perspicuous teaching. Teachers will find it an invaluable aid, and no student who has mastered it need fear to face the Science and Art Department."—*Educational News*.

"Any youth of average intelligence, with such a work in his hands, ought to find little difficulty in mastering the principles of perspective, or getting his certificate at South Kensington."—*Schoolmaster*.

FORSYTH—TEST PAPERS IN PERSPECTIVE, for Testing the Progress of Pupils, and for preparing them for the Second Grade Examination of the Science and Art Department. 26 different papers. Full Government size. Third Edition, Enlarged. 1s. 6d. per set.

"The test papers are admirably adapted to familiarize students with examination work."—*Educational News*.

"Can hardly fail to be acceptable to teachers."—*Athenæum*.

FREELAND — A BIRTH SONG AND OTHER POEMS. By WILLIAM FREELAND. Extra Foolscap 8vo. 6s.

GAIRDNER—THE PHYSICIAN AS NATURALIST, Memoirs bearing on the Progress of Medicine. By W. T. GAIRDNER, M.D., LL.D., Professor of Medicine in the University of Glasgow, Physician in Ordinary to H.M. the Queen in Scotland. Crown 8vo. 7s. 6d.

"It will doubtless be read with great interest by medical men, but it is to be hoped that this weighty volume, from the pen of one of the most scholarly physicians of the day, will be carefully read by the general public."—*Manchester Examiner*.

GLASGOW UNIVERSITY CALENDAR FOR THE YEAR 1890-91. *Published annually.* Crown 8vo, Cloth. 2s. 6d.

GLASGOW UNIVERSITY LOCAL EXAMINATIONS. Scheme of Examinations for 1891, and Report for 1890. *Published annually.* Crown 8vo. 6d.

GLASGOW ARCHÆOLOGICAL SOCIETY'S TRANS-ACTIONS. First Series. 8vo. Volume I. Parts II., III., IV., V. Volume II. Parts I., II., III. 5s. each. New Series. Foolscap 4to. Parts I., II., III., IV. 6s. each.

A few sets of the First Series of the Transactions, in eight parts, 8vo, have been completed for sale, price £2 per set. Two of the parts which had been long out of print were reprinted in order to complete a very limited number of sets.

GLASGOW—MEMOIRS AND PORTRAITS OF ONE HUNDRED GLASGOW MEN who have Died during the last Thirty Years, and who in their Lives did much to make the City what it now is. Two vols. Royal 4to. Half Red Morocco, gilt top. £7 7s.

This work contains memoirs of one hundred Glasgow men, with one hundred full-page engraved portraits which have all been specially engraved for this book. The memoirs have all been written by Glasgow gentlemen who, from personal knowledge, have been able to give accurate and life-like sketches, and thus to present a most graphic history of Glasgow for this century.

A full prospectus, with list of Memoirs and Portraits, will be sent on application to the Publishers. More than four-fifths of the whole Edition have been subscribed for.

GLASGOW—THE OLD COUNTRY HOUSES OF THE OLD GLASGOW GENTRY. Illustrated by permanent Photographs. Royal 4to. Half Red Morocco, gilt top. Second Edition. *Very scarce.* £10 10s.

This is a history of one hundred of the old houses in and around Glasgow, and of the families who owned and lived in them. To the local antiquary it is especially interesting as a memorial of the old burgher aristocracy, of their character and habits, and of the city in which they lived ; while to the descendants of the "old gentry" it is interesting as containing the history of their forefathers and the rise of their families.

GRANT—CATALOGUE OF 6415 STARS FOR THE EPOCH 1870, deduced from Observations made at the Glasgow University Observatory. By ROBERT GRANT, M.A., F.R.S., F.R.A.S., Professor of Astronomy in the University of Glasgow. 4to. 31s. 6d.

This volume has been printed at the expense of Her Majesty's Government as advised by the Council of the Royal Society.

GRANT—THE LORD'S SUPPER EXPLAINED. By the REV. WILLIAM GRANT, Ayr. Ninth Edition. 16mo. 4d.

GRAY, •David—THE LUGGIE, and other Poems. By DAVID GRAY. Edited by HENRY GLASSFORD BELL. Cheap Edition, extra Fcap. 8vo. 3s. 6d.

" Gems of poetry, exquisitely set."—*Glasgow News.*

HENLEY—A CENTURY OF ARTISTS : a Memorial of Loan Collection of the Glasgow International Exhibition, 1888. By W. E. HENLEY. With Descriptive Notices of the Pictures by ROBERT WALKER. Extra pott folio, £2 2s. nett. Large Paper Edition, with the plates on Japanese, • £5 5s. nett.

This Memorial Volume has taken the form of a series of brief critical Biographies of one hundred and three Artists, by Mr. W. E. Henley, and a description, by Mr. Robert Walker, of each of their pictures exhibited. A typical illustration of the work of each Artist is given.

The Etchings, after pictures by Bosboom, Corot, Israels, Macnee, Maris, Reynolds, Rousseau, Wilkie, and Thomson of Duddingston, are by Mr. William Hole, R.S.A., Mr. William Strang, Mr. F. Huth, and Mr. A. W. Henley. Other Illustrations are by Mr. Hugh Cameron, R.S.A., Mr. William Hole, R.S.A., Mr. A. Roche, Mr. J. Crawford Hamilton, Mr. Hector Chalmers, and Mr. D. Gauld.

" A noble memorial of an interesting collection."—*Times.*

" A handsome book, to which it would be more easy to find a rival abroad than at home."—*St. James' Gazette.*

" Nothing but the highest praise can be given to the style in which the volume has been produced."—*Scotsman.*

HAMILTON, Janet—POEMS, ESSAYS, AND SKETCHES. By JANET HAMILTON. New Edition, with portrait. Cr. 8vo. 6s.

"It is a book containing the Memoirs, Poems, and other Compositions of, to my mind, the most remarkable old woman I have ever heard of. Certainly if some of her poems were placed among the poems of Burns in a volume of his, no one would for a moment doubt that they were the productions of the greatest of all the Scottish Poets.

"Hers, I think, is an amazing story. I confess it has surprised me beyond anything I have read for a long time."—The Right Hon. JOHN BRIGHT, M.P.

"One of the most remarkable books that has fallen into our hands for a long time past. It is a book that ennobles life."—*Athenæum.*

"Our readers should buy the book (they will not repent of the bargain) and look out its good things for themselves."—*St. James' Gazette.*

HUNTER—HYMNS OF FAITH AND LIFE. Collected and Edited by the REV. JOHN HUNTER, Trinity Congregational Church, Glasgow. 656 pages. Fcap. 8vo. 3s. 6d.

"No more catholic collection of hymns has ever been given to the world. . . . . From whatever standpoint it is regarded, this latest addition to the hymnology of the Church must be pronounced a decided success, and Mr. Hunter's keen appreciation of literary beauty has enabled him to produce a volume of purely devotional verse which disproves the dictum of Mr. Goldwin Smith that hymns have rarely 'any serious value as poetry.'"— *The Christian World.*

"The ideal hymn-book is perhaps not yet in existence. We felt certain of that fact until we read and re-read this splendid collection by Mr. Hunter. We are not quite sure of it now. If this is not the ideal hymn-book it is not much behind. The melodious voices of all the sweetest singers blend here. The poets of all the churches meet together. The devout and cultured mind will rejoice in its pages. For private devotion it is above all price and praise. It should be on the same shelf as Thomas à Kempis."— *The Sheffield Independent.*

"Mr. Hunter's anthology of hymns is much superior to ordinary collections. It is truly catholic. The Psalms and Canticles are a novel feature, and are interesting. The printing and binding are neat and dainty." — *The Academy.*

HUNTER—DEVOTIONAL SERVICES FOR PUBLIC WORSHIP, including additional Services for Baptism, the Lord's Supper, Marriage, and the Burial of the Dead. Prepared by the REV. JOHN HUNTER. Crown 8vo. 2s. 6d.

JEBB—HOMER : AN INTRODUCTION TO THE ILIAD AND
THE ODYSSEY. For the use of Schools and Colleges.
By R. C. JEBB, Litt.D., LL.D., Professor of Greek in the
University of Cambridge. Third Edition. Crown 8vo. 3s. 6d.

"Professor Jebb has rendered a signal service to the scientific study of
Greek literature by the publication of this little book. So far as we are
aware, nothing of the same sort has been done of late years, even in
Germany. We heartily commend the handbook before us to the diligent
study of all beginners and many 'ripe scholars.'"—*Athenæum.*
"A trustworthy and indispensable guide to the study of the two great
poems."—*Classical Review.*
"We know of no work which will prove so interesting and useful an
introduction to the study of Homer."—*School Board Chronicle.*

JEBB—THE ANABASIS OF XENOPHON.—Books III. and IV.,
with the *Modern Greek Version* of Professor Michael Con-
stantinides, Edited by Professor JEBB. Fcap. 8vo. 4s. 6d.

JEFFREY—THE SALVATION OF THE GOSPEL. A Series of
Discourses. By REV. ROBERT T. JEFFREY, M.D. Crown
8vo. 6s.   [*This Day.*

KANT—THE PHILOSOPHY OF KANT, as contained in Extracts
from his own Writings. Selected and Translated by JOHN
WATSON, LL.D., Professor of Moral Philosophy in the
University of Queen's College, Kingston, Author of " Kant
and his English Critics." Crown 8vo. 7s. 6d.

"Cannot fail soon to recommend itself to all concerned."—*Mind.*

KANT. *See* CAIRD'S KANT.

KANT. *See* WATSON'S KANT AND HIS ENGLISH CRITICS.

KING—MEMOIR OF THE REV. DAVID KING, LL.D. By his
Wife and Daughter. Crown 8vo. With Portrait. 7s. 6d.

LECKIE—Sermons by Joseph Leckie, D.D., Ibrox, Glasgow. Crown 8vo. Second Edition. 6s.

"A new—new at least to us—and original preacher has appeared. There is a strange impress of power in these discourses. They combine a frequent beauty and finish of expression, of the newest kind."—*Expositor.*

"To those who want a volume of sound yet vigorous sermons, which will set their own minds thinking, we unhesitatingly say, get this without delay."—*Leeds Mercury.*

"Ere we had read a page it was evident that we were in the grasp of a mind of singular force and originality. There is nothing hackneyed, commonplace, or tedious in the volume."—*Christian World.*

LECKIE—Life and Religion. By the late Rev. Joseph Leckie, D.D., Ibrox, Glasgow. With Biographical Notice by his Son. Crown 8vo. With Portrait. 6s. [*This Day.*

LEISHMAN—A System of Midwifery, including the Diseases of Pregnancy and the Puerperal State. By William Leishman, M.D., Regius Professor of Midwifery in the University of Glasgow. Fourth Edition. Revised and Enlarged, with Additional Illustrations. 2 vols. Demy 8vo. 24s.

"We should counsel the student by all means to procure Dr. Leishman's work."—*London Medical Record.*

LEITCH—Practical Educationists and their Systems of Teaching. By James Leitch Crown 8vo. 6s.

LYTTON, EARL OF—National and Individual Morality Compared. Demy 8vo. 6d.

MACGEORGE—Papers on the Principles and Real Position of the Free Church. By Andrew Macgeorge. 8vo. 6s.

M'KENDRICK—TEXT-BOOK OF PHYSIOLOGY.   By J. G.
M'KENDRICK, M.D., LL.D., F.R.S., Professor of the
Institutes of Medicine in the University of Glasgow. 2 vols.
Demy 8vo.   40s.   (*The volumes are sold separately.*)
Vol. I.—General Physiology, including the Chemistry and
Histology of the Tissues and the Physiology of Muscle.
542 Pages, 400 Illustrations.   16s.
Vol II.—Special Physiology, including Nutrition, Innerva-
tion, and Reproduction. 830 Pages, 500 Illustrations. 24s.

" The clearness of the style, and the abundance and excellence of the
drawings, cannot fail to render the work, as it deserves to be, one of the
most popular text-books of Physiology in our language."—*Dublin Journal
of Medical Science.*
" The work will rank high in its own department, and, like all Professor
M'Kendrick's works, it is definite, clear, and precise, and ought to be
acceptable to the physiologist and the student."—*Scotsman.*

MACKENZIE—AN INTRODUCTION TO SOCIAL PHILOSOPHY.
By JOHN S. MACKENZIE, M.A.Glas., B.A. Cantab., Fellow
of Trinity College, Cambridge, and Lecturer on Philosophy
at Owens College, Manchester : formerly Shaw Philosophical
Fellow and Examiner in Philosophy in the University of
Glasgow. Demy 8vo. 10s. 6d.

" The style is fresh, clear, and attractive."—*Glasgow Herald.*
"This book may be safely commended to those who are interested in
the social problems of our time, and do not shrink from their study in a
comprehensive and philosophical manner. Mr. Mackenzie has read much
and writes well."—*The Times.*

MACKINTOSH—ESSAYS TOWARDS A NEW THEOLOGY. By
ROBERT MACKINTOSH, M.A., B.D., Author of " Christ and
the Jewish Law." Demy 8vo. 12s. 6d.

"This is a thoughtful book by a man earnestly sincere, inspired with a
high purpose, whose mind is both comprehensive and acute. It is an able
and important contribution to a revised theology."—*Spectator.*

MACKINTOSH—THE OBSOLETENESS OF THE WESTMINSTER CONFESSION OF FAITH. Demy 8vo. 1s.

MACKINTOSH—THE INSUFFICIENCY OF REVIVALISM AS A RELIGIOUS SYSTEM. Demy 8vo. 1s.

MACLEHOSE — TALES FROM SPENSER, chosen from The Faerie Queene. By SOPHIA H. MACLEHOSE. Second Edition. Fcap. 8vo. Ornamental Cloth, gilt top, 3s. 6d.

"The tales are charmingly and very dramatically told."—*Times.*
"This is a charming book of stories from the 'Faerie Queene,' It is just the sort of book for a good uncle to give to niece or nephew."—*Scots Observer.*
"The editor's performance of her task is in every way admirable and enjoyable."—*Manchester Examiner.*

MACMILLAN—OUR LORD'S THREE RAISINGS FROM THE DEAD. By the REV. HUGH MACMILLAN, LL.D., F.R.S.E., Author of "Bible Teachings in Nature." Crown 8vo. 6s.

"A spirit of earnest piety pervades the book ; its language is simple and unaffected, and it abounds in apt and felicitous illustrations."—*Scotsman.*

MÜLLER—OUTLINES OF HEBREW SYNTAX. By DR. AUGUST MÜLLER, Professor of Oriental Languages in the University of Könisberg. Translated and Edited by James Robertson, M.A., D.D., Professor of Oriental Languages in the University of Glasgow. Demy 8vo. Third Edition. 6s.

"It may be recommended as an able and thoroughly trustworthy introduction to Hebrew syntax."—Professor S. R. Driver in *The Academy.*
"The work supplies a real want for English students. The translation is excellent."—*Bibliotheca Sacra.*

MURRAY—THE PROPERTY OF MARRIED PERSONS, with an Appendix of Statutes. By DAVID MURRAY, M.A., LL.D., F.S.A.Scot. Demy 8vo. [*Immediately.*

MURRAY—OLD CARDROSS. By DAVID MURRAY, M.A., LL.D., F.S.A. SCOT. Crown 8vo, 1s. 6d. Large paper copies, 6s.

MURRAY—A NOTE ON SOME GLASGOW AND OTHER PROVINCIAL COINS AND TOKENS. Fcap. 4to. 3s. 6d.

NEWTON—SIR ISAAC NEWTON'S PRINCIPIA. Edited by SIR WILLIAM THOMSON, D.C.L., LL.D., F.R.S., Professor of Natural Philosophy in the University of Glasgow, and HUGH BLACKBURN, M.A. Crown 4to. 31s. 6d.

NICHOL—TABLES OF EUROPEAN HISTORY, LITERATURE, SCIENCE, AND ART, FROM A.D. 200 TO 1888, and of American History, Literature and Art. By JOHN NICHOL, M.A., Balliol, Oxon., LL.D., formerly Professor of English Language and Literature in the University of Glasgow. Fourth Edition, revised and greatly enlarged. Royal 8vo. Printed in Five Colours. 7s. 6d.

"The Tables are clear, and form an admirable companion to the student of history, or indeed to any one who desires to revise his recollection of facts."—*Times.*

"In a word, the great leading facts of European history for nearly seventeen hundred years are here compressed with wonderful clearness into a single slim volume. The book is a triumph of systematization; it embodies the result of great research, and will be found an admirable guide to the student, as well as useful for purposes of rapid reference."—*Scotsman.*

"About as convenient a book of reference as could be found."—*Spectator.*

"A great boon to students." –*Dundee Advertiser.*

NICHOL—TABLES OF ANCIENT LITERATURE AND HISTORY, FROM B.C. 1500 TO A.D. 200. 4to, Cloth. 4s. 6d.

"They constitute a most successful attempt to give interest to the chronology of literature, by setting before the eye the relation between the literature and the practical life of mankind."—*Observer.*

NICHOL—THE DEATH OF THEMISTOCLES, and other Poems. Extra fcap. 8vo. 3s. 6d.

OLIPHANT, MRS.—EFFIE OGILVIE; The Story of a Young Life. By Mrs. OLIPHANT. Crown 8vo. Cheap Edition. 5s.

OLRIG GRANGE. *See* SMITH.

PATRICK—MEDIÆVAL SCOTLAND. By R. W. COCHRAN PATRICK, LL.D., of Woodside, Author of "Records of the Coinage of Scotland." [*Shortly*.

QUEEN MARGARET COLLEGE CALENDAR, Session 1889-90. *Published annually*. Crown 8vo. 6d.

RANKINE—SONGS AND FABLES. By W. J. MACQUORN RANKINE, late Professor of Engineering in the University of Glasgow. With Portrait, and with Ten Illustrations by J. B. Second Edition. Extra fcap. 8vo. 6s.

REFORMERS (THE) : Lectures by Ministers of the United Presbyterian Church, Graduates of the University of Glasgow. Crown 8vo. 478 pages. 6s.

CONTENTS—Wyclif, Hus, Savonarola, Erasmus, Luther, Calvin, Lollards of Kyle, Hamilton and Wishart, John Knox.

"These lectures are scholarly, able, earnest, eloquent, and constitute a noble addition to the Reformation literature."—*Evangelical Magazine.*

ROBERTSON—HEBREW SYNTAX. *See* MÜLLER.

ROBERTSON—LIFE AND LETTERS OF REV. WILLIAM B. ROBERTSON, D.D., of Irvine. By JAMES BROWN, D.D. St. James', Paisley, author of "The Life of a Scottish Probationer." With Two Portraits. Fourth and Cheaper Edition. Crown 8vo. 5s.

"The book is both pleasant and easy reading. The letters are full of geniality, fervour, and sympathy." – *Saturday Review.*

"We advise our readers to go to the book itself; they will be very morose indeed if they do not laugh long and heartily many times, and very learned indeed if they do not pick up something from his descriptions of many out-of-the-way bits of history and art."—*Glasgow Herald.*

SCHLOMKA. — A· GERMAN GRAMMAR. With Copious Exercises, Dialogues, and a Vocabulary. By CLEMENS SCHLOMKA, M.A., Ph.D. Third Edition. Crown 8vo. 4s. 6d.

"Wonderfully clear, consecutive, and simple. We have no hesitation in strongly recommending this grammar."—*School Board Chronicle.*

SCHLOMKA—GERMAN READER. Exercises for translating German into English and English into German. With Vocabularies for both. Second Edition. Crown 8vo. 3s.

"Well arranged, and furnished with a good vocabulary. This work forms a worthy companion to its author's German Grammar."—*Scotsman.*

SCOTTISH NATIONAL MEMORIALS. Extra pott folio, with 30 full-page Plates, and 287 Illustrations in the Text. £2 12s. 6d. nett.

This volume is the outgrowth of the interest excited by the Historical and Archæological Collection which was brought together in the "Bishop's Castle" in Glasgow for the International Exhibition of 1888. The whole collection has been carefully examined by experts who have contributed most interesting accounts of many relics which are intimately bound up with Scottish history. This volume is not only a valuable contribution to the history of Scottish Antiquities, but affords a picture of Scottish Life which has rarely been equalled in interest.

The work is edited by Mr. James Paton, Superintendent of the Corporation Galleries of Art and the Kelvingrove Museum, Glasgow, with the assistance of the most eminent Antiquaries of Scotland.

Among those who have co-operated with the Editor in the production of the work are Sir Arthur Mitchell, K.C.B., Joseph Anderson, LL.D., the Rev. Father Joseph Stevenson, S.J., Editor of Nau's *Mary Stewart*, Mr. John M. Gray, Curator of the Scottish National Portrait Gallery, Mr. D. Hay Fleming, Mr. J. Dalrymple Duncan, F.S.A., Mr. Alex. J. S. Brook, David Murray, M.A., LL.D., Mr. J. O. Mitchell, Mr. C. D. Donald, and Professor John Ferguson, LL.D., F.S.A.

"It will be enjoyed in equal measure by the Scotchman who is a student of archæology and history, and by the Englishman who has time to saunter through the sections into which it is divided, to sit down here and there, and drink in the significance of the pictures of Scotch life in the past that are presented to him in rich abundance and under the most fascinating guise."—*Spectator.*

𝔑𝔢𝔴 𝔓𝔬𝔢𝔪 𝔟𝔶 𝔱𝔥𝔢 𝔄𝔲𝔱𝔥𝔬𝔯 𝔬𝔣 "𝔒𝔩𝔯𝔦𝔤 𝔊𝔯𝔞𝔫𝔤𝔢."

SMITH, WALTER C.—A HERETIC, AND OTHER POEMS. Extra fcap. 8vo. Cloth. 7s. 6d. [*This Day*.

SMITH, WALTER C.—NEW UNIFORM EDITION OF POEMS by WALTER C. SMITH, M.A., Author of " Olrig Grange." Fcap. 8vo., cloth, gilt top, 5s. each.

OLRIG GRANGE. Fourth Edition.

NORTH COUNTRY FOLK.

KILDROSTAN.

HILDA. Fourth Edition.

" That it is characterized by vigorous thinking, delicate fancy, and happy terms of expression, is admitted on all hands."— *Times.*

" A poem of remarkable power."—*British Quarterly Review.*

" It is to ' Hilda,' however, that we must turn for the most tragic conception of actual life that has hitherto been fashioned into verse. No modern poet, it may safely be said, has plunged so deeply into the innermost heart of living men and women, and none has used such remarkable materials for his drama."—*Scottish Review.*

" These poems are really dramatic, genuinely pathetic, and will bear reading over and over again."— *Westminster Review.*

" For rich variety alike in substance and form, for scathing exposure of all that is mean and base, and for the effective presentation of the loftiest ideals, for mingled humour and pathos, we do not know a volume in the whole range of Scottish verse that can be said to surpass ' North Country Folk '."—*Christian Leader.*

" ' Kildrostan ' has all the interest and excitement of a novel."—*Scotsman.*

SMITH--THOUGHTS AND FANCIES FOR SUNDAY EVENINGS. By WALTER C. SMITH, M.A., Author of " Olrig Grange." Second Edition. Fcap. 8vo. 2s. 6d.

" 'These poems are full of stimulating thought and wide sympathy, put in a refreshing manner. Dr. Smith has given us many poems, for which we are truly grateful, but none that will prove more helpful in the spiritual life than these song sermons."—*Dundee Advertiser.*

" A delightful little book of sacred poetry."—*Nottingham Express.*

SMITH, J. Guthrie—STRATHENDRICK, AND ITS INHABITANTS FROM EARLY TIMES : An account of the parishes of Fintry, Balfron, Killearn, Drymen, Buchanan, and Kilmaronock. By JOHN GUTHRIE SMITH, F.S.A.Scot., author of "The Parish of Strathblane."   [*In preparation.*

SPENS—EMPLOYERS AND EMPLOYED : an Exposition of the Law of Reparation for Physical Injury. By WALTER C. SPENS, Advocate, Sheriff-Substitute of Lanarkshire, and ROBERT T. YOUNGER, M.A., LL.B., Advocate. Cr. 8vo. 14s.

"This volume is a most complete compendium of the Law of Employers and Employed as regards reparation for physical injury."—*Glasgow Herald.*
"The law is very fully and clearly stated, and it will be a valuable aid to masters in dealing with claims made by workmen."—*Aberdeen Journal.*

SPENSER—TALES FROM SPENSER, CHOSEN FROM THE FAERIE QUEENE. By SOPHIA H. MACLEHOSE. Second Edition. Fcap. 8vo, ornamental cloth, gilt top, 3s. 6d.

"A delightful book for children. It could not have been better executed had it been the work of the Lambs.—*Saturday Review.*
"A dainty volume It makes a charming introduction to a great poem."—*Guardian.*

STANLEY, Dean—THE BURNING BUSH : a Sermon. 8vo. 1s.

STEVEN—OUTLINES OF PRACTICAL PATHOLOGY. An Introduction to the Practical Study of Morbid Anatomy and Histology. By J. LINDSAY STEVEN, M.D., Demonstrator of Pathology, Western Infirmary, Glasgow. Crown 8vo. 7s. 6d.

"To the earnest student bent on seeing for himself the facts of which he reads, such a manual as that of Dr. Steven's will be invaluable."—*Lancet.*
"The whole book is eminently practical. It will be found very useful not only by students but also by practitioners."—*Glasgow Medical Journal.*
"This is a sensible, practical, useful book. The work has evidently been prepared with great care ; nothing is superfluous ; there is no over-lapping of subjects ; and the matter has been rigorously subordinated to the wants of the practical student."—*Bristol Medico-Chirurgical Journal.*

STORY—CREED AND CONDUCT : Sermons preached in Rosneath Church. By ROBERT HERBERT STORY, D.D., Regius Professor of Church History in the University of Glasgow. Crown 8vo. Cheap Edition. 3s. 6d.

" In all respects this volume is worthy to be placed alongside of those of Caird and Guthrie, Tulloch and Service."—*Glasgow Herald.*

VEITCH—THE TWEED, AND OTHER POEMS. By JOHN VEITCH, LL.D., Professor of Logic and Rhetoric in the University of Glasgow. Extra fcap. 8vo. 6s. 6d.

VEITCH—LUCRETIUS AND THE ATOMIC THEORY. Crown 8vo. 3s. 6d.

VEITCH—HILLSIDE RHYMES. Extra fcap. 8vo. 5s.

WADDELL—OSSIAN AND THE CLYDE ; or, Ossian Historical and Authentic. By P. HATELY WADDELL, LL.D. 4to. 12s. 6d.

WADDELL—VERSES AND IMITATIONS IN GREEK AND LATIN. By WILLIAM WARDLAW WADDELL. Fcap. 8vo. 2s. 6d.

WATSON—KANT AND HIS ENGLISH CRITICS, a Comparison of Critical and Empirical Philosophy. By JOHN WATSON, M.A., LL.D., Professor of Moral Philosophy in Queen's University, Kingston, Canada. 8vo. 12s. 6d.

" Decidedly the best exposition of Kant which we have seen in English. We cannot too strongly commend it."—*Saturday Review.*

" C'est l'œuvre d'un penseur et d'un maître. . . . Nous avons lu le livre de M. Watson avec un vif intérêt et une grande sympathie."—*Revue Philosophique.*

WATSON—Selections from Kant. *See* Kant.

WHITELAW—The Gospel of St. John: an Exposition
Exegetical and Homiletical, for the use of Clergymen,
Students, and Teachers. By Thomas Whitelaw, M.A.,
D.D., author of "The Exposition and Homiletics in the
Pulpit Commentary on Genesis." 8vo. 528 pages. 14s.

"We have rarely opened a book which displayed more evidence of
expository and homiletical skill than this. In the homiletic sections of
his work, Dr. Whitelaw is particularly happy, sound, suggestive, and
practical; apt in his divisions, and never trivial. Altogether, this is one
of the most helpful commentaries for the preacher's use that we know of.
—*The Record.*

"Dr. Whitelaw's work is of sterling value. To all who desire a learned
and exhaustive exposition and commentary, this work may be confidently
recommended."—*The Christian.*

"To preachers and teachers this book will be invaluable. We cannot
too highly recommend it."—*English Churchman.*